# Bio-Medical Ethics

PHI 227
Northern Virginia Community College
ELI Distance Learning

Ronald Munson
Tom L Beauchamp
LeRoy Walters
Jeffrey P. Kahn
Anna C. Mastroianni

CENGAGE
Learning

Australia • Brazil • Japan • Korea • Mexico • Singapore • Spain • United Kingdom • United States

CENGAGE
Learning·

**Bio-Medical Ethics
PHI 227
Northern Virginia Community College,
ELI Distance Learning**

Intervention and Reflection: Basic Issues in Bioethics, Ninth Edition
Munson
© 2012, 2008, 2004 Cengage Learning. All rights reserved.

Contemporary Issues in Bioethics, Eighth Edition
Beauchamp/Walters/Kahn/Mastroianni
© 2014, 2008, 2003 Cengage Learning. All rights reserved.

Contemporay Issues in Bioethics, Seventh Edition
Beauchamp/Walters/Kahn/Mastroianni
© 2008, 2003 Cengage Learning. All rights reserved.

Senior Project Development Manager:
Linda deStefano

Market Development Manager:
Heather Kramer

Senior Production/
Manufacturing Manager:
Donna M. Brown

Production Editorial Manager:
Kim Fry

Sr. Rights Acquisition Account Manager:
Todd Osborne

For product information and technology assistance, contact us at
**Cengage Learning Customer & Sales Support, 1-800-354-9706**
For permission to use material from this text or product,
submit all requests online at **cengage.com/permissions**
Further permissions questions can be emailed to
**permissionrequest@cengage.com**

This book contains select works from existing Cengage Learning resources and
was produced by Cengage Learning Custom Solutions for collegiate use. As
such, those adopting and/or contributing to this work are responsible for
editorial content accuracy, continuity and completeness.

**Compilation © 2013 Cengage Learning**

ISBN-13: 978-1-285-90524-2

ISBN-10: 1-285-90524-5

**Cengage Learning**
5191 Natorp Boulevard
Mason, Ohio 45040
USA

Cengage Learning is a leading provider of customized learning solutions with
office locations around the globe, including Singapore, the United Kingdom,
Australia, Mexico, Brazil, and Japan. Locate your local office at:
**international.cengage.com/region.**
Cengage Learning products are represented in Canada by Nelson Education, Ltd.
For your lifelong learning solutions, visit **www.cengage.com /custom.**
Visit our corporate website at **www.cengage.com.**

Printed in the United States of America

# Custom Contents

(* Note – this is a "custom" textbook that has been designed specifically for this course in a joint effort between you instructor and the publisher.  Please note that some chapters have been removed intentionally.)

Ethical Theory and Bioethics          1

Telling the Truth to Patients: A Clinical Ethics
Exploration / David C. Thomasma          37

Confidentiality in Medicine---A Decrepit Concept / Mark Siegler          41

The Wisdom of Repugnance / Leon R. Kass          45

Roe v. Wade / United States Supreme Court, 1973          51

Planned Parenthood v. Casey / United States Supreme Court, 1992          56

Why Abortion is Immoral / Don Marquis          63

GONZALES v. CARHART / United States Supreme Court, 2007          72

A Defense of Abortion / Judith Jarvis Thomson          81

The Morality of Abortion / Baruch Brody          92

End of Life          100

An Alternative to Physician-Assisted Suicide / Bernard Gert,
Charles M. Culver, and K. Danner Clouser          109

When Self-Determination Runs Amok / Daniel Callahan          118

DENNIS C. VACCO ATTORNEY GENERAL OF NEW YORK, ET AL. v.
TIMOTHY E QUILL ET AL.  / United States Supreme Court, 1997          123

WASHINGTON ET AL v. HAROLD GLUCKSBERG ET AL / United States Supreme Court, 1997     125

Ballot Measure 16:  The Oregon Death with Dignity Act     129

ALBERTO R GONZALES, Attorney General ET AL.  v. OREGON ET AL / United States Supreme Court, 2006     133

Cruzan v. Director, Missouri Department of Health / United States Supreme Court, 1990     139

Case Presentation, Terri Schiavo     145

# Chapter 1
## Ethical Theory and Bioethics

The moral problems discussed in this book have emerged from professional practice in the fields of clinical medicine, biomedical and biotechnology research, nursing, public health, and the social and behavioral sciences. The goal of this first chapter is to provide a basis in language, norms, and theory sufficient for reading and critiquing the selections in the later chapters.

Everyone is aware that ethics in the biomedical professions has had a distinguished history. Among the most influential sources of medical and nursing ethics, in particular, are its traditions: the concepts, practices, and norms that have long guided conduct in these fields. The history and precise character of these traditions may be the logical starting point in reflecting on professional ethics, but great traditions such as Hippocratic ethics from ancient Greek medicine often fail to provide a comprehensive, unbiased, and adequately justified ethics. Indeed, the history of medical ethics over the last two thousand years is a disappointing history from the perspective of today's concerns in bioethics about the rights of patients and research subjects.

Prior to the early 1970s, there was no firm ground in which a commitment to principles outside of Hippocratic medical ethics could flourish. Particular ethical codes written for the medical, nursing, and research professions had always been written by their own members to govern their own conduct. To consult persons outside the profession was thought not only unnecessary, but dangerous. This conception has collapsed in the face of an exposed history of insularity and the pressures of the modern world. Such a professional morality has been judged inadequately comprehensive, at least somewhat incoherent, not nimble enough to address fast-changing issues, and insensitive to conflicts of interest. The birth of bioethics occurred as a result of an increasing awareness that this older ethic had become obsolete, if it was ever adequate.

Ethical theory has helped supply new concepts and forms of reasoning not found previously in the ethics of the health professions. But ethical theory is not the only source providing insights for understanding issues in bioethics, as we will see.

## FUNDAMENTAL PROBLEMS

### THE STUDY OF MORALITY

*Some Basic Concepts and Definitions.* The field of ethics includes the study of social morality as well as philosophical reflection on its norms and practices. The terms *ethical theory* and *moral philosophy* refer, in their most common usage, to philosophical reflection on morality. The term *morality*, by contrast, refers to traditions of belief about right and wrong human conduct. Morality is a social institution with a history and a code of learnable rules and conventions. Like natural languages and political constitutions, core parts of morality exist before we become instructed in the relevant rules and regulations. As we develop and mature, we learn moral responsibilities together with other social obligations, such as duties to abide by laws. Eventually we learn to distinguish general social rules of law and morals from rules binding only on members of special groups, such as those rules that bind only members of the veterinary profession. That is, we learn to distinguish general *social morality* from *professional moralities, institutional codes, traditional cultural moralities*, and the like.

We learn moral rules alongside other important social rules, making it difficult to distinguish between the two. For example, we are constantly reminded in our early years that we must observe social rules of etiquette, such as saying "Please" when we want something and "Thank you" when we receive it, as well as more specific rules such as "A judge is addressed as 'Judge'." We are also taught rules of prudence, such as "Don't touch a hot stove," together with rules of housekeeping, dressing, and the like.

Morality enters the picture when certain actions ought or ought not to be performed because of the considerable impact these actions can be expected to have on the interests of other people. We first learn maxims such as "It is better to give than to receive" and "Respect the rights of others." These are elementary instructions in morality; they express what society expects of us and of everyone in terms of taking the interests of other people into account. We thus learn about moral instructions and expectations, and gradually we come to understand morality as a set of normative standards about doing good, avoiding harm, respecting others, keeping promises, and acting fairly. We are also taught standards of character and moral excellence.

All persons living a moral life grasp the core dimensions of morality. They know not to lie, not to steal others' property, to keep promises, to respect the rights of others, not to kill or cause harm to innocent persons, and the like. All persons committed to morality are comfortable with these rules and do not doubt their relevance and importance. They know that to violate these norms is unethical and will likely generate feelings of remorse as well as subject violators to moral blame by others. Individuals do not create these moral norms, and morality therefore cannot be purely a personal policy or code.

*The Common Morality.* The set of norms shared by all persons committed to morality constitutes what will here be called "the common morality."[1] The common morality is not merely *a* morality, among *other* moralities. The common morality applies to everyone, and all persons are rightly judged by its standards. The following are examples of standards of action (rules of obligation) found in the common morality: Do not lie to others; keep promises; do not cause harm to others; and take account of the well-being of others. This background of shared rules in the common morality is the raw data for theory and is one reason why we can speak of the origins of moral principles as in the common morality that we all already share.

In recent years, the favored language to express the idea of universal morality has been human rights, but standards of obligation and virtue are no less important. It would of course be absurd to suppose that all persons do, in fact, accept the norms of the common morality. Many amoral, immoral, or selectively moral persons do not care about or identify with moral demands. Nonetheless, all persons in all cultures who are committed to *moral conduct* do accept the demands of the common morality.

The problem is that there are also many distinct moralities comprised of moral norms and positions that spring from particular cultural, philosophical, and religious sources. One reason that well-developed codes of medical ethics vary from society to society, and even from person to person, is that rules in these codes are not a part of universal morality. That is, no part of common morality has a specific focus on what doctors should and should not do. Universal common morality only supplies the core moral concepts and principles on the basis of which we can and should *reflect on* the more specific problems that arise in the health professions. For example, while everyone is obligated to tell the

truth, there may be occasions on which a doctor should not make a full disclosure to a patient or to a family.

Whereas the common morality contains general moral norms that are abstract, universal, and content-thin, particular moralities present concrete, nonuniversal, and content-rich norms. These moralities include the many responsibilities, aspirations, ideals, sympathies, attitudes, and sensitivities found in diverse cultural traditions, religious traditions, professional traditions, and institutional expectations.

Sometimes persons who suppose that they speak with an authoritative moral voice operate under the false belief that they have the force of the common morality (that is, universal morality) behind them. The particular moral viewpoints that such persons represent may be acceptable and even praiseworthy, but they also may not morally bind other persons or communities. For example, persons who believe that scarce medical resources such as transplantable organs should be allocated by lottery rather than by medical need or waiting time may have very good moral reasons for their views, but they cannot claim the force of the common morality for those views unless they make an explicit argument for why that is the case.

A theory of common morality does not hold that all *customary* moralities qualify as part of the *common* morality; and use of the common morality in moral reasoning need not lead to conclusions that are socially received. An important function of the general norms in the common morality is to provide a basis for the evaluation and criticism of groups or communities whose customary moral viewpoints are in some respects deficient. Critical reflection in light of the common morality may ultimately vindicate moral judgments that at the outset were not widely shared or appeared deficient.

*Four Approaches to the Study of Ethics.* Morality can be studied and developed in a variety of ways. In particular, four ways appear prominently in the literature of ethics. Two of these approaches describe and analyze morality without taking moral positions, and these approaches are therefore called *nonnormative*. Two other approaches do involve taking moral positions and are therefore called *normative* or *prescriptive*. These four approaches can be grouped as follows:

A. *Nonnormative approaches*
   1. Descriptive ethics
   2. Metaethics
B. *Normative approaches*
   1. General normative ethics
   2. Practical normative ethics

It would be a mistake to regard these categories as expressing rigid, sharply differentiated approaches. They are often undertaken at the same time, and they overlap in goal and content. Nonetheless, when understood as broad polar contrasts exemplifying models of inquiry, these distinctions are important.

First among the two nonnormative fields of inquiry into morality is *descriptive ethics*, or the factual description and explanation of moral behavior and beliefs. Anthropologists, sociologists, and historians who study moral behavior employ this approach when they explore how moral attitudes, codes, and beliefs differ from person to person and from society to society. Their works often dwell in detail on matters such as professional codes and practices, codes of honor, and rules governing permissible killing in a society. Although philosophers do not typically engage in descriptive ethics in their work, some have

combined descriptive ethics with philosophical ethics—for example, by analyzing the ethical practices of Native American tribes, or researching Nazi experimentation during World War II, and by writing case studies. In the broad field of bioethics, scholars and researchers may engage in either descriptive or normative ethics in their work, and some engage in both.

The second nonnormative field, *metaethics*, involves analysis of the meanings of central terms in ethics, such as *right*, *obligation*, *good*, *virtue*, and *responsibility*. The proper analysis of the term *morality* and the distinction between the moral and the nonmoral are common metaethical problems. Crucial terms in bioethics, including *physician-assisted suicide, informed consent, allocation of organs,* and *universal access* to health care, can be and should be given careful conceptual attention, and they are so treated in various chapters in this volume. (Descriptive ethics and metaethics may not be the only forms of nonnormative inquiry. In recent years there has been an active discussion of the biological bases of moral behavior and of the ways in which humans do and do not differ from animals.)

General normative ethics attempts to formulate and defend basic principles and virtues governing the moral life. Ideally, any ethical theory will provide a system of moral principles or virtues and reasons for adopting them and will defend claims about the range of their applicability. In the course of this chapter the most prominent of these theories will be examined, as will various principles of respect for autonomy, justice, and beneficence that have played a major role in some of these theories.

General normative theories are sometimes used to justify positions on particular moral problems such as abortion, euthanasia, the distribution of health care, research involving human subjects, human embryonic stem cell research, and policies governing organ procurement and allocation. Usually, however, no direct move can be made from moral theory and principles to particular judgments and actions, and theory and principles therefore typically only *facilitate* the development of policies, action guides, or judgments. In general, the attempts to delineate practical action guides are referred to as *practical ethics* (B.2 in the preceding outline).

Substantially the same general ethical theories and principles apply to problems across different professional fields and in areas beyond professional ethics as well. One might appeal to principles of justice, for example, in order to illuminate and resolve issues of taxation, health care distribution, criminal punishment, and affirmative action in hiring. Similarly, principles of veracity (truthfulness) are invoked to discuss secrecy and deception in international politics, misleading advertisements in business ethics, balanced reporting in journalistic ethics, and the disclosure of the nature and extent of an illness to a patient in medical ethics.

### MORAL DILEMMAS AND DISAGREEMENTS

In the teaching of ethics, moral problems are often examined through cases—in particular, law cases, clinical cases, and public policy cases. These cases, which appear in virtually every chapter in this book, vividly display dilemmas and disagreements that require students to identify and grapple with real moral problems.

*Moral Dilemmas.* In a case presented in Chapter 2, two judges on an appeals court became entangled in apparent moral disagreement when ruling in a murder trial. A woman named Tarasoff had been killed by a man who previously had confided to a therapist his intention to kill her as soon as she returned home from a summer vacation. Owing to obligations of confidentiality between patient and physician, a psychologist and a consulting

psychiatrist did not report the threat to the woman or to her family, though they did make one unsuccessful attempt to commit the man to a mental hospital.

One judge held that the therapist could not escape liability: "When a therapist determines, or pursuant to the standards of his profession should determine, that his patient presents a serious danger of violence to another, he incurs an obligation to use reasonable care to protect the intended victim against such danger." Notification of police and direct warnings to the family were mentioned as possible instances of due care. The judge argued that although medical confidentiality must generally be observed by physicians, it was overridden in this case by an obligation to the possible victim and to the "public interest in safety from violent assault."

In the minority opinion, a second judge stated his firm disagreement. He argued that a patient's rights are violated when rules of confidentiality are not observed, that psychiatric treatment would be frustrated by any failure to respect confidentiality, and that patients would subsequently lose confidence in psychiatrists and would fail to provide full disclosures. He also suggested that violent assaults would actually increase because mentally ill persons would be discouraged from seeking psychiatric aid.[2]

The Tarasoff case is an instance of a moral dilemma because strong moral reasons support the rival conclusions of the two judges. The most difficult and recalcitrant moral controversies that we encounter in this volume generally have at least some dilemmatic features. They may even involve what Guido Calabresi has called "tragic choices." Everyone who has been faced with a difficult decision—such as whether to have an abortion, to have a pet "put to sleep," to commit a family member to a mental institution, or to withdraw life support from a loved one—knows through deep anguish what is meant by a personal dilemma.

Dilemmas occur whenever one has good reasons for mutually exclusive alternatives; if one set of reasons is acted upon, events will result that are desirable in some respects but undesirable in others. Here it appears that an agent morally ought to do one thing and also morally ought to do another thing, but the agent is precluded by circumstances from doing both. Although the moral reasons behind each alternative are good reasons, neither set of reasons clearly outweighs the other. Parties on both sides of dilemmatic disagreements thus can *correctly* present moral reasons in support of their competing conclusions. The reasons behind each alternative are good and weighty, and neither set of reasons is obviously best. Most moral dilemmas therefore present a need to balance rival claims in untidy circumstances.

One possible response to the problem of public moral dilemmas and disputes is that we do not have and are not likely ever to have a single theory or method for resolving public disagreements. In any pluralistic culture there may be many sources of moral value and consequently a pluralism of moral points of view on many issues: bluffing in business deals, providing national health insurance to all citizens, involuntary isolation of patients during infectious disease outbreaks, the use of human embryos in research, civil disobedience in pursuit of justice, and so on. If this response is correct, we can understand why there seem to be intractable moral dilemmas and controversies. However, there also are ways to alleviate at least some dilemmas and disagreements, as we shall now see.

*The Resolution of Moral Disagreements.* No single set of considerations is an entirely reliable method for resolving disagreement and controversy, but several methods for dealing constructively with moral disagreements have been employed in the past. Each deserves recognition as a method of constructively contending with disagreement.

1. *Obtaining Objective Information.* First, many moral disagreements can be at least facilitated by obtaining factual information concerning points of moral controversy. It has often been assumed that moral disputes are produced solely by differences over moral principles or their interpretation and application, rather than by a lack of information. However, disputes over what morally ought or ought not to be done often have nonmoral elements as central ingredients. For example, debates about the justice of government allocation of health dollars to preventive and educational strategies have often bogged down over factual issues of whether these strategies actually do function to prevent illness and promote health.

In some cases new information facilitates negotiation and compromise. New information about the alleged dangers involved in certain kinds of scientific research, for instance, have turned public controversies regarding the risks of science and the rights of scientific researchers in unanticipated directions. In several controversies over research with a high level of uncertainty, it has been feared that the research might create an irreversible and dangerous situation—for example, by releasing a pathogen for which the population has no immunity and for which there is no effective treatment.

Controversies about sweetening agents for drinks, toxic substances in the workplace, pesticides in agriculture, radiation therapies, and vaccine dissemination, among others, have been laced with issues of both values and facts. The arguments used by disagreeing parties in these cases sometimes turn on a dispute about liberty or justice and therefore sometimes are primarily normative, but they may also rest on purely factual disagreements. The problem is that rarely, if ever, is all the information obtained that would be sufficient to settle such disagreements.

2. *Providing Definitional Clarity.* Second, controversies have been calmed by reaching conceptual or definitional agreement over the language used by disputing parties. Controversies about "euthanasia," "rationing" health care, "informed consent," and "mental health," for example, are often needlessly entangled because disputing parties use different senses of the terms and have invested heavily in their particular definitions. For example, it may be that one party equates "euthanasia" with mercy killing and another party equates it with voluntarily elected natural death. Some even hold that euthanasia is by definition *nonvoluntary* mercy killing. Any resulting moral controversy over the concept of euthanasia will then be ensnared in terminological problems, rendering it doubtful that the parties are even discussing the same concepts and problems. Accordingly, careful conceptual analysis may be essential to facilitate discussion of issues. Many essays in this volume dwell at some length on conceptual analysis.

3. *Adopting a Code.* Third, resolution of moral problems can be facilitated if disputing parties can come to agreement on a common set of specific moral guidelines, such as rules that define "conflict of interest," and then state obligations to avoid such conflicts. If this method requires a complete shift from one starkly different moral point of view to another, disputes will virtually never be eased. Differences that divide persons at the level of their most cherished views are deep divisions, and conversions are infrequent. Nonetheless, carefully articulated codes reached by discussion and negotiation can lead to the adoption of a new or changed moral framework that can serve as a common basis for evaluation of conduct.

Virtually every professional association in medicine and nursing has a code of ethics, and the reason for the existence of these codes is to give guidance in a circumstance of uncertainty or dispute. Their rules apply to all persons in the relevant professional roles in medicine, nursing, and research and often help resolve charges of unprofessional or unethical conduct. These codes contain general rules and cannot be expected to cover every possible case, but agreed-upon rules do provide an important starting point.

4. *Using Examples and Counterexamples.* Fourth, resolution of moral controversies can be aided by a constructive method of example and opposed counterexample. Cases or examples favorable to one point of view are brought forward, and counterexamples to these cases are thrown up against the examples and claims of the first. This form of debate occurred when a national commission once considered the level of risk that can justifiably be permitted in scientific research involving children as subjects, where no therapeutic benefit is offered to the child. On the basis of principles of acceptable risk used in their own previous deliberations, commissioners were at first inclined to accept the view that only low-risk or minimal-risk procedures could be justified in the case of children (where *minimal risk* refers analogically to the level of risk present in standard medical examinations of patients). Examples from the history of medicine were cited that revealed how certain significant diagnostic, therapeutic, and preventive advances in medicine would have been unlikely, or at least slowed, unless procedures that posed a higher level of risk had been employed. Counterexamples of overzealous researchers who placed children at too much risk were then thrown up against these examples, and the debate continued in this way for several months.

Eventually a majority of commissioners abandoned their original view that nontherapeutic research involving more than minimal risk was unjustified. The majority accepted the position that a somewhat higher level of risk can be justified by the benefits provided to other children, as when some terminally ill children become subjects of research in the hope that something will be learned about their disease that can be applied to other children. Once a consensus on this issue crystallized, resolution was achieved on the primary moral controversy about the involvement of children as research subjects in so-called nontherapeutic research (although two commissioners never agreed).

5. *Analyzing Arguments.* Fifth and finally, one of the most important methods of philosophical inquiry is the exposing of inadequacies, gaps, fallacies, and unexpected consequences of an argument. If an argument rests on accepting two incoherent points of view, then pointing out the incoherence will require a change in the argument. There are many subtle ways of attacking an argument. For example, in Chapters 4 and 5 there are discussions of the nature of "persons"—whether, for example, fetuses are persons and whether the irreversibly comatose are persons. Some writers on topics of abortion and the right to die have not appreciated that their arguments about persons were so broad that they carried important but unnoticed implications for other groups, such as infants and animals. Their arguments implicitly provided reasons they had not noticed for denying rights to infants (rights that adults have), or for granting (or denying) the same rights to fetuses that infants have, and in some cases for granting (or denying) the same rights to animals that infants have.

It may, of course, be correct to hold that infants have fewer rights than adults, or that fetuses and animals should be granted the same rights as infants. The present point is simply that if a moral argument leads to conclusions that a proponent is not prepared to defend and did not previously anticipate, the argument will probably have to be changed, and this process may reduce the distance between the parties who were initially in disagreement.

This style of argument may be supplemented by one or more of the other four ways of reducing moral disagreement. Much of the work published in journals takes the form of attacking arguments, using counterexamples, and proposing alternative principles.

The moral life will of course always be plagued by forms of conflict and incoherence. Our pragmatic goal should be methods that help alleviate and overcome disagreement, not methods that will always eradicate problems. We need not claim that moral disagreements can always be resolved, or even that every rational person must accept the same method for approaching problems. However, if something is to be done to alleviate disagreement, a resolution is more likely to occur if the methods outlined in this section are used.

### THE PROBLEM OF RELATIVISM

The fact of moral disagreement and the idea of a universal common morality raise questions about whether moral judgments can be reached impartially and hold for everyone, or instead lead to an inescapable relativism of moral belief.

*Cultural Relativism.* Relativists have often appealed to anthropological data indicating that moral rightness and wrongness vary from place to place and that there are no absolute or universal moral standards that could apply to all persons at all times. They maintain that rightness is contingent on cultural beliefs and that the concepts of rightness and wrongness are meaningless apart from the specific cultural and historical contexts in which they arise. The claim is that patterns of culture can only be understood as unique wholes and that moral beliefs are closely connected in a culture.

Although it is true that many cultural practices and individual beliefs vary, it does not follow that morally committed people in various parts of the world disagree about the moral standards that were described earlier in this chapter as norms in the common morality. Two cultures may agree about these norms and yet disagree about how to apply them in particular situations or practices. The two cultures may even agree on all the basic principles of morality yet disagree about how to live by these principles in particular circumstances.

For example, if personal payments for special services are common in one culture and punishable as bribery in another, then it is undeniable that these customs are different, but it does not follow that the moral principles underlying the customs are relative. One culture may exhibit a belief that practices of payments to "grease" the process produce a social good by eliminating government interference and by lowering the salaries paid to functionaries, while the people of another culture may believe that the overall social good is best promoted by eliminating all special favors. Both justifications rest on an appraisal of the overall social good, but the people of the two cultures apply this principle in disparate and apparently competing ways.

This possibility suggests that a basic or fundamental conflict between cultural values can only occur if apparent cultural disagreements about proper principles or rules occur at the level of ultimate moral principles. Otherwise, the apparent disagreements can be understood in terms of, and perhaps be arbitrated by, appeal to deeper shared values. If a moral conflict were truly fundamental, then the conflict could not be removed even if there were perfect agreement about the facts of a case, about the concepts involved, and about background beliefs.

We need, then, to distinguish *relativism of judgments* from *relativism of standards*: Judgments that differ across cultures and individuals may rely upon the same general standards for their justification. Relativism of judgment is so pervasive in human social life that it would be foolish to deny it. When people differ about whether one policy for keeping hospital information confidential is more acceptable than another, they differ in their judgments, but they need not have different moral standards about the importance of maintaining medical confidentiality. They may hold the same moral standard but differ over how to implement that standard.

Showing that a relativism of standards is morally incorrect is more than we can hope to achieve here, but we might make some headway in this direction. First, we can recall the earlier discussion of common morality, by contrast to other moralities such as cultural moralities, professional moralities, and individual moralities. The common morality, by definition (or by its very nature) is not relative; it applies to all equally. Second, we can show how difficult it would be to demonstrate that a relativism of standards is true. Suppose, for the sake of argument, that disagreement exists at the deepest level of moral belief; that is, suppose that two cultures disagree on one or more fundamental moral norms. It does not follow even from this cultural relativity of *standards* that there is no ultimate norm or set of norms in which everyone *ought* to believe. Consider an analogy to religious disagreement: From the fact that people have incompatible religious or atheistic beliefs, it does not follow that there is no single correct set of religious or atheistic propositions. Nothing more than skepticism is justified by the facts about religion that are adduced by anthropology; and, similarly, nothing more than this skepticism would be justified if fundamental conflicts of social belief were discovered in ethics.

*Normative Relativism.* Consider now a second type of relativism. Some relativists interpret "What is right at one place or time may be wrong at another" to mean that *it is right* in one context to act in a way that *it is wrong* to act in another. This thesis is normative, because it makes a value judgment; it delineates *which standards or norms correctly determine right and wrong behavior.* One form of this normative relativism asserts that one ought to do what one's society determines to be right (a group or social form of normative relativism), and a second form holds that one ought to do what one personally believes is right (an individual form of normative relativism).

This normative position has sometimes crudely been translated as "Anything is right or wrong whenever some individual or some group judges that it is right or wrong." However, less crude formulations of the position can be given, and more or less plausible examples can be adduced. One can hold the view, for example, that in order to be right something must be conscientiously and not merely customarily believed. Alternatively, it might be formulated as the view that whatever is believed to be right is right if it is part of a well-formed traditional moral code of rules in a society—for example, a medical code of ethics developed by a professional society.

However, this theory is very difficult to defend. The evident inconsistency of this form of relativism with many of our most cherished moral beliefs is a strong reason to be doubtful of it. No general theory of normative relativism is likely to convince us that a belief is acceptable merely because others believe it in a certain way, although that is exactly the commitment of this theory. At least some moral views seem relatively more enlightened, no matter how great the variability of beliefs. The idea that practices such as slavery, sexual exploitation under severe threat, quarantining persons while not treating their contagious diseases, and banning women from attending medical school cannot be evaluated across cultures by some common standard seems morally unacceptable, not morally enlightened. It is one thing to suggest that such beliefs might be *excused* (and persons found not culpable for holding those beliefs), still another to suggest that they are *right*.

We can also evaluate this second form of relativism by focusing on (1) the objectivity of morals within cultures, and (2) the stultifying consequences of a consistent commitment to moral relativism. (The first focus provides an argument against *individual* relativism, and the second provides an argument against a *cultural* source of relativism.)

We noted previously that the common morality provides one set of standards of objectivity that cuts across all cultures. In addition, we also said that particular moralities are concerned with practices of right and wrong transmitted within cultures from one generation to another. The terms of social life are set by these practices, whose rules are pervasively acknowledged and shared in that culture. Within the culture, then, there is both universal morality and a significant measure of moral agreement (objectivity) in the culture itself. Neither the common morality nor the culture's morality can be modified through a person's individual preferences.

For example, a hospital corporation cannot develop its professional ethics in any way it wishes. No hospital chain can draw up a code that brushes aside the need for confidentiality of patient information or that permits surgeons to proceed without adequate consents from patients, and a physician cannot make up his or her individual "code" of medical ethics. If codes deviate significantly from standard or accepted rules, they will rightly be rejected as subjective and mistaken.

Room for invention or alteration in morality is therefore restricted. Beliefs cannot become *moral* standards simply because an individual so labels them. Because individual (normative) relativism claims that moral standards can be invented or labeled, the theory seems *factually* mistaken. This critique of *individual* relativism does not count against *cultural* relativism, of course, because a cultural relativist could easily accept this critique. Our focus needs to shift, then, to a second argument, which is directed at cultural forms of normative relativism.

The problem is this: In circumstances of disagreement, moral reflection is needed to resolve moral issues, whether or not people accept different norms. When two parties argue about a serious, divisive, and contested moral issue—for example, conflicts of interest—most of us think that some fair and justified compromise may be reached despite the differences of belief causing the dispute. People seldom infer from the mere fact of a conflict between beliefs that there is no way to judge one view as correct or as better argued or fairer minded than the other. The more implausible the position advanced by one party, the more convinced others become that some views are mistaken or require supplementation.

People seldom conclude, then, that there is not a better and worse ethical perspective and body of argument. If cultural normative relativists deny this claim, they seem to deny one of our most cherished moral outlooks.

### THE ACCEPTABILITY OF MORAL DIVERSITY AND MORAL DISAGREEMENT

Even conscientious and reasonable moral agents who work diligently at moral reasoning sometimes disagree with other equally conscientious persons. They may disagree about whether disclosure to a fragile patient is appropriate, whether religious values about brain death have a central place in secular ethics, whether physician-assisted suicide should be legalized, and hundreds of other issues in bioethics. Such disagreement does not indicate moral ignorance or moral defect. We simply lack a single, entirely reliable way to resolve all disagreements.

This fact returns us to the questions about the common morality by contrast to particular moralities with which we opened this chapter. Neither the common morality nor ethical theory has the resources to provide a single solution to every moral problem. So-called "moral" disagreement can emerge for many reasons, including (1) factual disagreements (for example, about the level of suffering that an action will cause), (2) scope disagreements about who should be protected by a moral norm (for example, whether fetuses or animals are protected), (3) disagreements about which norms are relevant in the circumstances, (4) disagreements about appropriate specifications, (5) disagreements about the weight of the relevant norms in the circumstances, (6) disagreements about appropriate forms of balancing, (7) the presence of a genuine moral dilemma, and (8) insufficient information or evidence.

Different parties may emphasize different principles or assign different weights to principles even when they do not disagree over which principles are relevant. Such disagreement may persist among morally committed persons who conform to all the demands that morality makes upon them. In the face of this problem, when evidence is incomplete and different sets of evidence are available to different parties, one individual or group may be justified in reaching a conclusion that another individual or group is justified in rejecting. Even when both parties have incorrect beliefs, each party may be justified in holding those beliefs. We cannot hold persons to a higher standard in practice than to make judgments conscientiously in light of the relevant norms and the available and relevant evidence.

These facts about the moral life sometimes discourage those who must deal with practical problems, but the phenomenon of reasoned moral disagreement provides no basis for skepticism about morality or about moral thinking. Indeed, it offers a reason for taking morality seriously and using the best tools that we have to carry our moral projects as far as we can. After all, we frequently obtain near complete agreement in our moral judgments, and we always have the universal basis for morality (the common morality) considered earlier in this chapter.

When disagreements arise, a moral agent can—and often should—defend his or her decision without disparaging or reproaching others who reach different decisions. Recognition of legitimate diversity (by contrast to moral violations that call for criticism) is exceedingly important when we evaluate the actions of others. What one person does may not be what other persons should do when they face the same problem. Similarly, what one institution or government should do may not be what another institution or government should do. From this perspective, individuals and societies legitimately construct different requirements that comprise part of the moral life (consistent with what we have called morality in the broad sense), and we may not be able to judge one as better than another.[3]

### MORAL JUSTIFICATION

Typically we have no difficulty in deciding whether to act morally. We make moral judgments through a mix of appeals to rules, paradigm cases, role models, and the like. These moral beacons work well as long as we are not asked to deliberate about or justify our judgments. However, when we experience moral doubt or uncertainty, we are led to moral deliberation, and often from there to a need to justify our beliefs. As we deliberate, we usually consider which among the possible courses of action is morally justified—that is, which has the strongest moral reasons behind it. The reasons we finally accept express the conditions under which we believe some course of action is morally justified.

The objective of justification is to establish one's case by presenting a sufficient set of reasons for belief and action. Not all reasons, however, are good reasons, and even good reasons are not always sufficient for justification. There is, then, a need to distinguish a reason's *relevance* to a moral judgment from its final *adequacy* for that judgment, and also to distinguish an *attempted* justification from a *successful* justification. For example, a good reason for involuntarily committing certain mentally ill persons to institutions is that they present a clear and present danger to other persons. By contrast, a reason for commitment that is sometimes offered as a good reason, but that many people consider a bad reason (because it involves a deprivation of liberty), is that some mentally ill persons present a clear and present danger to themselves or that they require treatment for a serious mental disorder.

If someone holds that involuntary commitment on grounds of danger to self is a good reason and is solely sufficient to justify commitment, that person should be able to give some account of why this reason is good and sufficient. That is, the person should be able to give further justifying reasons for the belief that the reason offered is good and sufficient. The person might refer, for example, to the dire consequences for the mentally ill that will occur if no one intervenes. The person might also invoke certain principles about the moral importance of caring for the needs of the mentally ill. In short, the person is expected to give a set of reasons that amounts to an argued defense of his or her perspective. These appeals are usually either to a coherent group of moral principles or to consequences of actions, and they form the substantive basis of justification.

Many philosophers now defend the view that the relationship between general moral norms and particular moral judgments is bilateral (neither a unilateral "application" of general norms nor a unilateral abstraction from particular case judgments). John Rawls's celebrated account of *reflective equilibrium* has been the most influential model in this literature. In developing and refining a system of ethics, he argues, it is appropriate to start with the broadest possible set of *considered judgments* (see following) about a subject and to erect a provisional set of principles that reflects them. Reflective equilibrium views investigation in ethics (and theory construction) as a reflective testing of moral principles, theoretical postulates, and other relevant moral beliefs to render them as coherent as possible. Starting with paradigms of what is morally right or wrong, one searches for principles that are consistent with these paradigms as well as one another. Such principles and considered judgments are taken, as Rawls puts it, "provisionally as fixed points," but also as "liable to revision."

*Considered judgments* is a technical term referring to judgments in which moral beliefs and capacities are most likely to be presented without a distorting bias. Examples are judgments about the wrongness of racial discrimination, religious intolerance, and predatory sexual behavior. The goal of reflective equilibrium is to match, prune, and adjust considered judgments and principles so that they form a coherent moral outlook. This model demands the best approximation to full coherence under the assumption of a never-ending search for consistency and unanticipated situations. From this perspective, ethical theories and individual moral outlooks are never complete, always stand to be informed by practical contexts, and must be tested for adequacy by their practical implications.

Although the justification of particular moral *judgments* is often the issue, philosophers are as often concerned with the justification of general ethical *theories*. Which theory, we can now ask, is the best theory? Or do all theories fail tests for considered judgments and coherence?

TYPES OF ETHICAL THEORY

Many writers in bioethics believe that we would justifiably have more confidence in our individual and communal moral judgments if only we could justify them on the basis of a comprehensive ethical theory. The ambition of an ethical theory is to provide an adequate normative framework for processing, and ideally resolving, moral problems. However, our objective in this section is not to show how ethical theory actually can *resolve* problems, but only to present influential types of ethical theory.

These theories fall under the category that we earlier called general normative ethics. We will concentrate on utilitarianism, Kantianism, virtue (or character) ethics, the ethics of care, and casuistry. Some knowledge of these theories is indispensable for reflective study in bioethics because a sizable part of the field's literature draws on methods and conclusions found in these theories. It is also important to note that we do not address the role of religion as a source of influence in normative ethics or its relation to morality more generally. These are important questions and there are many sources for discussion of these relationships, but it is afield of this discussion of ethical theory.

### UTILITARIAN THEORIES

*Utilitarianism* is rooted in the thesis that an action or practice is right (when compared to any alternative action or practice) if it leads to the greatest possible balance of good consequences or to the least possible balance of bad consequences in the world as a whole. Utilitarians hold that there is one and only one basic principle of ethics: the principle of utility. This principle asserts that we ought always to produce the maximal balance of good consequences over bad consequences. The classical origins of this theory are found in the writings of Jeremy Bentham (1748–1832) and John Stuart Mill (1806–1873).

Utilitarians invite us to consider the larger objective or function of morality as a social institution, where *morality* is understood to include our shared rules of justice and other principles of the moral life. The point of the institution of morality, they insist, is to promote human welfare by minimizing harms and maximizing benefits: There would be no point to moral codes unless they served this purpose. Utilitarians thus see moral rules as the means to the fulfillment of individual needs as well as to the achievement of broad social goals.

*Mill's Utilitarianism.* In several types of ethical theory, classic works of enduring influence form the basis for development of the theory. The most influential presentation of utilitarianism is John Stuart Mill's book *Utilitarianism* (1863). In this work Mill refers to the principle of utility as the Greatest Happiness Principle: "Actions are right in proportion as they tend to promote happiness, wrong as they tend to produce the reverse of happiness." Mill's view seems to be that the purpose of morality is to tap natural human sympathies to benefit others while at the same time controlling unsympathetic attitudes that cause harm to others. The principle of utility is conceived as the best means to these basic human goals.

For Mill and other utilitarians, moral theory is grounded in a theory of the general goals of life, which they conceive as the pursuit of pleasure and the avoidance of pain. The production of pleasure and pain assumes moral and not merely personal significance when the consequences of our actions affect the pleasurable or painful states of others. Moral rules and moral and legal institutions, as they see it, must be grounded in a general theory of good or value, and morally good actions are alone determined by these final values.

*Essential Features of Utilitarianism.* Several essential features of utilitarianism are found in the theories of Mill and all other utilitarians. In particular, four conditions must be satisfied in order to qualify as a utilitarian theory.

1. *The Principle of Utility: Maximize the Good.* First, actors are obliged to maximize the good: We ought always to produce the greatest possible balance of value over disvalue (or the least possible balance of disvalue, if only bad results can be achieved), whatever that balance is and however it is distributed. For example, we ought to maximize the public benefits of scientific research, clinical medicine, public health measures, and so forth. But what is the good or the valuable? This question takes us to the second condition.

2. *A Theory of Value: The Standard of Goodness.* The goodness or badness of consequences is to be measured by items that count as the primary goods or utilities. Various theories of value (or theories of the good) held by utilitarians elevate the following goods to prominence: (1) happiness, (2) the satisfaction of desires and aims, and (3) the attainment of such conditions or states of affairs as autonomy, understanding, various kinds of functioning, achievement, and deep personal relationships. Put another way, utilitarians think of what is good or valuable in terms of basic conditions of well-being such as happiness, health, security, freedom, and companionship and attachment.

Many utilitarians agree that ultimately we ought to look to the production of *agent-neutral* or intrinsic values, those that do not vary from person to person. That is, we should look to the production of what is good in itself, not merely what is good as a means to something else. Bentham and Mill are hedonists; they believe that only pleasure or happiness (synonymous terms in this context) can be intrinsically good. Pluralistic utilitarian philosophers, by contrast, believe that no single goal or state constitutes the good and that many values besides happiness possess intrinsic worth—for example, the values of friendship, knowledge, love, personal achievement, culture, freedom, and liberties might all qualify in a utilitarian theory.

Both the hedonistic and the pluralistic approaches have seemed to some recent philosophers relatively problematic for purposes of objectively aggregating widely different interests in order to determine where maximal value, and therefore right action, lies. Many utilitarians interpret the good as that which is *subjectively* desired or wanted. The satisfaction of desires or wants is seen as the goal of our moral actions. To maximize an individual's utility, under this conception, is to maximize what he or she has chosen or would choose from the available alternatives.

3. *Consequentialism.* Whatever its precise value theory, any utilitarian theory decides which actions are right entirely by reference to the *consequences* of the actions, rather than by reference to any intrinsic moral features the actions may have, such as truthfulness or fidelity. Here the utilitarian need not demand that all future consequences or even all avoidable consequences be anticipated. A utilitarian demands only that we take account of what can reasonably be expected to produce the greatest balance of good or least balance of harm. In judging the *agent* of the action, we should assess whether the agent conscientiously attempts to produce the best utilitarian outcome.

4. *Impartiality (Universalism).* Finally, in the utilitarian approach all parties affected by an action must receive *impartial consideration.* Utilitarianism here stands in sharp contrast to egoism, which proposes maximizing consequences for oneself rather than for all parties

affected by an action. In seeking a blinded impartiality, utilitarianism aligns good and mature moral judgment with moral distance from the choices to be made. A moral point of view is *impartial* in the sense that a moral judgment is formed without regard to personal preference and interest and also without regard to the particular fortuitous advantages or disadvantages of persons such as special talents or handicaps, because these properties are morally arbitrary. The ideal, then, is unbiased evaluation without regard to a person's race, sex, nationality, and economic circumstances, none of which can be regarded as legitimate bases for treating persons differently from other persons.

*Act and Rule Utilitarianism.* Utilitarian moral philosophers are conventionally divided into several types, and it is best to think of "utilitarianism" as a label designating a family of theories that use a consequentialist, maximizing principle. A significant dispute has arisen among utilitarians over whether the principle of utility is to be applied to *particular acts* in particular circumstances or to *rules of conduct* that determine which acts are right and wrong. For the *rule utilitarian*, actions are justified by appeal to rules such as "Don't deceive" and "Don't break promises." These rules, in turn, are justified by appeal to the principle of utility. An *act utilitarian* simply justifies actions directly by appeal to the principle of utility. Act utilitarianism is thus characterized as a "direct" or "extreme" theory because the act utilitarian directly asks, "What good and evil consequences will result *directly* from this action in this circumstance?"—not "What good and evil consequences will result *generally* from this sort of action?"

Consider the following case, which occurred in the state of Kansas and which anticipates some issues about euthanasia encountered in Chapter 5. An elderly woman lay ill and dying. Her suffering came to be too much for her and her faithful husband of fifty-four years to endure, so she requested that he kill her. Stricken with grief and unable to bring himself to perform the act, the husband hired another man to kill his wife. An act utilitarian might reason that *in this case* hiring another person to kill the woman was justified, although *in general* we would not permit persons to perform such actions. After all, only this woman and her husband were directly affected, and relief of her pain was the main issue. It would be unfortunate, the act utilitarian might reason, if our "rules" against killing failed to allow for selective killings in extenuating circumstances, because it is extremely difficult to generalize from case to case. The jury, as it turned out, convicted not only the third party but also the husband of murder, and he was sentenced to twenty-five years in prison. An act utilitarian might maintain that a *rigid* application of rules inevitably leads to injustices and that rule utilitarianism cannot escape this problem of an undue rigidity of rules.

Many philosophers reject act utilitarianism, charging its exponents with basing morality on mere expediency. On act-utilitarian grounds, they say, it is desirable for a physician to kill babies with many kinds of birth defects if the death of the child would relieve the family and society of a burden and inconvenience and would lead to the greatest good for the greatest number. Many opponents of act utilitarianism have thus argued that strict rules, which cannot be set aside for the sake of convenience, must be maintained. Many of these apparently desirable rules can be justified by the principle of utility, so utilitarianism need not be abandoned if act utilitarianism is judged unworthy.

Rule utilitarians hold that rules have a central position in morality and cannot be compromised in particular situations. Compromise threatens the rules themselves. The rules' effectiveness is judged by determining whether the observance of a given rule would maximize social utility better than would any substitute rule (or having no rule). Utilitarian rules are, in theory, firm and protective of all classes of individuals, just as human rights firmly protect all individuals regardless of social convenience and momentary need.

Nonetheless, we can ask whether rule-utilitarian theories offer anything more than act utilitarianism. Dilemmas often arise that involve conflicts among moral rules—for example, rules of confidentiality conflict with rules protecting individual welfare, as in the Tarasoff case. If there are no rules to resolve these conflicts, perhaps the rule utilitarian cannot be distinguished from the act utilitarian.

### KANTIAN THEORIES

We have seen that utilitarianism conceives the moral life in terms of producing what is valuable. A second type of theory departs significantly from this approach. Often called *deontological* (i.e., a theory that some features of actions other than or in addition to consequences make actions obligatory), this type is now increasingly called *Kantian*, because of its origins in the theory of Immanuel Kant (1724–1804).

*Duty from Rules of Reason.* Kant believed that an act is morally praiseworthy only if done neither for self-interested reasons nor as the result of a natural disposition, but rather from *duty*. That is, the person's motive for acting must be a recognition of the act as resting on duty. It is not good enough, in Kant's view, that one merely performs the morally correct action, because one could perform one's duty for self-interested reasons having nothing to do with morality. For example, if an employer discloses a health hazard to an employee only because he or she fears a lawsuit, and not because of a belief in the importance of truth-telling, then this employer acts rightly but deserves no moral credit for the action.

Kant tries to establish the ultimate basis for the validity of moral rules in pure reason, not in intuition, conscience, or utility. He thinks all considerations of utility and self-interest morally unimportant, because the moral worth of an agent's action depends exclusively on the moral acceptability of the rule on the basis of which the person is acting. An action has moral worth only when performed by an agent who possesses a good will, and a person has a good will only if moral duty based on a universally valid rule is the sole motive for the action. Morality, then, provides a rational framework of principles and rules that constrain and guide everyone, without regard to their personal goals and interests.

Kant's supreme principle, *the categorical imperative*, also called *the moral law*, is expressed in several ways in his writings. His first formulation may be roughly paraphrased in this way: "Always act in such a way that you can will that everyone act in the same manner in similar situations." Kant's view is that wrongful practices, such as lying, theft, cheating, and failure to help someone in distress when you can easily do so, involve a kind of contradiction. Consider the example of cheating on exams. If everyone behaved as the cheater did, exams would not serve their essential function of testing mastery of relevant material, in which case there would effectively be no such thing as an exam. But cheating presupposes the background institution of taking exams, so the cheater cannot consistently will that everyone act as he or she does.

The categorical imperative is categorical, Kant says, because it admits of no exceptions and is absolutely binding. It is imperative because it gives instruction about how one must act. Kant draws a distinction between a *categorical imperative* and a *hypothetical imperative*. A hypothetical imperative takes the form, "If I want to achieve such and such a valued end, then I must do so and so." These prescriptions—so reminiscent of utilitarian and pragmatic thinking—tell us what we must do, provided that we already have certain desires, interests, or goals. An example is "If you want to regain your health, then you must take this medication," or "If you want to improve infant mortality rates, then you must improve your hospital facilities." These imperatives are not commanded for their own sakes. They are commanded as means to an end that has already been willed or accepted. Hypothetical imperatives are not moral imperatives in Kant's philosophy because moral imperatives tell us what must be done independently of our goals or desires.

Kant emphasizes the notion of *rule as universal law*. Rules that determine duty are made correct by their universality, that is, the fact that they apply to everyone. This criterion of universality offers some worthwhile lessons for bioethics. Some of the clearest cases of immoral behavior involve a person's trying to make a unique exception of himself or herself purely for personal reasons. This conduct could not be made universal, because the rules presupposed by the idea of "being an exception" would be destroyed. If carried out consistently by others, this conduct would violate the rules presupposed by the system of morality, thereby rendering the system inconsistent—that is, having inconsistent rules of operation.

Kant's view is that wrongful practices, including invasion of privacy, lying, theft, and manipulative suppression of information, are "contradictory"; that is, they are not consistent with the very duties and institutions they presuppose. In cases of lying, for example, the universalization of rules that allow lying would entitle everyone to lie to you, just as you would be entitled to lie to them. Such rules are inconsistent with the practice of truth-telling that they presuppose. Similarly, fraud in research is inconsistent with the practice of publishing the truth. All such practices are inconsistent with a rule or practice that they presuppose.

*The Requirement to Never Treat Persons as Means.* A second formulation of Kant's categorical imperative—one more frequently invoked in medical ethics—may be paraphrased in this way: "Treat every person as an end and never solely as a means."[4] This principle requires us to treat persons as having their own established goals. Deceiving prospective subjects in order to get them to consent to participate in nontherapeutic research is one example of a violation of this principle.

It has commonly been said that Kant is here arguing that we can never treat another as a means to our ends. This interpretation, however, misrepresents his views. He argues only that we must not treat another *exclusively* as a means to our own ends. When adult human research subjects are asked to volunteer, for example, they are treated as a means to a researcher's ends. However, they are not exclusively used for others' purposes, because they do not become mere servants or objects. Their consent justifies using them as means to the end of research.

Kant's imperative demands only that persons in such situations be treated with the respect and moral dignity to which all persons are always entitled, including the times when they are used as means to the ends of others. To treat persons merely as a means, strictly speaking, is to disregard their personhood by exploiting or otherwise using them without regard to their own thoughts, interests, and needs. It involves a failure to acknowledge that every person has a worth and dignity equal to that of every other person and that this worth and dignity cannot be compromised for utilitarian or any other reasons.

### CONTEMPORARY CHALLENGES TO THE TRADITIONAL THEORIES

Thus far we have treated only two types of theory: utilitarianism and Kantianism. These theories combine a variety of moral considerations into a surprisingly systematized framework, centered around a single major principle. Much is attractive in these theories, and they were the dominant models in ethical theory throughout much of the twentieth century. During the 1970s and 1980s, utilitarian and deontological approaches also dominated the theoretical literature and discourse of bioethics.

Although utilitarian and deontological arguments or patterns of reasoning are still common today, the theories themselves no longer dominate the field of bioethics. The reasons for the demotion of utilitarian and single-principle deontological theories concern the disadvantages of any approach that attempts to characterize the entire domain of morality with one supreme principle. Three disadvantages are especially worthy of note. First, there is a problem of authority. Despite myriad attempts by philosophers in recent centuries to justify the claim that some principle is morally authoritative—that is, correctly regarded as the supreme moral principle—no such effort at justification has persuaded a majority of philosophers or other thoughtful people that either the principle or the moral system is as authoritative as the common morality that supplies its roots. Thus to attempt to illuminate problems in bioethics with a single-principle theory has struck many as misguided and, at times, presumptuous or dogmatic.

Second, even if an individual working in this field is convinced that some such theory is correct (that is, authoritative), he or she needs to deal responsibly with the fact that many other morally serious individuals do not share this theory and give it little or no authority. Thus, problems of how to communicate and negotiate in the midst of disagreement do not favor appeals to rigid theories or inflexible principles, which can generate a gridlock of conflicting principled positions, rendering moral discussion hostile and alienating.

Third, there is the problem that a highly general principle is indeterminate in many contexts in which one might try to apply it. That is, the content of the principle itself does not always identify a unique course of action as right. It has increasingly become apparent that single-principle theories are significantly incomplete, frequently depending on independent moral considerations with the help of which the theories can serve as effective guides to action.

Much recent philosophical writing has focused on weaknesses in utilitarian and Kantian theories and on ways in which the two types of theory actually affirm some broader and less controversial conception of the moral life. Critics of utilitarian and Kantian models believe that these two types of theory need to be replaced with a better theory. Three accounts have been popular in bioethics as replacements for, or perhaps supplements to, utilitarian and Kantian theories: (1) virtue theory (which is character based), (2) the ethics of care (which is relationship based), and (3) casuistry (which is case based). These are the topics of the next three sections.

## VIRTUE ETHICS

In discussing utilitarian and Kantian theories, we have looked chiefly at obligations and rights. Beyond obligations and rights, we often reflect on the agents who perform actions, have motives, and follow principles. Here we commonly make judgments about good and evil character in persons. Virtue ethics gives good character a preeminent place.

*Virtue ethics* descends from the classical Hellenistic tradition represented by Plato and Aristotle. Here the cultivation of virtuous traits of character is viewed as morality's primary function. Moral virtues are understood as morally praiseworthy character traits, such as courage, compassion, sincerity, reliability, and industry. In virtue ethics, the primary concern is with what sort of person is ideal, while action is considered to have secondary importance. People are viewed as acquiring virtues much as they do skills such as carpentry, playing an instrument, or cooking. They become just by performing just actions and become temperate by performing temperate actions. Virtuous character is cultivated and made a part of the individual, much like a language or tradition.

However, an ethics of virtue is more than habitual training. One must also have a correct *motivational structure*. A conscientious person, for example, not only has a disposition to act conscientiously, but a morally appropriate desire to be conscientious. The person characteristically has a moral concern and reservation about acting in a way that would not be conscientious.

Imagine a person who always performs his or her obligation because it is an obligation but intensely dislikes having to allow the interests of others to be of importance. Such a person does not cherish, feel congenial toward, or think fondly of others, and respects them only because obligation requires it. This person can, on a theory of moral obligation such as Kant's or Mill's, perform a morally right action, have an ingrained disposition to perform that action, and act with obligation as the foremost motive. It is possible (1) to be disposed to do what is right, (2) to intend to do it, and (3) to do it, while also (4) yearning to be able to avoid doing it. If the motive is improper, a vital moral ingredient is missing and if a person *characteristically* lacks this motivational structure, a necessary condition of virtuous character is absent.

Consider a physician who meets his moral obligations because they are his obligations and yet has underlying motives that raise questions of character. This physician detests his job and hates having to spend time with every patient who comes through the door. He cares not about being of service to people or creating a better environment in the office. All he wants to do is make money, avoid malpractice suits, and meet his obligations. Although this man never acts immorally from the perspective of duty, something in his character is deeply defective morally. The admirable compassion and dedication guiding the lives of many health professionals is absent in this person, who merely engages in rule-following behavior.

Virtue ethics may seem only of intellectual interest, but it has practical value in that a morally good person with right desires or motives is more likely to understand what should be done, to perform required acts, and to form moral ideals than is a morally bad or indifferent person. A trusted person has an ingrained motivation and desire to do what is right and to care about whether it is done. Whenever the feelings, concerns, and attitudes of others are the morally relevant matters, rules and principles are not as likely as human warmth and sensitivity to lead a person to notice what should be done. From this perspective, virtue ethics is at least as fundamental in the moral life as principles of basic obligation.

We also often morally evaluate a person's emotional responses—which tend to reflect one's character—even where no particular action is called for. One might admire a social worker's genuine sorrow at the news that another social worker's patient committed suicide; her expression of sorrow reflects her caring and sympathy. Moreover, in practice, well-established virtues may prove at least as important as mastery of principles, rules, and other action guides. For example, it may be the case that being truthful, compassionate, perceptive, diligent, and so forth is a more reliable basis for good medical practice than knowledge of the principles and rules of bioethics.

A proponent of character ethics need not claim that analysis of the virtues subverts or discredits ethical principles, rules, or theories. It is enough to argue that ethical theory is more complete if the virtues are included and that moral motives deserve to be at center stage in a way some leading traditional theories have inadequately appreciated. It is not difficult to see the compatibility of virtue ethics and duty ethics.

Indeed, it is doubtful that virtue can be adequately conceptualized without some background assumptions about right action. For example, seeing truthfulness as a virtue seems inseparable from seeing truth-telling as a prima facie obligation. If we ask why one should generally be truthful, it seems evasive to say, "Because virtuous people are that way." A more adequate response would show how truthfulness displays respect for people's autonomy, tends to promote certain benefits, and ordinarily avoids certain kinds of harm.

## THE ETHICS OF CARE

Related to virtue ethics in vital respects is a body of moral reflection often called the "ethics of care." This theory develops some of the themes in virtue ethics about the centrality of character, but the ethics of care focuses on a set of character traits that people all deeply value in close personal relationships: sympathy, compassion, fidelity, love, friendship, and the like. Noticeably absent are universal moral rules and impartial utilitarian calculations such as those espoused by Kant and Mill.

To understand this approach, consider the traditional theories' criterion of impartiality in moral judgment. This criterion of distanced fairness and treating similar cases similarly makes eminently good sense for courts, but does it make good sense of intimate moral relationships? The care perspective views this criterion as cutting away too much of morality in order to get to a standpoint of detached fairness. Lost in the traditional *detachment* of impartiality is *attachment*—that which we care about most and which is closest to us. In seeking blindness, we may be made blind and indifferent to the special needs of others. So, although impartiality is a moral virtue in some contexts, it may be a moral vice in others. The care perspective is especially important for roles such as parent, friend, physician, and nurse, where contextual response, attentiveness to subtle clues, and discernment are likely to be more important morally than impartial treatment.

Being cautious about abstract principles of obligation—the instruments of impartiality— is also characteristic of the ethics of care. Defenders of the ethics of care find principles often to be irrelevant, vacuous, or ineffectual in the moral life. A defender of principles could say that principles of care, compassion, and kindness structure our understanding of when it is appropriate to respond in caring, compassionate, and kind ways, but there is something hollow about this claim. It seems to best capture our moral experience to say that we rely on our emotions, our capacity for sympathy, our sense of friendship, and our knowledge of how caring people behave.

Exponents of the ethics of care have also criticized the autonomous, unified, rational beings that typify both the Kantian and the utilitarian conception of the moral self. They argue that moral decisions often require a sensitivity to the situation as well as an awareness of the beliefs, feelings, attitudes, and concerns of each of the individuals involved and of the relationships of those individuals to one another.

Additional reasons exist for thinking that a morality centered on care and concern cannot be squeezed into a morality of rules. For example, it seems difficult to express the responsibilities of a health care professional adequately through principles and rules. We can generalize about how caring physicians and nurses respond in encounters with patients, but these generalizations do not amount to principles, nor will such generalizations be subtle enough to give sound guidance for the next patient. Each situation calls for a different set of responses, and behavior that in one context is caring seems to intrude on privacy or be offensive in another context.

A morality centered on care and concern can potentially serve health care ethics in a constructive and balanced fashion, because it is close to the processes of reason and feeling exhibited in clinical contexts. Disclosures, discussions, and decision making in health care typically become a family affair, with support from a health care team. The ethics of care maintains that many human relationships in health care and research involve persons who are vulnerable, dependent, ill, and frail and that the desirable moral response is attached attentiveness to needs, not detached respect for rights. Feeling for and being immersed in the other person establish vital aspects of the moral relationship. Accordingly, this approach features responsibilities and forms of empathy that a rights-based account may ignore in the attempt to protect persons from invasion by others.

CASUISTRY

A third alternative to classic theories has been labeled casuistry. It focuses on decision making using particular cases, where the judgments reached rely on judgments reached in prior cases. Casuists are skeptical of the power of principles and theory to resolve problems in specific cases. They think that many forms of moral thinking and judgment do not involve appeals to general guidelines, but rather to narratives, paradigm cases, and precedents established by previous cases.[5]

Casuists concentrate our attention on practical decision making in particular cases and on the implications of those cases for other cases. Here we proceed by identifying the specific features of, and problems present in, the case. We may attempt to identify the relevant precedents and prior experiences we have had with related cases, attempting to determine how similar and how different the present case is from other cases. For example, if the case involves a problem of medical confidentiality, analogous cases would be considered in which breaches of confidentiality were justified or unjustified in order to see whether such a breach is justified in the present case.

Consider the way a physician thinks in making a judgment and then a recommendation to a patient. Many individual factors, including the patient's medical history, the physician's successes with other similar patients, paradigms of expected outcomes, and the like will play a role in formulating a judgment and recommendation to this patient, which may be very different from the recommendation made to the next patient with the same malady. The casuist views moral judgments and recommendations similarly. One can make successful moral judgments of agents, actions, and policies, casuists say, only when one has an intimate understanding of particular situations and an appreciation of treating similar cases similarly.

An analogy to case law is helpful in understanding the casuist's point. In case law, the normative judgments made by courts of law become authoritative, and it is reasonable to hold that these judgments are primary for later judges who assess other cases—even though the particular features of each new case will be different. Matters are similar in ethics, say casuists. Normative judgments about certain cases emerge through case comparisons. A case currently being considered is placed in the context of a set of cases that shows a resemblance, and the similarities and differences are assessed. The relative weight of competing values is presumably determined by the comparisons to analogous cases. Moral guidance is provided by an accumulated mass of influential cases, which represent a consensus in society and in institutions reached by reflection on cases. That consensus then becomes authoritative and is extended to new cases.[6]

Cases like *Tarasoff* have been enormously influential in bioethics. Writers have used it as a form of authority for decisions in new cases. Features of their analyses have then been discussed throughout the literature of bioethics, and they become integral to the way we think and draw conclusions in the field. The leading cases become enduring and authoritative sources for reflection and decision making. Cases such as the so-called Tuskegee syphilis study (in which syphilis treatment was intentionally withheld from a group of African-American men in rural Alabama without their knowledge or consent in a government-sponsored experiment to follow the course of the disease) are routinely invoked to illustrate *unjustified* biomedical experimentation. Decisions reached about moral wrongs in this case serve as a form of authority for decisions in new cases. These cases profoundly influence our standards of fairness, negligence, paternalism, and the like. Just as case law (legal rules) develops incrementally from legal decisions in cases, so the moral law (moral rules) develops incrementally. From this perspective, principles are less important for moral reasoning than cases.

At first sight, casuistry seems strongly opposed to the frameworks of principles in traditional duty-based theory. However, closer inspection of casuistry shows that its primary concern (like the ethics of care) is with an excessive reliance in recent philosophy on impartial, universal action guides. Two casuists, Albert Jonsen and Stephen Toulmin, write that "*good* casuistry . . . applies general principles to particular cases with discernment." As a history of similar cases and similar judgments mounts, we become more confident in our general judgments. A "locus of moral certitude" arises in the judgments, and the stable elements crystallize into tentative principles. As confidence in these generalizations increases, they are accepted less tentatively and moral knowledge develops.[7]

Today's casuists have resourcefully argued for the importance of analogical reasoning, paradigm cases, and practical judgment. Bioethics, like ethical theory, has sometimes unduly minimized this avenue to moral knowledge. Casuists also have rightly pointed out that generalizations are often best learned, accommodated, and implemented by using cases, case discussion, and case methods. These insights can be utilized by connecting them to an appropriate set of concepts, principles, and theories that control the judgments we make about cases.

Nonetheless, casuists' emphases can be misleading. Casuists sometimes write as if cases lead to moral paradigms, analogies, or judgments entirely by their facts alone—or perhaps by appeal only to a few salient features of the cases. This premise is suspect. No matter how many facts are stacked up, we will still need some *value* premises in order to draw out moral conclusions from the case. The properties that we observe to be of moral importance in cases are picked out by the values that we have already accepted as being morally important. In short, the paradigm cases of the casuists are inherently value-laden.

The best way to understand this idea of paradigm cases is as a combination of (1) *facts* that can be generalized to other cases—for example, "The patient refused the recommended treatment"—and (2) *settled values*—for example, "Competent patients have a right to refuse treatment." In a principle-based system, these settled values are called principles, rules, rights claims, and the like; and they are analytically distinguished from the facts of particular cases. In casuistical appeals to cases, rather than keeping values distinct from facts, the two are bound together in the paradigm case; the central values are generalizable and therefore preserved from one case to the next.

## ETHICAL PRINCIPLES

Various basic principles are accepted in classical ethical theories and also seem to be presupposed in traditional codes of ethics. There is an "overlapping consensus" about the validity of these principles. But what is a principle, and which ones overlap the different theories?

A *principle* is a fundamental standard of conduct from which many other moral standards and judgments draw support for their defense and standing. For example, universal moral rights and basic professional duties can be delineated on the basis of moral principles. Ideally, a set of general principles will serve as an analytical framework of basic principles that expresses the general values underlying rules in the common morality and guidelines in professional ethics.

Three general moral principles have proved to be serviceable as a framework of principles for bioethics: respect for autonomy, beneficence, and justice. These three principles should not be construed as jointly forming a complete moral system or theory, but they can provide the beginnings of a framework through which we can begin to reason about problems in bioethics. Each is treated in a separate subsequent section.

One caution is in order about the nature and use of such principles. Moral thinking and judgment must take account of many considerations besides ethical principles and rules, and principles do not contain sufficient content to determine judgments in a great many cases. Often the most prudent course is to search for more information about cases and policies rather than trying to decide prematurely on the basis of either principles or some general theoretical commitments. More information sometimes will resolve problems and in other cases will help fix the principles that are most important in the circumstances.

Principles provide a starting point for moral judgment and policy evaluation, but, as we saw in the previous section and will see in the section on public policy (and its application in the context of public health), more content is needed than that supplied by principles alone. They are tested and reliable starting points, but they rarely are sufficient for moral thinking.

## RESPECT FOR AUTONOMY

One principle at the center of modern bioethics is *respect for autonomy*. It is rooted in the liberal moral and political tradition of the importance of individual freedom and choice. In moral philosophy *personal autonomy* refers to personal self-governance: personal rule of the self by adequate understanding while remaining free from controlling interferences by others and from personal limitations that prevent choice. *Autonomy* thus means freedom from external constraint and the presence of critical mental capacities such as understanding, intending, and voluntary decision-making capacity.[8]

To *respect* an autonomous agent is to recognize with due appreciation that person's capacities and perspective, including his or her right to hold certain views, to make certain choices, and to take certain actions based on personal values and beliefs. The moral demand that we respect the autonomy of persons can be expressed as a principle of respect for autonomy: Autonomy of action should not be subjected to control by others. The principle provides the basis for the right to make decisions, which in turn takes the form of specific autonomy-related rights.

For example, in the debate over whether autonomous, informed patients have the right to refuse self-regarding, life-sustaining medical interventions, the principle of respect for autonomy suggests a morally appropriate response. But the principle covers even simple exchanges in the medical world, such as listening carefully to patients' questions, answering the questions in the detail that respectfulness would demand, and not treating patients in a patronizing fashion.

Respect for autonomy has historically been connected to the idea that persons possess an intrinsic value independent of special circumstances that confer value. As expressed in Kantian ethics, autonomous persons are ends in themselves, determining their own destiny, and are not to be treated merely as means to the ends of others. Thus, the burden of moral justification rests on those who would restrict or prevent a person's exercise of autonomy.

To respect the autonomy of self-determining agents is to recognize them as *entitled* to determine their own destiny, with due regard to their considered evaluations and view of the world. They must be accorded the moral right to have their own opinions and to act on them (as long as those actions produce no moral violation). Thus, in evaluating the self-regarding actions of others, we are obligated to respect those people as persons with the same right to their judgments as we possess to our own, and they in turn are obligated to treat us in the same way.

Medical and nursing codes have begun in recent years to include rules that are explicitly based on this principle. For example, the first principle of the American Nurses Association Code reads as follows:

The nurse, in all professional relationships, practices with compassion and respect for the inherent dignity, worth and uniqueness of every individual, unrestricted by considerations of social or economic status, personal attributes, or the nature of health problems.[9]

The controversial problems with the noble-sounding principle of respect for autonomy, as with all moral principles, arise when we must interpret its significance for particular contexts and determine precise limits on its application and how to handle situations when it conflicts with such other moral principles as beneficence and justice. Some of the best-known problems of conflict are found in cases of overriding refusals of treatment by patients, as in Jehovah's Witnesses' refusals of blood transfusions.

Many controversies involve questions about the conditions under which a person's right to autonomous expression demands actions by others and also questions about the restrictions society may rightfully place on choices by patients or subjects when these choices conflict with other values. If an individual's choices endanger the public health, potentially harm another party, or involve a scarce resource for which a patient cannot pay, it may be justifiable to restrict exercises of autonomy. If restriction is in order, the justification will rest on some competing moral principle such as beneficence or justice. This issue of both specifying and balancing the demands made by conflicting moral principles can now be seen to apply to each of these principles.

## BENEFICENCE

The welfare of patients is the goal of health care. This welfare objective is medicine's context and justification: Clinical therapies are aimed at the promotion of health by cure or prevention of disease. This value has long been treated as a foundational value—and sometimes as *the* foundational value—in medical and nursing ethics. Among the most quoted principles in the history of codes of medical ethics is the maxim *primum non nocere*: "Above all, do no harm." Although the origins of this abstract principle are obscure and its implications often unclear, it has appeared in many medical writings and codes, and was present in nursing codes as early as Florence Nightingale's pledge for nurses (the Nightingale Pledge). Many current medical and nursing codes assert that the health professional's "primary commitment" is to protect the patient from harm and to promote the patient's welfare.

Other duties in medicine, nursing, public health, and research are expressed in terms of a *more positive* obligation to come to the assistance of those in need of treatment or in danger of injury. In the International Code of Nursing Ethics, for example, it is said that "[T]he nurse shares with other citizens the responsibility for initiating and supporting action to meet the health and social needs of the public."[10] Various sections of the *Principles of Medical Ethics* of the American Medical Association express a virtually identical point of view.

The range of duties requiring abstention from harm and positive assistance may be conveniently clustered under the single heading of *beneficence*. This term has a broad set of meanings, including the doing of good and the active promotion of good, kindness, and charity. But in the present context the principle of beneficence has a narrower meaning: It requires us to abstain from injuring others and to help others further their important and legitimate interests, largely by preventing or removing possible harms. Presumably such acts are required when they can be performed with minimal risk to the actors; one is not under an obligation of beneficence in all circumstances of risk.

According to William Frankena, the principle of beneficence can be expressed as including the following four elements: (1) One ought not to inflict evil or harm (a principle of nonmaleficence). (2) One ought to prevent evil or harm. (3) One ought to remove evil or harm. (4) One ought to do or promote good.[11] Frankena suggests that the fourth element may not be an obligation at all (being an act of benevolence that is over and above obligation) and contends that these elements appear in a hierarchical arrangement so that the first takes precedence over the second, the second over the third, and the third over the fourth.

There are philosophical reasons for separating passive nonmaleficence (as expressed in element 1) and active beneficence (as expressed in elements 2–4). Ordinary moral thinking often suggests that certain duties not to injure others are more compelling than duties to benefit them. For example, we do not consider it justifiable to kill a dying patient in order to use the patient's organs to save two others. Similarly, the obligation not to injure a patient by abandonment seems intuitively stronger than the obligation to prevent injury to a patient who has been abandoned by another (under the assumption that both are moral duties).

Despite the attractiveness of this hierarchical ordering rule, it is not firmly sanctioned by either morality or ethical theory. The obligation expressed in element 1 may not *always* outweigh those expressed in 2–4. For example, the harm inflicted in element 1 may be negligible or trivial, whereas the harm to be prevented in element 2 may be substantial: Saving a person's life by a blood transfusion clearly justifies the inflicted harm of venipuncture on the blood donor. One of the motivations for separating nonmaleficence from beneficence is that they themselves conflict when one must *either* avoid harm *or* bring aid. In such cases, one needs a decision procedure for choosing one alternative rather than another. But if the weights of the two principles can vary, as they can, there can be no mechanical decision rule asserting that one obligation must always outweigh the other.

One of the most vexing problems in ethical theory is the extent to which the principle of beneficence generates *general moral duties* that are incumbent on everyone—not because of a professional role but because morality itself makes a general demand of beneficence. Any analysis of beneficence, in the broad sense just delineated, would potentially demand severe sacrifice and extreme generosity in the moral life—giving a kidney for transplantation or donating bone marrow, for example. As a result, some philosophers have argued that this form of beneficent action is virtuous and a moral *ideal*, but not an obligation. We are not *required* by the general canons of morality to promote the good of persons, even if we are in a position to do so and the action is morally *justified*.

Several proposals have been offered in moral philosophy to resolve this problem by showing that beneficence *is* a principle of obligation, but these theoretical ventures are extraneous to our concerns here. The scope or range of acts required by the obligation of beneficence is an undecided issue, and perhaps an undecidable one. Fortunately, we do not need a resolution in the present context. That we are morally obligated on *some* occasions to assist others—at least in professional roles such as nursing, medicine, and research—is hardly a matter of moral controversy. Beneficent acts are demanded by the roles involved in fiduciary relationships between health care professionals and patients, lawyers and clients, researchers and subjects (at least in therapeutic research), bankers and customers, and so on.

We can treat the basic roles and concepts that give substance to the principle of beneficence in medicine as follows: The positive benefits that the physician and nurse are obligated to seek all involve the alleviation of disease and injury, if there is a reasonable hope of cure. The harms to be prevented, removed, or minimized are the pain, suffering, and disability of injury and disease. In addition, the physician and nurse are enjoined from *doing* harm if interventions inflict unnecessary pain and suffering on patients.

Those engaged in both medical practice and biomedical research know that risks of harm presented by interventions must be weighed against possible benefits for patients, subjects, and the public. The physician who professes to "do no harm" is not pledging never to cause harm, but rather to strive to create a positive balance of goods over inflicted harms. This is recognized in the Nuremberg Code, which enjoins: "The degree of risk to be taken should never exceed that determined by the humanitarian importance of the problem to be solved by the experiment."

### JUSTICE

Every civilized society is a cooperative venture structured by moral, legal, and cultural principles that define the terms of social cooperation. Beneficence and respect for autonomy are principles in this fabric of social order, but *justice* has been the subject of more treatises on the terms of social cooperation than any other principle. A person has been treated justly if treated according to what is fair, due, or owed. For example, if equal political rights are due all citizens, then justice is done when those rights are accorded.

The term *distributive justice* refers to fair, equitable, and appropriate distribution in society determined by justified norms of distribution that structure part of the terms of social cooperation. Usually this term refers to the distribution of primary social goods, such as economic goods and fundamental political rights. But burdens are also within its scope. Paying for forms of national health insurance is a distributed burden; Medicare checks and grants to do research are distributed benefits.[12]

Recent literature on distributive justice has tended to focus on considerations of fair economic distribution, especially unjust distributions in the form of inequalities of income between different classes of persons and unfair tax burdens on certain classes. But many problems of distributive justice exist besides issues about income and wealth, including the issues raised in prominent contemporary debates over health care distribution, as discussed in Chapter 8.

There is no single principle of justice. Somewhat like principles under the heading of beneficence, there are several *principles* of justice, each requiring specification in particular contexts. But common to almost all theories of justice is a minimal, beginning principle: Like cases should be treated alike, or, to use the language of equality, equals ought to be treated equally and unequals unequally. This elementary principle is referred to as the *formal principle of justice*, or sometimes as the *formal principle of equality*—formal because it states no particular respects in which people ought to be treated. It merely asserts that whatever respects are under consideration, if persons are equal in those respects, they should be treated alike. Thus, the formal principle of justice does not tell us how to determine equality or proportion in these matters, and it therefore lacks substance as a specific guide to conduct. Equality must here be understood as "equality in the relevant respects." Many controversies about justice arise over what should be considered the relevant characteristics for equal treatment. Principles that specify these relevant characteristics are often said to be *material* because they identify relevant properties for distribution.

The following is a sample list of major candidates for the position of valid material principles of distributive justice (though longer lists have been proposed): (1) to each person an equal share, (2) to each person according to individual need, (3) to each person according to acquisition in a free market, (4) to each person according to individual effort, (5) to each person according to societal contribution, and (6) to each person according to merit. There is no obvious barrier to acceptance of more than one of these principles, and some theories of justice accept all six as valid. Most societies use several principles in the belief that different rules are appropriate to different situations.

Because the formal and material principles leave space for differences in the interpretation of how justice applies to particular situations, philosophers have developed diverse *theories* of justice that provide material principles, specify the principles, and defend the choice of principles. These theories attempt to be more specific than the formal principle by elaborating how people are to be compared and what it means to give people their due. Egalitarian theories of justice emphasize equal access to primary goods; libertarian theories emphasize rights to social and economic liberty; and utilitarian theories emphasize a mixed use of such criteria so that public and private utility are maximized.

The *utilitarian theory* follows the main lines of the explanation of utilitarianism provided earlier, and thus economic justice is viewed as one among a number of problems concerning how to maximize value. The ideal economic distribution, utilitarians argue, is any arrangement that would have this maximizing effect.

*Egalitarianism* holds that distributions of burdens and benefits in a society are just to the extent they are equal, and deviations from equality in distribution are unjust. Most egalitarian accounts of justice are guardedly formulated, so that only *some* basic equalities among individuals take priority over their differences. In recent years an egalitarian theory discussed in the section on Kantian theories has enjoyed wide currency: John Rawls's *A Theory of Justice*. This book has as its central contention that we should distribute all economic goods and services equally except in those cases in which an unequal distribution would actually work to everyone's advantage, or at least would benefit the worst off in society.

Sharply opposed to egalitarianism is the *libertarian* theory of justice. What makes libertarian theories libertarian is the priority afforded to distinctive processes, procedures, or mechanisms for ensuring that liberty rights are recognized in economic practice—typically the rules and procedures governing social liberty and economic acquisition and exchange in free market systems. Because free choice is the pivotal goal, libertarians place a premium on the principle of respect for autonomy. In some libertarian systems, this principle is the sole basic moral principle, and there thus are no other principles of justice. We will see in Chapter 8 that many philosophers believe that this approach is fundamentally wrong because economic value is generated through an essentially communal process that our health policies must reflect if justice is to be done.

Libertarian theorists, however, explicitly reject the conclusion that egalitarian patterns of distribution represent a normative ideal. People may be equal in a host of morally significant respects (for example, entitled to equal treatment under the law and equally valued as ends in themselves), but the libertarian contends that it would be a basic violation of *justice* to regard people as deserving of equal economic returns. In particular, people are seen as having a fundamental right to own and dispense with the products of their labor as they choose, even if the exercise of this right leads to large inequalities of wealth in society. Equality and utility principles, from this libertarian perspective, sacrifice basic liberty rights to the larger public interest by coercively extracting financial resources through taxation.

These three theories of justice all capture some of our intuitive convictions about justice, and each exhibits strengths as a theory of justice. Perhaps, then, there are several equally valid, or at least equally defensible, theories of justice and just taxation. This problem will be studied further in Chapter 8.

*The Prima Facie Nature of Principles.* W. D. Ross, a prominent twentieth-century British philosopher, developed a theory intended to assist us in resolving problems of a conflict between principles. Ross's views are based on an account of what he calls prima facie duties, which he contrasts with actual duties. A *prima facie duty* is a duty that is always to be acted upon unless it conflicts on a particular occasion with an equal or stronger duty. A prima facie duty, then, is always right and binding, all other things being equal; it is conditional on not being overridden or outweighed by competing moral demands. One's *actual duty*, by contrast, is determined by an examination of the respective weights of competing prima facie duties.

Ross argues that several valid principles, all of which can conflict, express moral duties (that is, obligations). These principles do not, Ross argues, derive from either the principle of utility or Kant's categorical imperative. For example, our promises create duties of fidelity, wrongful actions create duties of reparation, and the generous gifts of our friends create duties of gratitude. Ross defends several additional duties, such as duties of self-improvement, nonmaleficence, beneficence, and justice. Unlike Kant's system and the utilitarian system, Ross's list of duties is not based on any overarching principle. He defends it simply as a reflection of our ordinary moral conventions and beliefs.

The idea that moral principles are absolute values that cannot be overridden has had a long, but troubled, history. It seems beyond serious dispute that all moral norms can be justifiably overridden in some circumstances. For example, we might withhold the truth in order to prevent someone from killing another person; and we might disclose confidential information about one person in order to protect the rights of another person. Principles, duties, and rights are not absolute or unconditional merely because they are universal. Both utilitarians and Kantians have defended their basic rule (the principle of utility and the categorical imperative) as absolute, but this claim to absoluteness is dubious. For Ross's reasons, among others, many moral philosophers have with increasing frequency come to regard principles, duties, and rights not as unbending standards but rather as strong prima facie moral demands that may be validly overridden in circumstances of competition with other moral claims.

Although no philosopher or professional code has successfully presented a system of moral rules that is free of conflicts and exceptions, this fact is no cause for either skepticism or alarm. Prima facie duties reflect the complexity of the moral life, in which a hierarchy of rules and principles is impossible. The problem of how to weight different moral principles remains unresolved, as does the best set of moral principles to form the framework of bioethics. Nonetheless, the general categories of prima facie principles discussed here have proven serviceable as a basic starting point and source for reflection on cases and problems. The main difficulty with these principles is that in most difficult contexts they must be specified.

*The Specification of Principles.* Practical moral problems often cannot, as we noticed earlier, be resolved by appeal to highly general principles. Practical problems typically require that we make our general norms suitably specific.[13] Universal norms are mere starting points that almost always must be transformed into a more specific and relevant form in order to create policies, bring controversial cases to closure, resolve conflicts, and the like. The implementation of the principles must take account of feasibility, efficiency, cultural pluralism, political procedures, uncertainty about risk, noncompliance by patients, moral dilemmas, and the like. In short, the principles must be specified for a context.

*Specification* is not a process of producing general norms; it assumes that they are already available. It is the process of making these norms concrete so that they can meaningfully guide conduct. This requires reducing the indeterminateness of the general norms to give them increased action-guiding capacity while retaining the moral commitments in the original norm. Filling out the commitments of the norms with which one starts is accomplished by narrowing the scope of the norms, not merely by explaining what the general norms mean. For example, without further specification the principle *respect the autonomy of competent persons* is too spare to handle complicated problems of what to say or ask for in clinical medicine and research involving human subjects. A mere definition of *respect for autonomy* (as, say, "allowing competent persons to exercise their liberty rights") might clarify one's meaning, but would not narrow the general norm or render it more specific. Specification is a different kind of spelling out than analysis of meaning. It adds content. For example, one possible specification of *respect the autonomy of competent persons* is "respect the autonomy of competent patients after they become incompetent by following their advance directives."

After this specification, when one subsequently encounters difficult cases of vague advance directives and must decide whether to observe them, one could further specify as follows: "Respect the autonomy of competent patients (after they become incompetent) by following their advance directives if and only if the directives are clear and relevant." As other problems and conflicts of norms emerge, the process of specification must continue. That is, already specified rules, guidelines, policies, and codes must be further specified to handle new or more complex circumstances. Such progressive specification is the way we do and should handle problems that arise in devising internal standards of medical morality.

A specification, by definition, must retain the initial norm while adding content to it. In the case of progressive specification, there must remain a transparent connection to the initial norm that gives moral authority to the string of norms that develop over time. Of course, there is always the possibility that more than one line of specification will issue from one or more initial norms. That is, different persons may offer different specifications. In this process of specification, overconfidence in one's specifications can lead to a dogmatic certainty of the sort found in the authoritative pronouncements of professional medical associations. Moral disagreement in the course of formulating specifications is inevitable and may not be eliminated by even the most conscientious specifications. In any given problematic or dilemmatic case, several competing specifications are virtually certain to be offered by reasonable parties. Alternative specifications are no more a matter of regret than are other contexts in which reflective persons offer alternative solutions to practical problems.

## POLICY AND LAW

Moral principles are often already embedded in public morality, public policies, and institutional practices, but if these values are already in place, how can moral reflection on philosophical theory assist us in the complicated task of forming and criticizing institutional policies, public policies, and laws?

### ETHICS AND PUBLIC AFFAIRS

Institutional and public policies are almost always motivated by and incorporate moral considerations. Policies such as those that fund health care for the indigent and those that protect subjects of biomedical research are examples. Moral analysis is part of good policy formation, not merely a method for evaluating already formed policy. A *policy*, in the relevant sense, is composed of a set of normative, enforceable guidelines that govern a particular area of conduct and that have been accepted by an official body, such as an institutional board of trustees, an agency of government, or a legislature. The policies of corporations, hospitals, trade groups, and professional societies are private rather than public, but the discussion that follows is directed at all forms of policy.

Many articles in this volume are concerned with the use of ethical theory for the formulation of public affairs. Joel Feinberg has made a suggestive comment about one way in which the problems raised in these essays might be viewed from an ideal vantage point:

> It is convenient to think of these problems as questions for some hypothetical and abstract political body. An answer to the question of when liberty should be limited or how wealth ideally should be distributed, for example, could be used to guide not only moralists, but also legislators and judges toward reasonable decisions in particular cases where interests, rules, or the liberties of different parties appear to conflict. . . . We must think of an ideal legislator as somewhat abstracted from the full legislative context, in that he is free to appeal directly to the public interest unencumbered by the need to please voters, to make "deals" with colleagues, or any other merely "political" considerations. . . . The principles of the ideal legislator . . . are still of the first practical importance, since they provide a target for our aspirations and a standard for judging our successes and failures.[14]

However, policy formation and criticism usually involve complex interactions between moral values and cultural and political values. A policy will be shaped by empirical data and information in relevant fields such as medicine, public health, economics, law, and the like. By taking into consideration factors such as efficiency, transparency, and public clientele acceptance, we interpret principles so that they provide a practical strategy for real-world problems that incorporate the demands of political procedures, legal constraints, uncertainty about risk, and the like.[15] For example, in this book we will consider policies pertaining to physician aid in dying, ethics committees in hospitals, public allocations for health care, regulation of risk in the workplace, protection of animal and human subjects of research, legislative definitions of death, liability for failures of disclosure and confidentiality, policies to control developments in genetics, the control of epidemics, and a host of other moral problems of institutional and public policy.

A specific example of ethics at work in the formulation of policy is found in the work of the National Commission for the Protection of Human Subjects of Biomedical and Behavioral Research, which was established in the mid-1970s by a federal law. Congress charged the commission with developing ethical guidelines for the conduct of research involving human subjects and making recommendations for policy implementation to the Department of Health, Education and Welfare (DHEW, a predecessor of the Department of Health and Human Services). To discharge its duties, the commission studied the nature and extent of various forms of research, its purposes, the ethical issues surrounding the research, present federal regulations, and the views of representatives of professional societies and federal agencies. The commission engaged in extensive public deliberations on these subjects, a process in which moral reasoning played as central a role as the information and methods supplied from other fields.

Subsequent government regulations regarding research issued by the relevant agency DHEW were developed on the basis of work provided by the commission. These public laws show the imprint of the commission in virtually every clause. The regulations cannot be regarded as exclusively ethical in orientation, but much distinctive ethical material is found in the commission documents, and ethical analysis provided the framework for its deliberations and recommendations. The commission also issued one exclusively philosophical volume, which sets forth the moral framework that underlies the various policy recommendations it made. It was and remains among the best examples of the use of moral frameworks for actual (not merely theoretical or programmatic) policy development and of a philosophical publication issued through a government-sponsored body.

Several U.S. federal branches, agencies, and courts regularly use ethical premises in the development of their health policies, rules, or decisions. These include the Centers for Disease Control and Prevention (CDC), the National Institutes of Health (NIH), the Agency for Healthcare Research and Quality (AHRQ), and the U.S. Supreme Court. Ethical analysis also often plays a prominent role in policy formation in bioethics. Examples include the widely examined work of the Oregon legislature on rationing in health care, bioethics commissions in other states, and the various iterations of federal-level bioethics commissions both in the United States and abroad. Their reports and legislative actions raise vital questions explored at various points in this book about the proper relation between government and professional groups in formulating standards of practice.

## MORALITY AND LAW

The "morality" of many actions that have a public impact is commonly gauged by whether the law prohibits that form of conduct. Law is the public's agent for translating morality into explicit social guidelines and practices and for determining punishments for offenses. Case law (judge-made law expressed in court decisions), statutory law (federal and state statutes and their accompanying administrative regulations), and international law (law from treaties and agreements among nations) set standards for science, medicine, and health care, and these sources have deeply influenced bioethics.

In these forms law has placed many issues before the public. Case law, in particular, has established influential precedents that provide material for reflection on both legal and moral questions. Prominent examples include judicial decisions about informed consent and terminating life-sustaining treatment. The line of court decisions since the Karen Ann Quinlan case in the mid-1970s, for example, constitutes an important body of material for moral reflection. Many of the chapters in this book contain selections from case law, and selections in the chapters frequently mention actual or proposed statutory law.

*Moral* evaluation is, nonetheless, very different from *legal* evaluation. Issues of legal liability, costs to the system, practicability within the litigation process, and questions of compensation demand that legal requirements be different from moral requirements.

The law is not the repository of our moral standards and values, even when the law is directly concerned with moral problems. A law-abiding person is not necessarily morally sensitive or virtuous, and from the fact that an act is legally acceptable, it does not follow that the act is morally acceptable. For example, when women and slaves were denied rights, including the right to make medical decisions, in the United States, these acts were morally unjust, despite whatever law supported them. Currently in the United States, the doctrine of employment at will permits employers such as hospitals to fire employees for unjust reasons and is (within certain limits) legal, though such dismissals are often morally unjustifiable. In short, many actions that are not illegal are morally unsustainable.

The judgment that an act is morally acceptable also does not imply that the law should permit it. For example, the position that various forms of euthanasia are morally justified is consistent with the thesis that the government should legally prohibit these acts, on grounds that it would not be possible to control potential abuses.

Bioethics in many countries is currently involved in a complex and mutually stimulating relationship with the law. The law often appeals to moral duties and rights, places sanctions on violators, and in general strengthens the social importance of moral beliefs. Morality and law share concerns over matters of basic social importance and often acknowledge the same principles, obligations, and criteria of evidence. Nevertheless, the law rightly backs away from attempting to legislate against everything that is morally wrong.

### LEGAL AND MORAL RIGHTS

Much of the modern ethical discussion that we encounter throughout this volume turns on ideas about rights, and many public policy issues concern rights or attempts to secure what are now generally called "human rights." Our political tradition itself has developed from various conceptions of natural rights or human rights. However, until the seventeenth and eighteenth centuries, problems of social and political philosophy were rarely discussed in terms of rights. New political views took root at this point in history, including the notion of universal rights. Rights came to be understood as powerful assertions of claims that demand respect and status.

Substantial differences exist between *moral* (or *human* or *natural*) *rights* and *legal rights*, because legal systems do not formally require reference to moral systems for their understanding or grounding, nor do moral systems formally require reference to legal systems. One may have a legal right to do something patently immoral or have a moral right without any corresponding legal guarantee. Legal rights are derived from political constitutions, legislative enactments, case law, and the executive orders of the highest state official. Moral rights, by contrast, exist independently of, and form a basis for, criticizing or justifying legal rights.

Philosophers have often drawn a distinction between positive and negative rights. A right to well-being—that is, a right to receive goods and services—is a *positive right*, and a right to liberty—a right not to be interfered with—is a *negative right*. The right to liberty is a negative right because no one has to do anything to honor it. Presumably all that must be done to honor negative rights is to leave people alone. The same is not true of positive rights. To honor those rights, someone has to provide something. For example, if a person has a human right to well-being and is starving, then someone has an obligation to provide that person with food.

This important distinction between positive and negative rights appears in Chapter 8 in a discussion of various rights pertaining to health and health care. Positive rights place an obligation to provide something on others, who can respond that this requirement interferes with their rights to use their resources for their chosen ends. This point has recently become a major issue in bioethics in light of the rise of theories of justice that address global poverty and that seek to restructure the global order. Assuming, as the United Nations does, that humans have a human right to have access to basic goods including housing, food, and health care, it can be argued that ensuring these rights to basic goods requires that coercive institutions such as governments, the World Health Organization, and the World Bank be designed to guarantee these positive rights to everyone. Bioethics approaches based on respect for human rights are an increasingly important part of the literature, particularly in relation to the ethics of public health. Human rights as an approach to bioethics is in large part motivated by the desire for an ethical foundation that is global, transcending the pluralistic influences and expressions of cultures, religions, societies, and communities. It would offer a broader approach than one focused on individual rights or relying on a particular ethical theory. This begs the question about the source or foundation of such transcendental rights, which remains a challenge for human rights approaches. One attempt to answer this concern is the United Nations' Declaration of Human Rights, which proposes in its preamble that human rights and dignity are self-evident.[16]

As an example of the foundation for individual rights, negative rights (rights of non-interference) have a direct connection to individual self-determination. Because general positive rights require that all members of the community yield some of their resources to advance the welfare of others by providing social goods and services, there is a natural connection in theories that emphasize positive rights to a sense of *the commons* that limits the scope of individualism. The broader the scope of positive rights in a theory, the more it will take on features of a human rights approach and the more likely it is to emphasize a scheme of social justice that confers positive rights to redistributions of resources. Several authors in this volume propose such a view, again most prominently in Chapter 8.

Accordingly, a moral system composed of a powerful set of negative obligations and rights is antithetical to a moral system composed of a powerful set of positive obligations and rights, just as a strong individualism is opposed to a strong communitarianism. Many of the conflicts that we encounter throughout this book spring from these basic differences over the existence and scope of negative and positive rights and obligations, especially regarding the number, types, and weight of positive rights and obligations.

### LAW, AUTHORITY, AND AUTONOMY

As important as autonomy rights are, no autonomy right is strong enough to entail a right to unrestricted exercises of autonomy. Acceptable liberty must be distinguished from unacceptable, but how are we to do so?

*Liberty-Limiting Principles.* Various principles have been advanced in the attempt to establish valid grounds for the limitation of autonomy. The following four "liberty-limiting principles" have all been defended.

1. *The Harm Principle:* A person's liberty is justifiably restricted to prevent harm to others caused by that person.
2. *The Principle of Paternalism:* A person's liberty is justifiably restricted to prevent harm to self caused by that person.
3. *The Principle of Legal Moralism:* A person's liberty is justifiably restricted to prevent that person's immoral behavior.
4. *The Offense Principle:* A person's liberty is justifiably restricted to prevent offense to others caused by that person.

Each of these four principles represents an attempt to balance liberty and other values. The harm principle is universally accepted as a valid liberty-limiting principle, but the other three principles are highly controversial. Only one of these controversial principles is pertinent to the controversies that arise in this volume: paternalism. Here the central problem is whether this form of justification for a restriction of liberty may ever validly be invoked, and, if so, how the principle is to be formulated.

*Paternalism.* The word *paternalism* refers to treating individuals in the way that a parent treats his or her child. Paternalism is the intentional limitation of the autonomy of one person by another, where the person who limits autonomy appeals exclusively to grounds of benefit for the person whose autonomy is limited. The essence of paternalism is an overriding of a person's autonomy on grounds of providing that person with a benefit—in medicine, a medical benefit.

Examples in medicine include involuntary commitment to institutions for treatment, intervention to stop "rational" suicides, resuscitating patients who have asked not to be resuscitated, withholding medical information that patients have requested, compulsory care, denial of an innovative therapy to patients who wish to try it, and some government efforts to promote health. Other health-related examples include laws requiring motorcyclists to wear helmets and motorists to wear seat belts and the regulations of governmental agencies such as the Food and Drug Administration that prevent people from purchasing possibly harmful or inefficacious drugs. In all cases, the motivation is the beneficent promotion of individuals' health and welfare.

Paternalism has been under attack in recent years, especially by defenders of the autonomy rights of patients. The latter hold that physicians and government officials intervene too often and assume too much paternalistic control over patients' choices. Philosophers and lawyers have generally supported the view that the autonomy of patients is the decisive factor in the patient–physician relationship and that interventions can be valid only when patients are in some measure unable to make voluntary choices or to perform autonomous actions. The point is that patients can be so ill that their judgments or voluntary abilities are significantly affected, or they may be incapable of grasping important information about their case, thus being in no position to reach carefully reasoned decisions about their medical treatment or their purchase of drugs. Beyond this form of intervention, many have argued, paternalism is not warranted.

However, paternalism also has defenders, even under some conditions in which autonomous choice is overridden. Any careful proponent of a principle of paternalism will specify precisely which goods and needs deserve paternalistic protection and the conditions under which intervention is warranted. Some writers have argued that one is justified in interfering with a person's autonomy only if the interference protects the person against his or her own actions where those actions are extremely and unreasonably risky (for example, refusing a life-saving therapy in nonterminal situations) or are potentially dangerous and irreversible in effect (as are some drugs). According to this position, paternalism is justified if and only if the harms prevented from occurring to the person are greater than the harms or indignities (if any) caused by interference with his or her liberty and if it can be universally justified, under relevantly similar circumstances, always to treat persons in this way.

This moderate formulation of paternalism still leaves many critics resolutely opposed to all possible uses of this principle. Their arguments against paternalism turn on some defense of the importance of the principle of respect for autonomy. We will many times encounter such appeals in this volume, especially as applied to rightful state intervention in order to benefit patients or subjects without their authorization.

T. L. B.

J. P. K.

## NOTES

1. See, for example, Tom L. Beauchamp and James F. Childress, *Principles of Biomedical Ethics*, 6th ed. (New York: Oxford University Press, 2008), especially chap. 10; Bernard Gert, Charles M. Culver, and Danner K. Clouser, *Bioethics: A Return to Fundamentals* (New York: Oxford University Press, 1997); Sissela Bok, *Common Values* (Columbia, MO: University of Missouri Press, 1995), 13–23, 50–59; Leigh Turner, "Zones of Consensus and Zones of Conflict: Questioning the 'Common Morality' Presumption in Bioethics," *Kennedy Institute of Ethics Journal* 13, no. 3 (2003), 193–218.

2. *Tarasoff v. Regents of the University of California*, California Supreme Court (17 California Reports, 3d Series, 425. Decided July 1, 1976).

3. Cf. Walter Sinnott-Armstrong, *Moral Dilemmas* (Oxford: Basil Blackwell, 1988), 216–27; D. D. Raphael, *Moral Philosophy* (Oxford: Oxford University Press, 1981), 64–65; Daniel Statman, "Hard Cases and Moral Dilemmas," *Law and Philosophy* 15 (1996), 117–48.

4. Immanuel Kant, *Foundations of the Metaphysics of Morals*, 2nd ed., trans. Lewis White Beck (New York: Macmillan, 1990), 46.

5. Albert R. Jonsen, "Casuistry as Methodology in Clinical Ethics," *Theoretical Medicine* 12 (December 1991), 295–307; Jonsen and Stephen Toulmin, *Abuse of Casuistry* (Berkeley, CA: University of California Press, 1988); Jonsen, "Casuistry: An Alternative or Complement to Principles?" *Kennedy Institute of Ethics Journal* 5 (1995), 237–51.

6. John D. Arras, "Principles and Particularity: The Role of Cases in Bioethics," *Indiana Law Journal* 69 (Fall 1994), 983–1014 (with two replies); and "Getting Down to Cases: The Revival of Casuistry in Bioethics," *Journal of Medicine and Philosophy* 16 (1991), 29–51.

7. Jonsen and Toulmin, *Abuse of Casuistry*, 16–19, 66–67; Jonsen, "Casuistry and Clinical Ethics," 67, 71.

8. For strikingly different autonomy-based theories, see H. Tristram Engelhardt Jr., *The Foundations of Bioethics*, 2nd ed. (New York: Oxford University Press, 1996); Joel Feinberg, *The Moral Limits of the Criminal Law* (New York: Oxford University Press, 1984–87); Jay Katz, *The Silent World of Doctor and Patient* (New York: The Free Press, 1984); and various essays in James S. Taylor, ed., *Personal Autonomy* (New York: Cambridge University Press, 2005).

9. American Nurses Association, *Code of Ethics for Nurses with Interpretive Statements* (Silver Spring, MD: American Nurses Publishing, 2001), quoted from the statement at http://nursingworld.org/ethics/chcode.htm (as posted February 15, 2007).

10. 1953 and 1973 International Codes of Nursing Ethics of the International Council of Nurses.

11. William Frankena, *Ethics*, 2nd ed. (Englewood Cliffs, NJ: Prentice-Hall, 1973), 47.

12. For accounts of justice that have influenced contemporary bioethics, see John Rawls, *A Theory of Justice* (Cambridge, MA: Harvard University Press, 1971); Norman Daniels, "Equity and Population Health: Toward a Broader Bioethics Agenda," *Hastings Center Report* 36, no. 4 (2006), 22–35; Madison Powers and Ruth Faden, *Social Justice: The Moral Foundations of Public Health and Health Policy* (New York: Oxford University Press, 2006); Thomas W. Pogge, *Freedom from Poverty as a Human Right: Who Owes What to the Very Poor?* (Oxford: Oxford University Press, 2007).

13. Henry S. Richardson, "Specifying Norms as a Way to Resolve Concrete Ethical Problems," *Philosophy and Public Affairs* 19 (Fall 1990), 279–310; and "Specifying, Balancing, and Interpreting Bioethical Principles," *Journal of Medicine and Philosophy* 25 (2000), 285–307.

14. Joel Feinberg, *Social Philosophy* (Englewood Cliffs, NJ: Prentice-Hall, 1973), 2–3.

15. Dennis Thompson, "Philosophy and Policy," *Philosophy and Public Affairs* 14 (Spring 1985), 205–18.

16. United Nations, *Universal Declaration of Human Rights*, 1948.

# DAVID C. THOMASMA

## Telling the Truth to Patients: A Clinical Ethics Exploration

David Thomasma was professor of medical ethics in the Neiswanger Institute for Bioethics and Health Policy at Loyola University Chicago Medical Center, where he directed the Medical Humanities Program. His many publications focused heavily on the Doctor-Patient Relationship. His collaborations with Dr. Edmund Pellegrino produced several books, including *For the Patient's Good: The Restoration of Beneficence in Health Care* (Oxford).

### REASONS FOR TELLING THE TRUTH

. . . In all human relationships, the truth is told for a myriad of reasons. A summary of the prominent reasons are that it is a right, a utility, and a kindness.

It is a right to be told the truth because respect for the person demands it. As Kant argued, human society would soon collapse without truth telling, because it is the basis of interpersonal trust, covenants, contracts, and promises.

The truth is a utility as well, because persons need to make informed judgments about their actions. It is a mark of maturity that individuals advance and grow morally by becoming more and more self-aware of their needs, their motives, and their limitations. All these steps toward maturity require honest and forthright communication, first from parents and later also from siblings, friends, lovers, spouses, children, colleagues, co-workers, and caregivers.[1]

Finally, it is a kindness to be told the truth, a kindness rooted in virtue precisely because persons to whom lies are told will of necessity withdraw from important, sometimes life-sustaining and life-saving relationships. Similarly, those who tell lies poison not only their relationships but themselves, rendering themselves incapable of virtue and moral growth.[2] . . .

### OVERRIDING THE TRUTH

. . . Not all of us act rationally and autonomously at all times. Sometimes we are under sufficient stress

From *Cambridge Quarterly of Healthcare Ethics* 3 (1994), 375–82. Copyright © 1994 Cambridge University Press. Reprinted with permission.

that others must act to protect us from harm. This is called necessary paternalism. Should we become seriously ill, others must step in and rescue us if we are incapable of doing it ourselves. . . .

#### IN GENERAL RELATIONSHIPS

In each of the three main reasons why the truth must be told, as a right, a utility, and a kindness, lurk values that may from time to time become more important than the truth. When this occurs, the rule of truth telling is trumped, that is, overridden by a temporarily more important principle. The ultimate value in all instances is the survival of the community and/or the well-being of the individual. Does this mean for paternalistic reasons, without the person's consent, the right to the truth, the utility, and the kindness, can be shunted aside? The answer is "yes." The truth in a relationship responds to a multivariate complexity of values, the context for which helps determine which values in that relationship should predominate.

Nothing I have said thus far suggests that the truth may be treated in a cavalier fashion or that it can be withheld from those who deserve it for frivolous reasons. The only values that can trump the truth are recipient survival, community survival, and the ability to absorb the full impact of the truth at a particular time. All these are only temporary trump cards in any event. They only can be played under certain limited conditions because respect for persons is a foundational value in all relationships.

It is time to look more carefully at one particular form of human relationship, the relationship between the doctor and the patient or sometimes between other healthcare providers and the patient.

Early in the 1960s, studies were done that revealed the majority of physicians would not disclose a diagnosis of cancer to a patient. Reasons cited were mostly those that derived from nonmaleficence. Physicians were concerned that such a diagnosis might disturb the equanimity of a patient and might lead to desperate acts. Primarily physicians did not want to destroy their patients' hope. By the middle 1970s, however, repeat studies brought to light a radical shift in physician attitudes. Unlike earlier views, physicians now emphasized patient autonomy and informed consent over paternalism. In the doctor–patient relation, this meant the majority of physicians stressed the patient's right to full disclosure of diagnosis and prognosis.

One might be tempted to ascribe this shift of attitudes to the growing patients' rights and autonomy movements in the philosophy of medicine and in public affairs. No doubt some of the change can be attributed to this movement. But also treatment interventions for cancer led to greater optimism about modalities that could offer some hope to patients. Thus, to offer them full disclosure of their diagnosis no longer was equivalent to a death sentence. Former powerlessness of the healer was supplanted with technological and pharmaceutical potentialities.

A more philosophical analysis of the reasons for a shift comes from a consideration of the goal of medicine. The goal of all healthcare relations is to receive/ provide help for an illness such that no further harm is done to the patient, especially in that patient's vulnerable state.[3] The vulnerability arises because of increased dependency. Presumably, the doctor will not take advantage of this vulnerable condition by adding to it through inappropriate use of power or the lack of compassion. Instead, the vulnerable person should be assisted back to a state of human equality, if possible, free from the prior dependency.[4]

First, the goal of the healthcare giver–patient relation is essentially to restore the patient's autonomy. Thus, respect for the right of the patient to the truth is measured against this goal. If nothing toward that goal can be gained by telling the truth at a particular time, still it must be told for other reasons. Yet, if the truth would impair the restoration of autonomy, then it may be withheld on grounds of potential harm. Thus the goal of the healing relationship enters into the calculus of values that are to be protected.

Second, most healthcare relationships of an interventionist character are temporary, whereas relationships involving primary care, prevention, and chronic or dying care are more permanent. These differences also have a bearing on truth telling. During a short encounter with healthcare strangers, patients and healthcare providers will of necessity require the truth more readily than during a long-term relation among near friends. In the short term, decisions, often dramatically important ones, need to be made in a compressed period. There is less opportunity to maneuver or delay for other reasons, even if there are concerns about the truth's impact on the person.

Over a longer period, the truth may be withheld for compassionate reasons more readily. Here, the patient and physician or nurse know one another. They are more likely to have shared some of their values. In this context, it is more justifiable to withhold the truth temporarily in favor of more important long-term values, which are known in the relationship.

Finally, the goal of healthcare relations is treatment of an illness. An illness is far broader than its subset, disease. Illness can be viewed as a disturbance in the life of an individual, perhaps due to many nonmedical factors. A disease, by contrast, is a medically caused event that may respond to more interventionist strategies.[5]

Helping one through an illness is a far greater personal task than doing so for a disease. A greater, more enduring bond is formed. The strength of this bond may justify withholding the truth as well, although in the end "the truth will always out."

## CLINICAL CASE CATEGORIES

The general principles about truth telling have been reviewed, as well as possible modifications formed from the particularities of the healthcare professional–patient relationship. Now I turn to some contemporary examples of how clinical ethics might analyze the hierarchy of values surrounding truth telling.

There are at least five clinical case categories in which truth telling becomes problematic: intervention cases, long-term care cases, cases of dying patients, prevention cases, and nonintervention cases.

### INTERVENTION CASES

Of all clinically difficult times to tell the truth, two typical cases stand out. The first usually involves a mother of advanced age with cancer. The family might beg the surgeon not to tell her what has been discovered for fear that "Mom might just go off the deep end." The movie *Dad*, starring Jack Lemmon, had as its centerpiece the notion that Dad could not tolerate the idea of cancer. Once told, he went into a psychotic shock that ruptured standard relationships with the doctors, the hospital, and the family. However, because this diagnosis requires patient participation for chemotherapeutic interventions and the time is short, the truth must be faced directly. Only if there is not to be intervention might one withhold the truth from the patient for a while, at the family's request, until the patient is able to cope with the reality. A contract about the time allowed before telling the truth might be a good idea.

The second case is that of ambiguous genitalia. A woman, 19 years old, comes for a checkup because she plans to get married and has not yet had a period. She is very mildly retarded. It turns out that she has no vagina, uterus, or ovaries but does have an undescended testicle in her abdomen. She is actually a he. Should she be told this fundamental truth about herself? Those who argue for the truth do so on grounds that she will eventually find out, and more of her subsequent life will have been ruined by the lies and disingenuousness of others. Those who argue against the truth usually prevail. National standards exist in this regard. The young woman is told that she has something like a "gonadal mass" in her abdomen that might turn into cancer if not removed, and an operation is performed. She is assisted to remain a female.

More complicated still is a case of a young Hispanic woman, a trauma accident victim, who is gradually coming out of a coma. She responds only to commands such as "move your toes." Because she is now incompetent, her mother and father are making all care decisions in her case. Her boyfriend is a welcome addition to the large, extended family. However, the physicians discover that she is pregnant. The fetus is about 5 weeks old. Eventually, if she does not recover, her surrogate decision makers will have to be told about the pregnancy, because they will be involved in the terrible decisions about continuing the life of the fetus even if it is a risk to the mother's recovery from the coma. This revelation will almost certainly disrupt current family relationships and the role of the boyfriend. Further, if the mother is incompetent to decide, should not the boyfriend, as presumed father, have a say in the decision about his own child?

In this case, revelation of the truth must be carefully managed. The pregnancy should be revealed

only on a "need to know" basis, that is, only when the survival of the young woman becomes critical. She is still progressing moderately towards a stable state.

## LONG-TERM CASES

Rehabilitation medicine provides one problem of truth telling in this category. If a young man has been paralyzed by a football accident, his recovery to some level of function will depend upon holding out hope. As he struggles to strengthen himself, the motivation might be a hope that caregivers know to be false, that he may someday be able to walk again. Yet this falsehood is not corrected, lest he slip into despair. Hence, because this is a long-term relationship, the truth will be gradually discovered by the patient under the aegis of encouragement by his physical therapists, nurses, and physicians, who enter his life as near friends.

## CASES OF DYING PATIENTS

Sometimes, during the dying process, the patient asks directly, "Doctor, am I dying?" Physicians are frequently reluctant to "play God" and tell the patient how many days or months or years they have left. This reluctance sometimes bleeds over into a less-than-forthright answer to the question just asked. A surgeon with whom I make rounds once answered this question posed by a terminally ill cancer patient by telling her that she did not have to worry about her insurance running out!

Yet in every case of dying patients, the truth can be gradually revealed such that the patient learns about dying even before the family or others who are resisting telling the truth. Sometimes, without directly saying "you are dying," we are able to use interpretative truth and comfort the patient. If a car driver who has been in an accident and is dying asks about other family members in the car who are already dead, there is no necessity to tell him the truth. Instead, he can be told that "they are being cared for" and that the important thing right now is that he be comfortable and not in pain. One avoids the awful truth because he may feel responsible and guilt ridden during his own dying hours if he knew that the rest of his family were already dead.

## PREVENTION CASES

A good example of problems associated with truth telling in preventive medicine might come from screening. The high prevalence of prostate cancer among men over 50 years old may suggest the utility of cancer screening. An annual checkup for men over

40 years old is recommended. Latent and asymptomatic prostate cancer is often clinically unsuspected and is present in approximately 30% of men over 50 years of age. If screening were to take place, about 16.5 million men in the United States alone would be diagnosed with prostate cancer, or about 2.4 million men each year. As of now, only 120,000 cases are newly diagnosed each year. Thus, as Timothy Moon noted in a recent sketch of the disease, "a majority of patients with prostate cancer that is not clinically diagnosed will experience a benign course throughout their lifetime."[6]

The high incidence of prostate cancer coupled with a very low malignant potential would entail a whole host of problems if subjected to screening. Detection would force patients and physicians to make very difficult and life-altering treatment decisions. Among them are removal of the gland (with impotence a possible outcome), radiation treatment, and most effective of all, surgical removal of the gonads (orchiectomy). But why consider these rather violent interventions if the probable outcome of neglect will overwhelmingly be benign? For this reason the U.S. Preventive Services Task Force does not recommend either for or against screening for prostate cancer.[7] Quality-of-life issues would take precedence over the need to know.

### NONINTERVENTION CASES

This last example more closely approximates the kind of information one might receive as a result of gene mapping. This information could tell you of the likelihood or probability of encountering a number of diseases through genetic heritage, for example, adult onset or type II diabetes, but could not offer major interventions for most of them (unlike a probability for diabetes).

Some evidence exists from recent studies that the principle of truth telling now predominates in the doctor–patient relationship. Doctors were asked about revealing diagnosis for Huntington's disease and multiple sclerosis, neither of which is subject to a cure at present. An overwhelming majority would consider full disclosure. This means that, even in the face of diseases for which we have no cure, truth telling seems to take precedence over protecting the patient from imagined harms.

The question of full disclosure acquires greater poignancy in today's medicine, especially with respect to Alzheimer's disease and genetic disorders that may be diagnosed in utero. There are times when our own

scientific endeavors lack a sufficient conceptual and cultural framework around which to assemble facts. The facts can overwhelm us without such conceptual frameworks. The future of genetics poses just such a problem. In consideration of the new genetics, this might be the time to stress values over the truth.

### CONCLUSION

Truth in the clinical relationship is factored in with knowledge and values.

First, truth is contextual. Its revelation depends upon the nature of the relationship between the doctor and patient and the duration of that relationship.

Second, truth is a secondary good. Although important, other primary values take precedence over the truth. The most important of these values is survival of the individual and the community. A close second would be preservation of the relationship itself.

Third, truth is essential for healing an illness. It may not be as important for curing a disease. That is why, for example, we might withhold the truth from the woman with ambiguous genitalia, curing her disease (having a gonad) in favor of maintaining her health (being a woman).

Fourth, withholding the truth is only a temporary measure. *In vino, veritas* it is said. The truth will eventually come out, even if in a slip of the tongue. Its revelation, if it is to be controlled, must always aim at the good of the patient for the moment.

At all times, the default mode should be that the truth is told. If, for some important reason, it is not to be immediately revealed in a particular case, a truth-management protocol should be instituted so that all caregivers on the team understand how the truth will eventually be revealed.

### NOTES

1. Bok, S. *Lying: Moral Choice in Public and Personal Life.* New York: Vintage Books, 1989.

2. Pellegrino, E. D., Thomasma, D. C. *The Virtues in Medical Practice.* New York: Oxford University Press, 1993.

3. Pellegrino, E. D., Thomasma, D. C. *For the Patient's Good: The Restoration of Beneficence in Health Care.* New York: Oxford University Press, 1998.

4. Cassell, E. The nature of suffering and the goals of medicine. *New England Journal of Medicine* 1982; 306(11): 639–45.

5. See Nordenfelt, L., issue editor. Concepts of health and their consequences for health care. *Theoretical Medicine* 1993; 14(4).

6. Moon, T. D. Prostate cancer. *Journal of the American Geriatrics Society* 1992; 40: 622–7 (quote from 626).

7. See note 6. Moon. 1992; 40: 622–7.

# Section 3:  Confidentiality

## Confidentiality in Medicine—A Decrepit Concept

### Mark Siegler

Mark Siegler calls attention to the impossibility of preserving the confidentiality traditionally associated with the physician–patient relationship. In the modern hospital, a great many people have legitimate access to a patient's chart and so to all medical, social, and financial information the patient has provided. Yet the loss of confidentiality is a threat to good medical care. Confidentiality protects a patient at a time of vulnerability and promotes the trust that is necessary for effective diagnosis and treatment. Siegler concludes by suggesting some possible solutions for preserving confidentiality while meeting the needs of others to know certain things about the patient.

Medical confidentiality, as it has traditionally been understood by patients and doctors, no longer exists. This ancient medical principle, which has been included in every physician's oath and code of ethics since Hippocratic times, has become old, worn-out, and useless; it is a decrepit concept. Efforts to preserve it appear doomed to failure and often give rise to more problems than solutions. Psychiatrists have tacitly acknowledged the impossibility of ensuring the confidentiality of medical records by choosing to establish a separate, more secret record. The following case illustrates how the confidentiality principle is compromised systematically in the course of routine medical care.

A patient of mine with mild chronic obstructive pulmonary disease was transferred from the surgical intensive-care unit to a surgical nursing floor two days after an elective cholecystectonomy. On the day of transfer, the patient saw a respiratory therapist writing in his medical chart (the therapist was recording the results of an arterial blood gas analysis) and became concerned about the confidentiality of his hospital records. The patient threatened to leave the hospital prematurely unless I could guarantee that the confidentiality of his hospital record would be respected.

Supported by a grant (OSS-8018097) from the National Science Foundation and by the National Endowment for the Humanities. The views expressed are those of the author and do not necessarily reflect those of the National Science Foundation or the National Endowment for the Humanities. Mark Siegler. From "Confidentiality in Medicine- A Decrepit Concept," *New England Journal of Medicine*, Vol. 307, no. 24. (1982):1518–521. Copyright © 1982 MASSACHUSETTS MEDICAL SOCIETY. All rights reserved. Reproduced by permission.

The patient's complaint prompted me to enumerate the number of persons who had both access to his hospital record and a reason to examine it. I was amazed to learn that at least 25 and possibly as many as 100 health professionals and administrative personnel at our university hospital had access to the patient's record and that all of them had a legitimate need, indeed a professional responsibility, to open and use that chart. These persons included 6 attending physicians (the primary physician, the surgeon, the pulmonary consultant and others); 12 house officers (medical, surgical, intensive-care unit, and "covering" house staff); 20 nursing personnel (on three shifts); 6 respiratory therapists; 3 nutritionists; 2 clinical pharmacists; 15 students (from medicine, nursing, respiratory therapy, and clinical pharmacy); 4 unit secretaries; 4 hospital financial officers; and 4 chart reviewers (utilization review, quality assurance review, tissue review, and insurance auditor). It is of interest that this patient's problem was straightforward, and he therefore did not require many other technical and support services that the modern hospital provides. For example, he did not need multiple consultants and fellows, such specialized procedures as dialysis, or social workers, chaplains, physical therapists, occupational therapists, and the like.

Upon completing my survey I reported to the patient that I estimated that at least 75 health professionals and hospital personnel had access to his medical record. I suggested to the patient that these people were all involved in providing or supporting his health-care services. They were, I assured him, working for him. Despite my reassurances the patient was obviously distressed and retorted, "I always believed that medical confidentiality was part of a doctor's code of ethics. Perhaps you should tell me just what you people mean by 'confidentiality'!"

## Two Aspects of Medical Confidentiality

### Confidentiality and Third-Party Interests

Previous discussions of medical confidentiality usually have focused on the tension between a physician's responsibility to keep information divulged by patients secret and a physician's legal and moral duty, on occasion, to reveal such confidences to third parties, such as families, employers, public health authorities, or police authorities. In all these instances, the central question relates to the stringency of the physician's obligation to maintain patient confidentiality when the health, well-being, and safety of identifiable others or of society in general would be threatened by a failure to reveal information about the patient. The tension in such cases is between the good of the patient and the good of others.

### Confidentiality and the Patient's Interest

As the example above illustrates, further challenges to confidentiality arise because the patient's personal interest in maintaining confidentiality comes into conflict with his personal interest in receiving the best possible health care. Modern high-technology health care is available principally in hospitals (often, teaching hospitals), requires many trained and specialized workers (a "health-care team"), and is very costly. The existence of such teams means that information that previously had been held in confidence by an individual physician will now necessarily be disseminated to many members of the team. Furthermore, since health-care teams are expensive and few patients can afford to pay such costs directly, it becomes essential to grant access to the patient's medical record to persons who are responsible for obtaining third-party payment. These persons include chart reviewers, financial officers, insurance auditors, and quality-of-care assessors. Finally, as medicine expands from a narrow, disease-based model to a model that encompasses psychological, social, and economic problems, not only will the size of the health-care team and medical costs increase, but more sensitive information (such as one's personal habits and financial condition) will now be

included in the medical record and will no longer be confidential.

The point I wish to establish is that hospital medicine, the rise of health-care teams, the existence of third-party insurance programs, and the expanding limits of medicine all appear to be responses to the wishes of people for better and more comprehensive medical care. But each of these developments necessarily modifies our traditional understanding of medical confidentiality.

## The Role of Confidentiality in Medicine

Confidentiality serves a dual purpose in medicine. In the first place, it acknowledges respect for the patient's sense of individuality and privacy. The patient's most personal physical and psychological secrets are kept confidential in order to decrease a sense of shame and vulnerability. Secondly, confidentiality is important in improving the patient's health care—a basic goal of medicine. The promise of confidentiality permits people to trust (i.e., have confidence) that information revealed to a physician in the course of a medical encounter will not be disseminated further. In this way patients are encouraged to communicate honestly and forthrightly with their doctors. This bond of trust between patient and doctor is vitally important both in the diagnostic process (which relies on an accurate history) and subsequently in the treatment phase, which often depends as much on the patient's trust in the physician as it does on medications and surgery. These two important functions of confidentiality are as important now as they were in the past. They will not be supplanted entirely either by improvements in medical technology or by recent changes in relations between some patients and doctors toward a rights-based, consumerist model.

## Possible Solutions to the Confidentiality Problem

First of all, in all nonbureaucratic, noninstitutional medical encounters—that is, in the millions of doctor–patient encounters that take place in physicians' offices, where more privacy can be preserved—meticulous care should be taken to guarantee that patients' medical and personal information will be kept confidential.

Secondly, in such settings as hospitals or large-scale group practices, where many persons have opportunities to examine the medical record, we should aim to provide access only to those who have "a need to know." This could be accomplished through such administrative changes as dividing the entire record into several sections—for example, a medical and financial section—and permitting only health professionals access to the medical information.

The approach favored by many psychiatrists—that of keeping a psychiatric record separate from the general medical record—is an understandable strategy but one that is not entirely satisfactory and that should not be generalized. The keeping of separate psychiatric records implies that psychiatry and medicine are different undertakings and thus drives deeper the wedge between them and between physical and psychological illness. Furthermore, it is often vitally important for internists or surgeons to know that a patient is being seen by a psychiatrist or is taking a particular medication. When separate records are kept, this information may not be available. Finally, if generalized, the practice of keeping a separate psychiatric record could lead to the unacceptable consequence of having a separate record for each type of medical problem.

Patients should be informed about what is meant by "medical confidentiality." We should establish the distinction between information about the patient that generally will be kept confidential regardless of the interest of third parties and information that will be exchanged among members of the health-care team in order to provide care for the patient. Patients should be made aware of the large number of persons in the modern hospital who require access to the medical record in order to serve the patient's medical and financial interests.

Finally, at some point most patients should have an opportunity to review their medical record and to make informed choices about whether their entire record is to be available to everyone or whether certain portions of the record are privileged and should be accessible only to their principal physician or to others designated explicitly by the patient. This approach would rely on traditional informed-consent procedural standards and might permit the patient to balance the personal value of medical confidentiality against the personal value of high-technology, team health care. There is no reason that the same procedure should not be used with psychiatric records instead of the arbitrary system now employed, in which everything related to psychiatry is kept secret.

## Afterthought: Confidentiality and Indiscretion

There is one additional aspect of confidentiality that is rarely included in discussions of the subject. I am referring here to the wanton, often inadvertent, but avoidable exchanges of confidential information that occur frequently in hospital rooms, elevators, cafeterias, doctors' offices, and at cocktail parties. Of course, as more people have access to medical information about the patient the potential for this irresponsible abuse of confidentiality increases geometrically.

Such mundane breaches of confidentiality are probably of greater concern to most patients than the broader issue of whether their medical records may be entered into a computerized data bank or whether a respiratory therapist is reviewing the results of an arterial blood gas determination. Somehow, privacy is violated and a sense of shame is heightened when intimate secrets are revealed to people one knows or is close to—friends, neighbors, acquaintances, or hospital roommates—rather than when they are disclosed to an anonymous bureaucrat sitting at a computer terminal in a distant city or to a health professional who is acting in an official capacity.

I suspect that the principles of medical confidentiality, particularly those reflected in most medical codes of ethics, were designed principally to prevent just this sort of embarrassing personal indiscretion rather than to maintain (for social, political, or economic reasons) the absolute secrecy of doctor–patient communications. In this regard, it is worth noting that Percival's Code of Medical Ethics (1803) includes the following admonition: "Patients should be interrogated concerning their complaint in a tone of voice which cannot be overheard" [Leake, C. D., ed., *Percival's Medical Ethics*, Baltimore: Williams and Wilkins, 1927]. We in the medical profession frequently neglect these simple courtesies.

## Conclusion

The principle of medical confidentiality described in medical codes of ethics and still believed in by patients no longer exists. In this respect, it is a decrepit concept. Rather than perpetuate the myth of confidentiality and invest energy vainly to preserve it, the public and the profession would be better served if they devoted their attention to determining which aspects of the original principle of confidentiality are worth retaining. Efforts could then be directed to salvaging those.

---

# Section 3:  Human Reproductive Cloning

---

## The Wisdom of Repugnance

Leon R. Kass

Leon Kass argues that the repulsion many people feel about the possibility of human cloning springs from a recognition that it violates our nature as embodied, engendered, and engendering beings and the social relations we have because of that nature. First, cloning would distort the cloned person's sense of individuality and social identity. Second, like IVF and prenatal genetic testing, cloning would transform procreation into manufacture and children into commodities. Third, cloning would encourage parents to regard children as property.

In contrast to those who see cloning as simply another technique, like AI and IVF, for helping individuals exercise their "right" to reproduce, Kass regards cloning as a significant slide down the slippery slope toward the "sperm to term" production of genetically designed children. In view of all these considerations, Kass urges an international legal ban on human cloning.

From *The New Republic*, 2 June 1997, pp. 17–26. Reprinted by permission of the author.

..."Offensive." "Grotesque." "Revolting." "Repugnant." "Repulsive." These are the words most commonly heard regarding the prospect of human cloning. Such reactions come both from the man or woman in the street and from the intellectuals, from believers and atheists, from humanists and scientists. Even Dolly's creator has said he "would find it offensive" to clone a human being.

People are repelled by many aspects of human cloning. They recoil from the prospect of mass production of human beings, with large clones of look-alikes, compromised in their individuality, the idea of father–son or mother–daughter twins; the bizarre prospects of a woman giving birth to and rearing a genetic copy of herself, her spouse or even her deceased father or mother; the grotesqueness of conceiving a child as an exact replacement for another who has died; the utilitarian creation of embryonic genetic duplicates of oneself, to be frozen away or created when necessary, in case of need for homologous tissues or organs for transplantation; the narcissism of those who would clone themselves and the arrogance of others who think they know who deserves to be cloned or which genotype any child-to-be should be thrilled to receive; the Frankensteinian hubris to create human life and increasingly to control its destiny; man playing God. Almost no one finds any of the suggested reasons for human cloning compelling; almost everyone anticipates its possible misuses and abuses. Moreover, many people feel oppressed by the sense that there is probably nothing we can do to prevent it from happening. This makes the prospect all the more revolting.

Revulsion is not an argument; and some of yesterday's repugnances are today calmly accepted—though, one must add, not always for the better. In crucial cases, however, repugnance is the emotional expression of deep wisdom, beyond reason's powerfully to articulate it. Can anyone really give an argument fully adequate to the horror which is father–daughter incest (even with consent), or having sex with animals, or mutilating a corpse, or eating human flesh, or even just (just!) raping or murdering another human being?

Would anybody's failure to give full rational justification for his or her revulsion at these practices make that revulsion ethically suspect? Not at all. On the contrary, we are suspicious of those who think that they can rationalize away our horror, say, by trying to explain the enormity of incest with arguments only about the genetic risks of inbreeding.

The repugnance at human cloning belongs in this category. We are repelled by the prospect of cloning human beings not because of the strangeness or novelty of the undertaking, but because we intuit and feel, immediately and without argument, the violation of things that we rightfully hold dear. Repugnance, here as elsewhere, revolts against the excesses of human willfulness, warning us not to transgress what is unspeakably profound. Indeed, in this age in which everything is held to be permissible so long as it is freely done, in which our given human nature no longer commands respect, in which our bodies are regarded as mere instruments of our autonomous rational wills, repugnance may be the only voice left that speaks up to defend the central core of our humanity. Shallow are the souls that have forgotten how to shudder.

The goods protected by repugnance are generally overlooked by our customary ways of approaching all new biomedical technologies. The way we evaluate cloning ethically will in fact be shaped by how we characterize it descriptively, by the context into which we place it, and by the perspective from which we view it. The first task for ethics is proper description. And here is where our failure begins.

Typically, cloning is discussed in one or more of three familiar contexts, which one might call the technological, the liberal and the meliorist. Under the first, cloning will be seen as an extension of existing techniques for assisting reproduction and determining the genetic makeup of children. Like them, cloning is to be regarded as a neutral technique, with no inherent meaning or goodness, but subject to multiple uses, some good, some bad. The morality of cloning thus depends absolutely on the goodness or badness of the motives and intentions of the cloners: as one bioethicist defender of cloning puts it, "the ethics must be judged [only] by the way the parents nurture and rear their resulting child and whether they bestow the same love and affection on a child brought into existence by a technique of assisted reproduction as they would on a child born in the usual way."

The liberal (or libertarian or liberationist) perspective sets cloning in the context of rights, freedoms and personal empowerment. Cloning is just a new option for exercising an individual's right to reproduce or to have the kind of child that he or she wants. Alternatively, cloning enhances our liberation (especially women's liberation) from the confines of nature, the vagaries of chance, or the necessity for sexual mating. Indeed, it liberates women from the need for men altogether, for the process requires only eggs, nuclei and (for the time being) uteri—plus, of course, a healthy dose of our (allegedly "masculine") manipulative science that likes to do all these things to mother nature and nature's mothers. For those who hold this outlook, the only moral restraints on cloning are adequately informed consent and the avoidance of bodily harm. If no one is cloned without her consent, and if the clonant is not physically damaged, then the liberal conditions for licit, hence moral, conduct are met. Worries that go beyond violating the will or maiming the body are dismissed as "symbolic"—which is to say, unreal. . . .

The meliorist perspective embraces valetudinarians and also eugenicists. The latter were formerly more vocal in these discussions, but they are now generally happy to see their goals advanced under the less threatening banners of freedom and technological growth. These people see in cloning a new prospect for improving human beings—minimally, by ensuring the perpetuation of healthy individuals by avoiding the risks of genetic disease inherent in the lottery of sex, and maximally, by producing "optimum babies," preserving outstanding genetic material, and (with the help of soon-to-come techniques for precise genetic engineering) enhancing inborn human capacities on many fronts. Here the morality of cloning as a means is justified solely by the excellence of the end, that is, by the outstanding traits or individuals cloned—beauty, or brawn, or brains. . . .

The technical, liberal and meliorist approaches all ignore the deeper anthropological, social and, indeed, ontological meanings of bringing forth new life. To this more fitting and profound point of view, cloning shows itself to be a major alteration, indeed, a major violation, of our given nature as embodied, gendered and engendering beings—and of the social relations built on this natural ground. Once this perspective is recognized, the ethical judgment on cloning can no longer be reduced to a matter of motives and intentions, rights and freedoms, benefits and harms, or even means and ends. It must be regarded primarily as a matter of meaning: Is cloning a fulfillment of human begetting and belonging? Or is cloning rather, as I contend, their pollution and perversion? To pollution and perversion, the fitting response can only be horror and revulsion; and conversely, generalized horror and revulsion are prima facie evidence of foulness and violation. The burden of moral argument must fall entirely on those who want to declare the widespread repugnances of humankind to be mere timidity or superstition.

Yet repugnance need not stand naked before the bar of reason. The wisdom of our horror at human cloning can be partially articulated, even if this is finally one of those instances about which the heart has its reasons that reason cannot entirely know. . . .

## The Perversities of Cloning

Cloning creates serious issues of identity and individuality. The cloned person may experience concerns about his distinctive identity not only because he will be in genotype and appearance identical to another human being, but, in this case, because he may also be twin to the person who is his "father" or "mother"—if one can still call them that. What would be the psychic burdens of being the "child" or "parent" of your twin? The cloned individual moreover, will be saddled with a genotype that has already lived. He will not be fully a surprise to the world. People are likely always to compare his performances in life with that of his alter ego. True, his nurture and his circumstance in life will be different; genotype is not exactly destiny. Still, one must also expect parental and other efforts to shape this new life after the original—or at least to view the child with the original version always firmly in mind. Why else did they clone from the star basketball player, mathematician and beauty queen—or even dear old dad—in the first place?. . .

Troubled psychic identity (distinctiveness), based on all-too-evident genetic identity (sameness), will be made much worse by the utter confusion of social identity and kinship ties: For, as already noted, cloning radically confounds lineage and social relations, for "offspring" as for "parents." As bioethicist James Nelson has pointed out, a female child cloned from her "mother" might develop a desire for a relationship to her "father," and might understandably seek out the father of her "mother," who is after all also her biological twin sister. Would "Grandpa," who thought his paternal duties concluded, be pleased to discover that the clonant looked to him for paternal attention and support?

Social identity and social ties of relationship and responsibility are widely connected to, and supported by, biological kinship. Social taboos on incest (and adultery) everywhere serve to keep clear who is related to whom (and especially which child belongs to which parents), as well as to avoid confounding the social identity of parent-and-child (or brother-and-sister) with the social identity of lovers, spouses and co-parents. True, social identity is altered by adoption (but as a matter of the best interest of already living children: we do not deliberately produce children for adoption). True, artificial insemination and in vitro fertilization with donor sperm, or whole embryo donation, are in some way forms of "prenatal adoption"—a not altogether unproblematic practice. Even here, though, there is in each case (as in all sexual reproduction) a known male source of sperm and a known single female source of egg—a genetic father and a genetic mother—should anyone care to know (as adopted children often do) who is genetically related to whom.

In the case of cloning, however, there is but one "parent." The usually sad situation of the "single-parent child" is here deliberately planned, and with a vengeance. In the case of self-cloning, the "offspring" is, in addition, one's twin; and so the dreaded result of incest—to be parent to one's sibling—is here brought about deliberately, albeit without any act of coitus. Moreover, all other relationships will be confounded. What will father, grandfather, aunt, cousin, sister mean? Who will bear what ties and what burdens? What sort of social identity will someone have with one whole side—"father's" or "mother's"—necessarily excluded? It is no answer to say that our society, with its high incidence of divorce, remarriage, adoption, extramarital childbearing and the rest, already confounds lineage and confuses kinship and responsibility for children (and everyone else), unless one also wants to argue that this is, for children, a preferable state of affairs.

Human cloning would also represent a giant step toward turning begetting into making, procreation into manufacture (literally, something "handmade"), a process already begun with in vitro fertilization and genetic testing of embryos. With cloning, not only is the process in hand, but the total genetic blueprint of the cloned individual is selected and determined by the human artisans. To be sure, subsequent development will take place according to natural processes; and the resulting children will still be recognizably human. But we here would be taking a major step into making man himself simply another one of the man-made things. Human nature becomes merely the last part of nature to succumb to the technological project, which turns all of nature into raw material at human disposal, to be homogenized by our rationalized technique according to the subjective prejudices of the day.

How does begetting differ from making? In natural procreation, human beings come together, complementarily male and female, to give existence to another being who is formed, exactly as we were, *by what we are*: living, hence perishable, hence aspiringly erotic, human beings. In clonal reproduction, by contrast, and in the more advanced forms of manufacture to which it leads, we give existence to a being not by what we are but by what we intend and design. As with any product of our making, no matter how excellent, the artificer stands above it, not as an equal but as a superior, transcending it by his will and creative prowess. Scientists who clone animals make it perfectly clear that they are engaged in instrumental making; the animals are, from the start, designed as means to serve rational human purposes. In human cloning, scientists and prospective "parents" would be adopting the same technocratic mentality to human children: human children would be their artifacts.

Such an arrangement is profoundly dehumanizing, no matter how good the product. Mass-scale cloning of the same individual makes the point vividly; but the violation of human equality, freedom and dignity are present even in a single planned clone. And procreation dehumanized into manufacture is further degraded by commodification, a virtually inescapable result of allowing babymaking to proceed under the banner of commerce. Genetic and reproductive biotechnology companies are already growth industries, but they will go into commercial orbit once the Human Genome Project nears completion. Supply will create enormous demand. Even before the capacity for human cloning arrives, established companies will have invested in the harvesting of eggs from ovaries obtained at autopsy or through ovarian surgery, practiced embryonic genetic alteration, and initiated the stockpiling of prospective donor tissues. Through the rental of surrogate-womb services, and through the buying and selling of tissues and embryos, priced according to the merit of the donor, the commodification of nascent human life will be unstoppable.

Finally, and perhaps most important, the practice of human cloning by nuclear transfer—like other anticipated forms of genetic engineering of the next generation—would enshrine and aggravate a profound and mischievous misunderstanding of the meaning of having children and of the parent–child relationship. When a couple now chooses to procreate, the partners are saying yes to the emergence of new life in its novelty, saying yes not only to having a child but also, tacitly, to having whatever child this child turns out to be. In accepting our finitude and opening ourselves to our replacement, we are tacitly confessing the limits of our control. In this ubiquitous way of nature, embracing the future by procreating means precisely that we are relinquishing our grip, in the very activity of taking up our own share in what we hope will be the immortality of human life and the human species. This means that our children are not *our* children: they are not our property, not our possessions. Neither are they supposed to live our lives for us, or anyone else's life but their own. To be sure, we seek to guide them on their way, imparting to them not just life but nurturing love, and a way of life; to be sure, they bear our hopes that they will live fine and flourishing lives, enabling us in small measure to transcend our own limitations. Still, their genetic distinctiveness and independence are the natural foreshadowing of the deep truth that they have their own and never-before-enacted life to live. They are sprung from a past, but they take an uncharted course into the future.

Much harm is already done by parents who try to live vicariously through their children. Children are sometimes compelled to fulfill the broken dreams of unhappy parents; John Doe Jr. or the III is under the burden of having to live up to his forebear's name. Still, if most parents have hopes for their children, cloning parents will have expectations. In cloning, such overbearing parents take at the start a decisive step which contradicts the entire meaning of the open and forward-looking nature of parent–child relations. The child is given a genotype that has already lived, with full expectation that this blueprint of a past life ought to be controlling of the life that is to come. Cloning is inherently despotic, for it seeks to make one's children (or someone else's children) after one's own image (or an image of one's choosing) and their fixture according to one's will. In some cases, the despotism may be mild and benevolent. In other cases, it will be mischievous and downright tyrannical. But despotism—the control of another through one's will—it inevitably will be.

## Meeting Some Objections

The defenders of cloning, of course, are not wittingly friends of despotism. Indeed, they regard themselves mainly as friends of freedom: the freedom of individuals to reproduce, the freedom of scientists and inventors to discover and devise and to foster "progress" in genetic knowledge and technique. They want large-scale cloning only for animals, but they wish to preserve cloning as a human option for exercising our "right to reproduce"—our right to have children, and children with "desirable genes." As law professor John Robertson points out, under our "right to reproduce" we already practice early forms of unnatural, artificial and extramarital reproduction, and we already practice early forms of eugenic choice. For this reason, he argues, cloning is no big deal.

We have here a perfect example of the logic of the slippery slope, and the slippery way in which it already works in this area. Only a few years ago, slippery slope arguments were used to oppose artificial insemination and in vitro fertilization using unrelated sperm donors. Principles used to justify these practices, it was said, will be used to justify more artificial and more eugenic practices, including cloning. Not so, the defenders retorted, since we can make the necessary distinctions. And now, without even a gesture at making the necessary distinctions, the continuity of practice is held by itself to be justificatory.

The principle of reproductive freedom as currently enunciated by the proponents of cloning logically embraces the ethical acceptability of sliding down the entire rest of the slope—to producing children ectogenetically from sperm to term (should it become feasible) and to producing children whose entire genetic makeup will be the product of parental eugenic planning and choice. If reproductive freedom means the right to have a child of one's own choosing, by whatever means, it knows and accepts no limits.

But, far from being legitimated by a "right to reproduce," the emergence of techniques of assisted reproduction and genetic engineering should compel us to reconsider the meaning and limits of such a putative right. In truth, a "right to reproduce" has always been a peculiar and problematic notion. Rights generally belong to individuals, but this is a right which (before cloning) no one can exercise alone. Does the right then inhere only in couples? Only in married couples? Is it a (woman's) right to carry or deliver or a right (of one or more parents) to nurture and rear? Is it a right to have your own biological child? Is it a right only to attempt reproduction, or a right also to succeed? Is it a right to acquire the baby of one's choice?

The assertion of a negative "right to reproduce" certainly makes sense when it claims protection against state interference with procreative liberty, say, through a program of compulsory sterilization. But surely it cannot be the basis of a tort claim against nature, to be made good by technology, should free efforts at natural procreation fail. Some insist that the right to reproduce embraces also the right against state interference with the free use of all technological means to obtain a child. Yet such a position cannot be sustained: for reasons having to do with the means employed, any community may rightfully prohibit surrogate pregnancy, or polygamy, or the sale of babies to infertile couples, without violating anyone's basic human "right to reproduce." When the exercise of a previously innocuous freedom now involves or impinges on troublesome practices that the original freedom never was intended to reach, the general presumption of liberty needs to be reconsidered.

We do indeed already practice negative eugenic selection, through genetic screening and prenatal diagnosis. Yet our practices are governed by a norm of health. We seek to prevent the birth of children who suffer from known (serious) genetic diseases. When and if gene therapy becomes possible, such diseases could then be treated, in utero or even before implantation—I have no ethical objection in principle to such a practice (though I have some practical worries), precisely because it serves the medical goal of healing existing individuals. But therapy, to be therapy, implies not only an existing "patient." It also implies a norm of health. In this respect, even germline gene "therapy," though practiced not on a human being but on egg and sperm, is less radical than cloning, which is in no way therapeutic. But once one blurs the distinction between health promotion and genetic enhancement, between so-called negative and positive eugenics, one opens the door to all future eugenic designs. "To make sure that a child will be healthy and have good chances in life": this is Robertson's principle, and owing to its latter clause it is an utterly elastic principle, with no boundaries. Being over eight feet tall will likely produce some very good chances in life, and so will having the looks of Marilyn Monroe, and so will a genius-level intelligence. . . .

## Ban the Cloning of Humans

What, then, should we do? We should declare that human cloning is unethical in itself and dangerous in its likely consequences. In so doing, we shall have the backing of the overwhelming majority of our fellow Americans, and of the human race, and (I believe) of most practicing scientists. Next, we should do all that we can to prevent the cloning of human beings. We should do this by means of an international legal ban if possible, and by a unilateral national ban, at a minimum. Scientists may secretly undertake to violate such a law, but they will be deterred by not being able to stand up proudly to claim the credit for their technological bravado and success. Such a ban on clonal baby-making, moreover, will not harm the progress of basic genetic science and technology. On the contrary, it will reassure the public that scientists are happy to proceed without violating the deep ethical norms and intuitions of the human community. . . .

The president's call for a moratorium on human cloning has given us an important opportunity. In a truly unprecedented way, we can strike a blow for the human control of the technological project, for wisdom, prudence and human dignity. The prospect of human cloning, so repulsive to contemplate, is the occasion for deciding whether we shall be slaves of unregulated progress, and ultimately its artifacts, or whether we shall remain free human beings who guide our technique toward the enhancement of human dignity.

*Landmark Court Cases on Abortion*

# ROE v. WADE

## United States Supreme Court, 1973

JUSTICE BLACKMUN delivered the opinion of the Court.

It is . . . apparent that at common law, at the time of the adoption of our Constitution, and throughout the major portion of the nineteenth century, abortion was viewed with less disfavor than under most American statutes currently in effect. Phrasing it another way, a woman enjoyed a substantially broader right to terminate a pregnancy than she does in most states today. At least with respect to the early stage of pregnancy, and very possibly without such a limitation, the opportunity to make this choice was present in this country well into the nineteenth century. Even later, the law continued for some time to treat less punitively an abortion procured in early pregnancy. . . .

Excerpted from 410 U.S. 113 (1973). Some notes and references omitted.

Three reasons have been advanced to explain historically the enactment of criminal abortion laws in the nineteenth century and to justify their continued existence.

It has been argued occasionally that these laws were the product of a Victorian social concern to discourage illicit sexual conduct. Texas, however, does not advance this justification in the present case, and it appears that no court or commentator has taken the argument seriously. . . .

A second reason is concerned with abortion as a medical procedure. When most criminal abortion laws were first enacted, the procedure was a hazardous one for the woman. This was particularly true prior to the development of antisepsis. Antiseptic techniques, of course, were based on discoveries by Lister, Pasteur, and others first announced in 1867, but were not generally accepted and employed until about the turn of the century. Abortion mortality was high. Even after 1900, and perhaps until as late as the development of antibiotics in the 1940s, standard modern techniques such as dilation and curettage were not nearly so safe as they are today. Thus it has been argued that a state's real concern in enacting a criminal abortion law was to protect the pregnant woman, that is, to restrain her from submitting to a procedure that placed her life in serious jeopardy.

Modern medical techniques have altered this situation. Appellants and various *amici* refer to medical data indicating that abortion in early pregnancy, that is, prior to the end of first trimester, although not without its risk, is now relatively safe. Mortality rates for women undergoing early abortions, where the procedure is legal, appear to be as low as or lower than the rates for normal childbirth. Consequently, any interest of the state in protecting the woman from an inherently hazardous procedure, except when it would be equally dangerous for her to forgo it, has largely disappeared. Of course, important state interests in the area of health and medical standards do remain. The state has a legitimate interest in seeing to it that abortion, like any other medical procedure, is performed under circumstances that insure maximum safety for the patient. This interest obviously extends at least to the performing physician and his staff, to the facilities involved, to the availability of after-care, and to adequate provision for any complication or emergency that might arise. The prevalence of high mortality rates at illegal "abortion mills" strengthens, rather than weakens, the state's interest in regulating the conditions under which abortions are performed. Moreover, the risk to the woman increases as her pregnancy continues. Thus the state retains a definite interest in protecting the woman's own health and safety when an abortion is performed at a late stage of pregnancy.

The third reason is the state's interest—some phrase it in terms of duty—in protecting prenatal life. Some of the argument for this justification rests on the theory that a new human life is present from the moment of conception. The state's interest and general obligation to protect life then extends, it is argued, to prenatal life. Only when the life of the pregnant mother herself is at stake, balanced against the life she carries within her, should the interest of the embryo or fetus not prevail. Logically, of course, a legitimate

state interest in this area need not stand or fall on acceptance of the belief that life begins at conception or at some other point prior to live birth. In assessing the state's interest, recognition may be given to the less rigid claim that as long as at least *potential* life is involved, the state may assert interests beyond the protection of the pregnant woman alone.

Parties challenging state abortion laws have sharply disputed in some courts the contention that a purpose of these laws, when enacted, was to protect prenatal life. Pointing to the absence of legislative history to support the contention, they claim that most state laws were designed solely to protect the woman. Because medical advances have lessened this concern, at least with respect to abortion in early pregnancy, they argue that with respect to such abortions the laws can no longer be justified by any state interest. There is some scholarly support for this view of original purpose. The few states courts called upon to interpret their laws in the late nineteenth and early twentieth centuries did focus on the state's interest in protecting the woman's health rather than in preserving the embryo and fetus. . . .

The Constitution does not explicitly mention any right of privacy. In a line of decisions, however, going back perhaps as far as *Union Pacific R. Co. v. Botsford* (1891), the Court has recognized that a right of personal privacy, or a guarantee of certain areas or zones of privacy, does exist under the Constitution. In varying contexts the Court or individual Justices have indeed found at least the roots of that right in the First Amendment, . . . in the Fourth and Fifth Amendments, . . . in the penumbras of the Bill of Rights, . . . in the Ninth Amendment, . . . or in the concept of liberty guaranteed by the first section of the Fourteenth Amendment. . . . These decisions make it clear that only personal rights that can be deemed "fundamental" or "implicit in the concept of ordered liberty" . . . are included in this guarantee of personal privacy. They also make it clear that the right has some extension to activities relating to marriage, . . . procreation, . . . contraception, . . . family relationships, . . . and child rearing and education. . . .

This right of privacy, whether it be founded in the Fourteenth Amendment's concept of personal liberty and restrictions upon state action, as we feel it is, or, as the District Court determined, in the Ninth Amendment's reservation of rights to the people, is broad enough to encompass a woman's decision whether or not to terminate her pregnancy. . . .

Appellants and some *amici* argue that the woman's right is absolute and that she is entitled to terminate her pregnancy at whatever time, in whatever way, and for whatever reason she alone chooses. With this we do not agree. Appellants' arguments that Texas either has no valid interest at all in regulating the abortion decision, or no interest strong enough to support any limitation upon the woman's sole determination, is unpersuasive. The Court's decisions recognizing a right of privacy also acknowledge that some state regulation in areas protected by that right is appropriate. As noted above, a state may properly assert important interests in safeguarding health, in maintaining medical standards, and in protecting potential life. At some point in pregnancy, these respective interests become sufficiently compelling to sustain regulation of the factors that govern the abortion decision. The privacy rights involved, therefore, cannot be said to be absolute. . . .

We therefore conclude that the right of personal privacy includes the abortion decision, but that this right is not unqualified and must be considered against important state interests in regulation.

We note that those federal and state courts that have recently considered abortion law challenges have reached the same conclusion. . . .

Although the results are divided, most of these courts have agreed that the right of privacy, however based, is broad enough to cover the abortion decision; that the right, nonetheless, is not absolute and is subject to some limitations; and that at some point the state interests as to protection of health, medical standards, and prenatal life, become dominant. We agree with this approach. . . .

The appellee and certain *amici* argue that the fetus is a "person" within the language and meaning of the Fourteenth Amendment. In support of this they outline at length and in detail the well-known facts of fetal development. If this suggestion of personhood is established, the appellant's case, of course, collapses, for the fetus's right to life is then guaranteed specifically by the Amendment. The appellant conceded as much on reargument. On the other hand, the appellee conceded on reargument that no case could be cited that holds that a fetus is a person within the meaning of the Fourteenth Amendment. . . .

All this, together with our observation, *supra*, that throughout the major portion of the nineteenth century prevailing legal abortion practices were far freer than they are today, persuades us that the word "person," as used in the Fourteenth Amendment, does not include the unborn. . . . Indeed, our decision in *United States v. Vuitch* (1971), inferentially is to the same effect, for we there would not have indulged in statutory interpretation favorable to abortion in specified circumstances if the necessary consequence was the termination of life entitled to Fourteenth Amendment protection.

. . . As we have intimated above, it is reasonable and appropriate for a state to decide that at some point in time another interest, that of health of the mother or that of potential human life, becomes significantly involved. The woman's privacy is no longer sole and any right of privacy she possesses must be measured accordingly.

Texas urges that, apart from the Fourteenth Amendment, life begins at conception and is present throughout pregnancy, and that, therefore, the state has a compelling interest in protecting that life from and after conception. We need not resolve the difficult question of when life begins. When those trained in the respective disciplines of medicine, philosophy, and theology are unable to arrive at any consensus, the judiciary, at this point in the development of man's knowledge, is not in a position to speculate as to the answer.

It should be sufficient to note briefly the wide divergence of thinking on this most sensitive and difficult question. There has always been strong support for the view that life does not begin until live birth. This was the belief of the Stoics. It appears to be the predominant, though not the unanimous, attitude of the Jewish faith. It may be taken to represent also the position of a large segment of the Protestant community, insofar as that can be ascertained; organized groups that have taken a formal position on the abortion issue have generally regarded abortion as a matter for the conscience of the individual and her family. As we have noted, the common law found greater significance in quickening. Physicians and their scientific colleagues have regarded that event with less interest and have tended to focus either upon conception or upon live birth or upon the interim point at which the fetus becomes "viable," that is, potentially able to live outside the mother's womb, albeit with artificial aid. Viability is usually placed at about seven months (28 weeks) but may occur earlier, even at 24 weeks. . . .

In areas other than criminal abortion the law has been reluctant to endorse any theory that life, as we recognize it, begins before live birth or to accord legal rights to the unborn except in narrowly defined situations and except when the rights are contingent upon live birth. . . . In short, the unborn have never been recognized in the law as persons in the whole sense.

In view of all this, we do not agree that, by adopting one theory of life, Texas may override the rights of the pregnant woman that are at stake. We repeat, however, that the state does have an important and legitimate interest in preserving and protecting the health of the pregnant woman, whether she be a resident of the state or a nonresident who seeks medical consultation and treatment there, and that it has still *another* important and legitimate interest in protecting the potentiality of human life. These interests are separate and distinct. Each grows in substantiality as the woman approaches term and, at a point during pregnancy, each becomes "compelling."

With respect to the state's important and legitimate interest in the health of the mother, the "compelling" point, in the light of present medical knowledge, is at approximately the end of the first trimester. This is so because of the now established medical fact . . . that until the end of the first trimester mortality in abortion is less than mortality in normal childbirth. It follows that, from and after this point, a state may regulate the abortion procedure to the extent that the regulation reasonably relates to the preservation and protection of maternal health. Examples of permissible state regulation in this area are requirements as to the qualifications of the person who is to perform the abortion; as to the licensure of that person; as to the facility in which the procedure is to be performed, that is, whether it must be a hospital or may be a clinic or some other place of less than hospital status; as to the licensing of the facility; and the like.

This means, on the other hand, that, for the period of pregnancy prior to this "compelling" point, the attending physician, in consultation with his patient, is free to determine, without regulation by the state, that in his medical judgment the patient's pregnancy should be terminated. If that decision is reached, the judgment may be effectuated by an abortion free of interference by the state.

With respect to the state's important and legitimate interest in potential life, the "compelling" point is at viability. This is so because the fetus then presumably has the capability of meaningful life outside the mother's womb. State regulation protective of fetal life after viability thus has both logical and biological justifications. If the state is interested in protecting fetal life after viability, it may go so far as to proscribe abortion during that period except when it is necessary to preserve the life or health of the mother. . . .

To summarize and repeat:

1. A state criminal abortion statute of the current Texas type, that excepts from criminality only a *life-saving* procedure on behalf of the mother, without regard to pregnancy stage and without recognition of the other interests involved, is violative of the Due Process Clause of the Fourteenth Amendment.

  (a) For the stage prior to approximately the end of the first trimester, the abortion decision and its effectuation must be left to the medical judgment of the pregnant woman's attending physician.

  (b) For the stage subsequent to approximately the end of the first trimester, the state, in promoting its interest in the health of the mother, may, if it chooses, regulate the abortion procedure in ways that are reasonably related to maternal health.

  (c) For the stage subsequent to viability the state, in promoting its interest in the potentiality of human life, may, if it chooses, regulate, and even proscribe, abortion except where it is necessary, in appropriate medical judgment, for the preservation of the life or health of the mother.

2. The state may define the term "physician" . . . to mean only a physician currently licensed by the state, and may proscribe any abortion by a person who is not a physician as so defined.

. . . The decision leaves the state free to place increasing restrictions on abortion as the period of pregnancy lengthens, so long as those restrictions are tailored to the recognized state interests. The decision vindicates the right of the physician to administer medical treatment according to his professional judgment up to the points where important state interests provide compelling justifications for intervention. Up to those points the abortion decision in all its aspects is inherently, and primarily, a medical decision, and basic responsibility for it must rest with the physician. If an individual practitioner abuses the privilege of exercising proper medical judgment, the usual remedies, judicial and intraprofessional, are available. . . .

JUSTICE WHITE, with whom JUSTICE REHNQUIST joins, dissenting.

At the heart of the controversy in these cases are those recurring pregnancies that pose no danger whatsoever to the life or health of the mother but are, nevertheless, unwanted for any one or more of a variety of reasons—convenience, family planning, economics, dislike of children, the embarrassment of illegitimacy, etc. The common claim before us is that for any one of such reasons, or for no reason at all, and without asserting or claiming any threat to life or health, any woman is entitled to an abortion at her request if she is able to find a medical advisor willing to undertake the procedure.

The Court for the most part sustains this position: During the period prior to the time the fetus becomes viable, the Constitution of the United States values the convenience, whim, or caprice of the putative mother more than the life or potential life of the fetus; the Constitution, therefore, guarantees the right to an abortion as against any state law or policy seeking to protect the fetus from an abortion not prompted by more compelling reasons of the mother.

With all due respect, I dissent. I find nothing in the language or history of the Constitution to support the Court's judgment. The Court simply fashions and announces a new constitutional right for pregnant mothers and, with scarcely any reason or authority for its action, invests that right with sufficient substance to override most existing state abortion statutes. The upshot is that the people and the legislatures of the 50 states are constitutionally disentitled to weigh the relative importance of the continued existence and development of the fetus, on the one hand, against a spectrum of possible impacts on the mother, on the other hand. As an exercise of raw judicial power, the Court perhaps has authority to do what it does today; but in my view its judgment is an improvident and extravagant exercise of the power of judicial review that the Constitution extends to this Court.

The Court apparently values the convenience of the pregnant mother more than the continued existence and development of the life or potential life that she carries. Whether or not I might agree with that marshaling of values, I can in no event join the Court's judgment because I find no constitutional warrant for imposing such an order of priorities on the people and legislatures of the states. In a sensitive area such as this, involving as it does issues over which reasonable men may easily and heatedly differ, I cannot accept the Court's exercise of its clear power of choice by interposing a constitutional barrier to state efforts to protect human life and by investing mothers and doctors with the constitutionally protected right to exterminate it. This issue, for the most part, should be left with the people and to the political processes the people have devised to govern their affairs.

It is my view, therefore, that the Texas statute is not constitutionally infirm because it denies abortions to those who seek to serve only their convenience rather than to protect their life or health. Nor is this plaintiff, who claims no threat to her mental or physical health, entitled to assert the possible rights of those women whose pregnancy assertedly implicated their health. This, together with *United States v. Vuitch*, 402 U.S. 62 (1971), dictates reversal of the judgment of the District Court.

Editor's note: The vote in *Roe* was 7–2, with Justices Rehnquist and White dissenting.

# *PLANNED PARENTHOOD v. CASEY*

## United States Supreme Court, 1992

JUSTICE O'CONNOR, JUSTICE KENNEDY, and JUSTICE SOUTER announced the judgment of the Court and delivered the opinion of the Court.

### I

Liberty finds no refuge in a jurisprudence of doubt. Yet 19 years after our holding that the Constitution protects a woman's right to terminate her pregnancy in its early stages, *Roe v. Wade*, 410 U.S. 113 (1973), that definition of liberty is still questioned. Joining the respondents as *amicus curiae*, the United States, as it has done in five other cases in the last decade, again asks us to overrule *Roe*. . . .

At issue in these cases are five provisions of the Pennsylvania Abortion Control Act of 1982 as amended in 1988 and 1989. . . . The Act requires that a woman seeking an abortion give her informed consent prior to the abortion procedure, and specifies that she be provided with certain information at least 24 hours before the abortion is performed. For a minor to obtain an abortion, the Act requires the informed consent of one of her parents, but provides for a judicial bypass option if the minor does not wish to or cannot obtain a parent's consent. Another provision of the Act requires that, unless certain exceptions apply, a married woman seeking an abortion must sign a statement indicating that she has notified her husband of her intended abortion. The Act exempts compliance with these three requirements in the event of a "medical emergency," which is defined in § 3203 of the Act. In addition to the above provisions regulating the performance of abortions, the Act imposes certain reporting requirements on facilities that provide abortion services. . . .

We find it imperative to review once more the principles that define the rights of the woman and the legitimate authority of the State respecting the termination of pregnancies by abortion procedures.

After considering the fundamental constitutional questions resolved by *Roe*, principles of institutional integrity, and the rule of *stare decisis*, we are led to conclude this: the essential holding of *Roe v. Wade* should be retained and once again reaffirmed.

It must be stated at the outset and with clarity that *Roe*'s essential holding, the holding we reaffirm, has three parts. First is a recognition of the right of the woman to choose to have an abortion before viability and to obtain it without undue interference from the State. Before viability, the State's interests are not strong enough to support a prohibition of abortion or the imposition of a substantial obstacle to the woman's effective right to elect the procedure. Second is a confirmation of the State's power to restrict abortions after fetal viability, if the law contains exceptions for pregnancies which endanger a woman's life or health. And third is the principle that the State has legitimate interests from the outset of the pregnancy in protecting the health of the woman and the life of the fetus that may become a child. These principles do not contradict one another; and we adhere to each.

### II

Constitutional protection of the woman's decision to terminate her pregnancy derives from the Due Process Clause of the Fourteenth Amendment. It declares that no State shall "deprive any person of life, liberty, or property, without due process of law." The controlling word in the case before us is "liberty." . . .

It is a promise of the Constitution that there is a realm of personal liberty which the government may not enter. We have vindicated this principle before. Marriage is mentioned nowhere in the Bill of Rights

Excerpted from 505 U.S. 833 (1992). Some notes and references omitted.

and interracial marriage was illegal in most States in the 19th century, but the Court was no doubt correct in finding it to be an aspect of liberty protected against state interference by the substantive component of the Due Process Clause. . . .

In *Griswold*, we held that the Constitution does not permit a State to forbid a married couple to use contraceptives. That same freedom was later guaranteed, under the Equal Protection Clause, for unmarried couples. See *Eisenstadt v. Baird*, 405 U.S. 438 (1972). Constitutional protection was extended to the sale and distribution of contraceptives in *Carey v. Population Services International*. It is settled now, as it was when the Court heard arguments in *Roe v. Wade*, that the Constitution places limits on a State's right to interfere with a person's most basic decisions about family and parenthood. . . .

The inescapable fact is that adjudication of substantive due process claims may call upon the Court in interpreting the Constitution to exercise that same capacity which by tradition courts always have exercised: reasoned judgment. Its boundaries are not susceptible of expression as a simple rule. That does not mean we are free to invalidate state policy choices with which we disagree; yet neither does it permit us to shrink from the duties of our office. . . .

It should be recognized, moreover, that in some critical respects the abortion decision is of the same character as the decision to use contraception, to which *Griswold v. Connecticut, Eisenstadt v. Baird*, and *Carey v. Population Services International*, afford constitutional protection. We have no doubt as to the correctness of those decisions. They support the reasoning in *Roe* relating to the woman's liberty because they involve personal decisions concerning not only the meaning of procreation but also human responsibility and respect for it. As with abortion, reasonable people will have differences of opinion about these matters. One view is based on such reverence for the wonder of creation that any pregnancy ought to be welcomed and carried to full term no matter how difficult it will be to provide for the child and ensure its well-being. Another is that the inability to provide for the nurture and care of the infant is a cruelty to the child and an anguish to the parent. These are intimate views with infinite variations, and their deep, personal character underlay our decisions in *Griswold, Eisenstadt*, and *Carey*. The same concerns are present where the woman confronts the reality that, perhaps despite her attempts to avoid it, she has become pregnant. . . .

III

. . . No evolution of legal principle has left *Roe's* doctrinal footings weaker than they were in 1973. No development of constitutional law since the case was decided has implicitly or explicitly left *Roe* behind as a mere survivor of obsolete constitutional thinking. . . .

The *Roe* Court itself placed its holding in the succession of cases most prominently exemplified by *Griswold v. Connecticut*, see *Roe*, 410 U.S., at 152–153. When it is so seen, *Roe* is clearly in no jeopardy, since subsequent constitutional developments have neither disturbed, nor do they threaten to diminish, the scope of recognized protection accorded to the liberty relating to intimate relationships, the family, and decisions about whether or not to beget or bear a child. . . .

[However], time has overtaken some of *Roe's* factual assumptions: advances in maternal health care allow for abortions safe to the mother later in pregnancy than was true in 1973, and advances in neonatal care have advanced viability to a point somewhat earlier. . . . But these facts go only to the scheme of time limits on the realization of competing interests, and the divergences from the factual premises of 1973 have no bearing on the validity of *Roe's* central holding, that viability marks the earliest point at which the State's interest in fetal life is constitutionally adequate to justify a legislative ban on nontherapeutic abortions. The soundness or unsoundness of that constitutional judgment in no sense turns on whether viability occurs at approximately 28 weeks, as was usual at the time of *Roe*, at 23 to 24 weeks, as it sometimes does today, or at some moment even slightly earlier in pregnancy, as it may if fetal respiratory capacity can somehow be enhanced in the future. Whenever it may occur, the attainment of viability may continue to serve as the critical fact, just as it has done since *Roe* was decided; which is to say that no change in *Roe's* factual underpinning has left its central holding obsolete, and none supports an argument for overruling it. . . .

. . . Liberty must not be extinguished for want of a line that is clear. And it falls to us to give some real substance to the woman's liberty to determine whether to carry her pregnancy to full term.

We conclude the line should be drawn at viability, so that before that time the woman has a right to choose to terminate her pregnancy. We adhere to this principle for two reasons. First . . . is the doctrine of *stare decisis*. Any judicial act of line-drawing may seem somewhat arbitrary, but *Roe* was a reasoned statement, elaborated with great care. We have twice reaffirmed it in the face of great opposition. . . .

The second reason is that the concept of viability, as we noted in *Roe*, is the time at which there is a realistic possibility of maintaining and nourishing a life outside the womb, so that the independent existence of a second life can in reason and all fairness be the object of state protection that now overrides the rights of the woman. See *Roe*, at 163. Consistent with other constitutional norms, legislatures may draw lines which appear arbitrary without the necessity of offering a justification. But courts may not. We must justify the lines we draw. And there is no line other than viability which is more workable. To be sure, as we have said, there may be some medical developments that affect the precise point of viability, but this is an imprecision within tolerable limits given that the medical community and all those who must apply its discoveries will continue to explore the matter. The viability line also has, as a practical matter, an element of fairness. In some broad sense it might be said that a woman who fails to act before viability has consented to the State's intervention on behalf of the developing child.

The woman's right to terminate her pregnancy before viability is the most central principle of *Roe v. Wade*. It is a rule of law and a component of liberty we cannot renounce.

On the other side of the equation is the interest of the State in the protection of potential life. The *Roe* Court recognized the State's "important and legitimate interest in protecting the potentiality of human life." *Roe*, at 162. The weight to be given this state interest, not the strength of the woman's interest, was the difficult question faced in *Roe*. We do not need to say whether each of us, had we been Members of the Court when the valuation of the State interest came before it as an original matter, would have concluded, as the *Roe* Court did, that its weight is insufficient to justify a ban on abortions prior to viability even when it is subject to certain exceptions. The matter is not before us in the first instance, and coming as it does after nearly 20 years of litigation in *Roe*'s wake we

are satisfied that the immediate question is not the soundness of *Roe*'s resolution of the issue, but the precedential force that must be accorded to its holding. And we have concluded that the essential holding of *Roe* should be reaffirmed.

Yet it must be remembered that *Roe v. Wade* speaks with clarity in establishing not only the woman's liberty but also the State's "important and legitimate interest in potential life." *Roe*, *supra*, at 163. That portion of the decision in *Roe* has been given too little acknowledgement and implementation by the Court in its subsequent cases. . . .

*Roe* established a trimester framework to govern abortion regulations. Under this elaborate but rigid construct, almost no regulation at all is permitted during the first trimester of pregnancy; regulations designed to protect the woman's health, but not to further the State's interest in potential life, are permitted during the second trimester; and during the third trimester, when the fetus is viable, prohibitions are permitted provided the life or health of the mother is not at stake. *Roe v. Wade*, at 163–166. Most of our cases since *Roe* have involved the application of rules derived from the trimester framework. . . .

The trimester framework no doubt was erected to ensure that the woman's right to choose not become so subordinate to the State's interest in promoting fetal life that her choice exists in theory but not in fact. We do not agree, however, that the trimester approach is necessary to accomplish this objective. A framework of this rigidity was unnecessary and in its later interpretation sometimes contradicted the State's permissible exercise of its powers.

Though the woman has a right to choose to terminate or continue her pregnancy before viability, it does not at all follow that the State is prohibited from taking steps to ensure that this choice is thoughtful and informed. Even in the earliest stages of pregnancy, the State may enact rules and regulations designed to encourage her to know that there are philosophic and social arguments of great weight that can be brought to bear in favor of continuing the pregnancy to full term and that there are procedures and institutions to allow adoption of unwanted children as well as a certain degree of state assistance if the mother chooses to raise the child herself. . . .

Numerous forms of state regulation might have the incidental effect of increasing the cost or decreasing the availability of medical care, whether for abortion or any other medical procedure. The fact that a law which serves a valid purpose, one not designed to strike at the right itself, has the incidental effect of making it more difficult or more expensive to procure an abortion cannot be enough to invalidate it. Only where state regulation imposes an undue burden on a woman's ability to make this decision does the power of the State reach into the heart of the liberty protected by the Due Process Clause. . . .

These considerations of the nature of the abortion right illustrate that it is an overstatement to describe it as a right to decide whether to have an abortion "without interference from the State," *Planned Parenthood of Central Mo. v. Danforth*, 428 U.S. 52, 61 (1976). All abortion regulations interfere to some degree with a woman's ability to decide whether to terminate her pregnancy. . . .

*Roe v. Wade* was express in its recognition of the State's "important and legitimate interest[s] in preserving and protecting the health of the pregnant woman [and] in protecting the potentiality of human life." 410 U.S., at 162. The trimester framework, however, does not fulfill *Roe*'s own promise that the State has an interest in protecting fetal life or potential life. *Roe* began the contradiction by using the trimester framework to forbid any regulation of abortion designed to advance that interest before viability. *Id.*, at 163. Before viability, *Roe* and subsequent cases treat all governmental attempts to influence a woman's decision on behalf of the potential life within her as unwarranted. This treatment is, in our judgment, incompatible with the recognition that there is a substantial state interest in potential life throughout pregnancy.

The very notion that the State has a substantial interest in potential life leads to the conclusion that not all regulations must be deemed unwarranted. Not all burdens on the right to decide whether to terminate a pregnancy will be undue. In our view, the undue burden standard is the appropriate means of reconciling the State's interest with the woman's constitutionally protected liberty. . . .

A finding of an undue burden is a shorthand for the conclusion that a state regulation has the purpose or effect of placing a substantial obstacle in the path of a woman seeking an abortion of a nonviable fetus. A statute with this purpose is invalid because the means chosen by the State to further the interest in potential life must be calculated to inform the woman's free choice, not hinder it. . . . That is to be expected in the application of any legal standard which must accommodate life's complexity. We do not expect it to be otherwise with respect to the undue burden standard. We give this summary:

(a) To protect the central right recognized by *Roe v. Wade* while at the same time accommodating the State's profound interest in potential life, we will employ the undue burden analysis as explained in this opinion. An undue burden exists, and therefore a provision of law is invalid, if its purpose or effect is to place a substantial obstacle in the path of a woman seeking an abortion before the fetus attains viability.

(b) We reject the rigid trimester framework of *Roe v. Wade*. To promote the State's profound interest in potential life, throughout pregnancy the State may take measures to ensure that the woman's choice is informed, and measures designed to advance this interest will not be invalidated as long as their purpose is to persuade the woman to choose childbirth over abortion. These measures must not be an undue burden on the right.

(c) As with any medical procedure, the State may enact regulations to further the health or safety of a woman seeking an abortion. Unnecessary health regulations that have the purpose or effect of presenting a substantial obstacle to a woman seeking an abortion impose an undue burden on the right.

(d) Our adoption of the undue burden analysis does not disturb the central holding of *Roe v. Wade*, and we reaffirm that holding. Regardless of whether exceptions are made for particular circumstances, a State may not prohibit any woman from making the ultimate decision to terminate her pregnancy before viability.

(e) We also reaffirm *Roe*'s holding that "subsequent to viability, the State in promoting its interest in the potentiality of human life may, if it chooses, regulate, and even proscribe, abortion except where it is necessary, in appropriate medical judgment, for the preservation of the life or health of the mother." *Roe v. Wade*, 410 U.S., at 164–165.

These principles control our assessment of the Pennsylvania statute, and we now turn to the issue of the validity of its challenged provisions.

## IV

The Court of Appeals applied what it believed to be the undue burden standard and upheld each of the provisions except for the husband notification requirement. We agree generally with this conclusion, but refine the undue burden analysis in accordance with the principles articulated above . . .

B

We next consider the informed consent requirement. 18 Pa. Cons. Stat. Ann. § 3205. Except in a medical emergency, the statute requires that at least 24 hours before performing an abortion a physician inform the woman of the nature of the procedure, the health risks of the abortion and of childbirth, and the "probable gestational age of the unborn child." The physician or a qualified nonphysician must inform the woman of the availability of printed materials published by the State describing the fetus and providing information about medical assistance for childbirth, information about child support from the father, and a list of agencies which provide adoption and other services as alternatives to abortion. An abortion may not be performed unless the woman certifies in writing that she has been informed of the availability of these printed materials and has been provided them if she chooses to view them.

Our prior decisions establish that as with any medical procedure, the State may require a woman to give her written informed consent to an abortion. . . .

In *Akron I*, 462 U.S. 416 (1983), we invalidated an ordinance which required that a woman seeking an abortion be provided by her physician with specific information "designed to influence the woman's informed choice between abortion or childbirth." *Id.*, at 444. As we later described the *Akron I* holding in *Thornburgh v. American College of Obstetricians and Gynecologists*, 476 U.S., at 762, there were two purported flaws in the Akron ordinance: the information was designed to dissuade the woman from having an abortion and the ordinance imposed "a rigid requirement that a specific body of information be given in all cases, irrespective of the particular needs of the patient. . . ." *Ibid.* . . .

In attempting to ensure that a woman apprehend the full consequences of her decision, the State furthers the legitimate purpose of reducing the risk that a woman may elect an abortion, only to discover later, with devastating psychological consequences, that her decision was not fully informed. If the information the State requires to be made available to the woman is truthful and not misleading, the requirement may be permissible.

We also see no reason why the State may not require doctors to inform a woman seeking an abortion of the availability of materials relating to the consequences to the fetus, even when those consequences have no direct relation to her health. An example illustrates the point. We would think it constitutional for the State to require that in order for there to be informed consent to a kidney transplant operation the recipient must be supplied with information about risks to the donor as well as risks to himself or herself. . . .

Whether the mandatory 24-hour waiting period is nonetheless invalid because in practice it is a substantial obstacle to a woman's choice to terminate her pregnancy is a closer question. The findings of fact by the District Court indicate that because of the distances many women must travel to reach an abortion provider, the practical effect will often be a delay of much more than a day because the waiting period requires that a woman seeking an abortion make at least two visits to the doctor. The District Court also found that in many instances this will increase the exposure of women seeking abortions to "the harassment and hostility of anti-abortion protestors demonstrating outside a clinic." 744 F. Supp., at 1351. As a result, the District Court found that for those women who have the fewest financial resources, those who must travel long distances, and those who have difficulty explaining their whereabouts to husbands, employers, or others, the 24-hour waiting period will be "particularly burdensome." . . .

We are left with the argument that the various aspects of the informed consent requirement are unconstitutional because they place barriers in the way of abortion on demand. Even the broadest reading of *Roe*, however, has not suggested that there is a constitutional right to abortion on demand. See, e.g., *Doe v. Bolton*, 410 U.S., at 189. Rather, the right protected by *Roe* is a right to decide to terminate a pregnancy free of undue interference by the State. Because the informed consent requirement facilitates the wise exercise of that right it cannot be classified as an interference with the right *Roe* protects. The informed consent requirement is not an undue burden on that right.

C

Section 3209 of Pennsylvania's abortion law provides, except in cases of medical emergency, that no physician shall perform an abortion on a married woman without receiving a signed statement from the woman that she has notified her spouse that she is about to undergo an abortion. The woman has the option of providing an alternative signed statement certifying that her husband is not the man who impregnated her; that her husband could not be located; that the pregnancy is the result of spousal sexual assault which she has reported; or that the woman believes that notifying her husband will cause him or someone else to inflict bodily injury upon her. A physician who performs an abortion on a married woman without receiving the appropriate signed statement will have his or her license revoked, and is liable to the husband for damages. . . .

The American Medical Association (AMA) has published a summary of the recent research in this field, which indicates that in an average 12-month period in this country, approximately two million women are the victims of severe assaults by their male partners. In a 1985 survey, women reported that nearly one of every eight husbands had assaulted their wives during the past year. The AMA views these figures as "marked underestimates," because the nature of these incidents discourages women from reporting them, and because surveys typically exclude the very poor, those who do not speak English well, and women who are homeless or in institutions or hospitals when the survey is conducted. According to the AMA, "[r]esearchers on family violence agree that the true incidence of partner violence is probably *double* the above estimates; or four million severely assaulted women per year. Studies suggest that from one-fifth to one-third of all women will be physically assaulted by a partner or ex-partner during their lifetime." AMA Council on Scientific Affairs, Violence Against Women 7 (1991) (emphasis in original). Thus on an average day in the United States, nearly 11,000 women are severely assaulted by their male partners. Many of these incidents involve sexual assault. . . .

In families where wife-beating takes place, moreover, child abuse is often present as well. . . .

In well-functioning marriages, spouses discuss important intimate decisions such as whether to bear a child. But there are millions of women in this country who are the victims of regular physical and psychological abuse at the hands of their husbands. Should these women become pregnant, they may have very good reasons for not wishing to inform their husbands of their decision to obtain an abortion. Many may have justifiable fears of physical abuse, but may be no less fearful of the consequences of reporting prior abuse to the Commonwealth of Pennsylvania. Many may have a reasonable fear that notifying their husbands will provoke further instances of child abuse; these women are not exempt from § 3209's notification requirement. . . . If anything in this field is certain, it is that victims of spousal sexual assault are extremely reluctant to report the abuse to the government; hence, a great many spousal rape victims will not be exempt from the notification requirement imposed by § 3209.

The spousal notification requirement is thus likely to prevent a significant number of women from obtaining an abortion. It does not merely make abortions a little more difficult or expensive to obtain; for many women, it will impose a substantial obstacle. We must not blind ourselves to the fact that the significant number of women who fear for their safety and the safety of their children are likely to be deterred from procuring an abortion as surely as if the Commonwealth had outlawed abortion in all cases. . . .

This conclusion is in no way inconsistent with our decisions upholding parental notification or consent requirements. Those enactments, and our judgment that they are constitutional, are based on the quite reasonable assumption that minors will benefit from consultation with their parents and that children will often not realize that their parents have their best interests at heart. We cannot adopt a parallel assumption about adult women. . . .

Our cases establish, and we reaffirm today, that a State may require a minor seeking an abortion to obtain the consent of a parent or guardian, provided that there is an adequate judicial bypass procedure. Under these precedents, in our view, the one-parent consent requirement and judicial bypass procedure are constitutional. . . .

V

Our Constitution is a covenant running from the first generation of Americans to us and then to future generations. It is a coherent succession. Each generation must learn anew that the Constitution's written terms embody ideas and aspirations that must survive more ages than one. We accept our responsibility not to retreat from interpreting the full meaning of the covenant in light of all of our precedents. We invoke it once again to define the freedom guaranteed by the Constitution's own promise, the promise of liberty. . . .

Editor's note: Casey is a plurality decision, which means that the opinion issued by Justices O'Connor, Kennedy, and Souter was not supported in its totality by a majority of the nine Supreme Court justices. Parts of the opinion, however, were each joined by at least two other justices, creating a majority on those parts.

*The Problem of Justifying Abortion*

# DON MARQUIS

## Why Abortion is Immoral

Don Marquis is professor of philosophy at the University of Kansas. His research
interests include the history of ethics as well as problems of abortion, social ethics,
and research ethics, on which he has published widely.

The view that abortion is, with rare exceptions, seriously immoral has received little support in the recent
philosophical literature. No doubt most philosophers
affiliated with secular institutions of higher education believe that the anti-abortion position is either a
symptom of irrational religious dogma or a conclusion generated by seriously confused philosophical
argument. The purpose of this essay is to undermine
this general belief. This essay sets out an argument
that purports to show, as well as any argument in ethics can show, that abortion is, except possibly in rare
cases, seriously immoral, that it is in the same moral
category as killing an innocent adult human being.

The argument is based on a major assumption.
Many of the most insightful and careful writers on the
ethics of abortion . . . believe that whether or not abortion is morally permissible stands or falls on whether
or not a fetus is the sort of being whose life it is seriously wrong to end. The argument of this essay will
assume, but not argue, that they are correct.

Also, this essay will neglect issues of great importance to a complete ethics of abortion. Some anti-
abortionists will allow that certain abortions, such as
abortion before implantation or abortion when the life
of a woman is threatened by a pregnancy or abortion
after rape, may be morally permissible. This essay

From *Journal of Philosophy* LXXXVI(4):183–202; 1989. Used
with permission.

will not explore the casuistry of these hard cases. The
purpose of this essay is to develop a general argument
for the claim that the overwhelming majority of deliberate abortions are seriously immoral. . . .

### I

Passions in the abortion debate run high. There are
both plausibilities and difficulties with the standard positions. Accordingly, it is hardly surprising
that partisans of either side embrace with fervor the
moral generalizations that support the conclusions
they preanalytically favor, and reject with disdain
the moral generalizations of their opponents as being subject to inescapable difficulties. It is easy to
believe that the counterexamples to one's own moral
principles are merely temporary difficulties that
will dissolve in the wake of further philosophical
research, and that the counterexamples to the principles of one's opponents are as straightforward as
the contradiction between *A* and *O* propositions in
traditional logic. This might suggest to an impartial
observer (if there are any) that the abortion issue is
unresolvable.

There is a way out of this apparent dialectical
quandary. The moral generalizations of both sides
are not quite correct. The generalizations hold for
the most part, for the usual cases. This suggests that
they are all *accidental* generalizations, that the moral
claims made by those on both sides of the dispute do
not touch on the *essence* of the matter.

This use of the distinction between essence and accident is not meant to invoke obscure metaphysical categories. Rather, it is intended to reflect the rather atheoretical nature of the abortion discussion. If the generalization a partisan in the abortion dispute adopts were derived from the reason why ending the life of a human being is wrong, then there could not be exceptions to that generalization unless some special case obtains in which there are even more powerful countervailing reasons. Such generalizations would not be merely accidental generalizations; they would point to, or be based upon, the essence of the wrongness of killing, what it is that makes killing wrong. All this suggests that a necessary condition of resolving the abortion controversy is a more theoretical account of the wrongness of killing. After all, if we merely believe, but do not understand, why killing adult human beings such as ourselves is wrong, how could we conceivably show that abortion is either immoral or permissible?

## II

In order to develop such an account, we can start from the following unproblematic assumption concerning our own case: It is wrong to kill *us*. Why is it wrong? Some answers can be easily eliminated. It might be said that what makes killing us wrong is that a killing brutalizes the one who kills. But the brutalization consists of being inured to the performance of an act that is hideously immoral; hence, the brutalization does not explain the immorality. It might be said that what makes killing us wrong is the great loss others would experience due to our absence. Although such hubris is understandable, such an explanation does not account for the wrongness of killing hermits, or those whose lives are relatively independent and whose friends find it easy to make new friends.

A more obvious answer is better. What primarily makes killing wrong is neither its effect on the murderer nor its effect on the victim's friends and relatives, but its effect on the victim. The loss of one's life is one of the greatest losses one can suffer. The loss of one's life deprives one of all the experiences, activities, projects, and enjoyments that would otherwise have constituted one's future. Therefore, killing someone is wrong, primarily because the killing inflicts (one of) the greatest possible losses on the victim. To describe this as the loss of life can be misleading, however. The change in my biological state does not by itself make killing me wrong. The effect of the loss of my biological life is the loss to me of all those activities, projects, experiences, and enjoyments which would otherwise have constituted my future personal life. These activities, projects, experiences, and enjoyments are either valuable for their own sakes or are means to something else that is valuable for its own sake. Some parts of my future are not valued by me now, but will come to be valued by me as I grow older and as my values and capacities change. When I am killed, I am deprived both of what I now value which would have been part of my future personal life, but also what I would come to value. Therefore, when I die, I am deprived of all of the value of my future. Inflicting this loss on me is ultimately what makes killing me wrong. This being the case, it would seem that what makes killing *any* adult human being prima facie seriously wrong is the loss of his or her future.

How should this rudimentary theory of the wrongness of killing be evaluated? It cannot be faulted for deriving an "ought" from an "is," for it does not. The analysis assumes that killing me (or you, reader) is prima facie seriously wrong. The point of the analysis is to establish which natural property ultimately explains the wrongness of the killing, given that it is wrong. A natural property will ultimately explain the wrongness of killing, only if (1) the explanation fits with our intuitions about the matter and (2) there is no other natural property that provides the basis for a better explanation of the wrongness of killing. This analysis rests on the intuition that what makes killing a particular human or animal wrong is what it does to that particular human or animal. What makes killing wrong is some natural effect or other of the killing. Some would deny this. For instance, a divine-command theorist in ethics would deny it. Surely this denial is, however, one of those features of divine-command theory which renders it so implausible.

The claim that what makes killing wrong is the loss of the victim's future is directly supported by two considerations. In the first place, this theory explains why we regard killing as one of the worst of crimes. Killing is especially wrong, because it deprives the victim of more than perhaps any other crime. In the second place, people with AIDS or cancer who know they are dying believe, of course, that dying is a very bad thing for them. They believe that the loss of a future to them that they would otherwise have experienced is what makes their premature death a very bad thing for them. A better theory of the wrongness of killing would require a different natural property associated with killing which better fits with the attitudes of the dying. What could it be?

The view that what makes killing wrong is the loss to the victim of the value of the victim's future gains additional support when some of its implications are examined. In the first place, it is incompatible with the view that it is wrong to kill only beings who are biologically human. It is possible that there exists a different species from another planet whose members have a future like ours. Since having a future like that is what makes killing someone wrong, this theory entails that it would be wrong to kill members of such a species. Hence, this theory is opposed to the claim that only life that is biologically human has great moral worth, a claim which many anti-abortionists have seemed to adopt. This opposition, which this theory has in common with personhood theories, seems to be a merit of the theory.

In the second place, the claim that the loss of one's future is the wrong-making feature of one's being killed entails the possibility that the futures of some actual nonhuman mammals on our own planet are sufficiently like ours that it is seriously wrong to kill them also. Whether some animals do have the same right to life as human beings depends on adding to the account of the wrongness of killing some additional account of just what it is about my future or the futures of other adult human beings which makes it wrong to kill us. No such additional account will be offered in this essay. Undoubtedly, the provision of such an account would be a very difficult matter. Undoubtedly, any such account would be quite controversial. Hence, it surely should not reflect badly on this sketch of an elementary theory of the wrongness of killing that it is indeterminate with respect to some very difficult issues regarding animal rights.

In the third place, the claim that the loss of one's future is the wrong-making feature of one's being killed does not entail, as sanctity of human life theories do, that active euthanasia is wrong. Persons who are severely and incurably ill, who face a future of pain and despair, and who wish to die will not have suffered a loss if they are killed. It is, strictly speaking, the value of a human's future which makes killing wrong in this theory. This being so, killing does not necessarily wrong some persons who are sick and dying. Of course, there may be other reasons for a prohibition of active euthanasia, but that is another matter. Sanctity-of-human-life theories seem to hold that active euthanasia is seriously wrong even in an individual case where there seems to be good reason for it independently of public policy considerations. This consequence is most implausible, and it is a plus for the claim that the loss of a future of value is what makes killing wrong that it does not share this consequence.

In the fourth place, the account of the wrongness of killing defended in this essay does straightforwardly entail that it is prima facie seriously wrong to kill children and infants, for we do presume that they have futures of value. Since we do believe that it is wrong to kill defenseless little babies, it is important that a theory of the wrongness of killing easily account for this. Personhood theories of the wrongness of killing, on the other hand, cannot straightforwardly account for the wrongness of killing infants and young children. Hence, such theories must add special ad hoc accounts of the wrongness of killing the young. The plausibility of such ad hoc theories seems to be a function of how desperately one wants such theories to work. The claim that the primary wrong-making feature of a killing is the loss to the victim of the value of its future accounts for the wrongness of killing young children and infants directly; it makes the wrongness of such acts as obvious as we actually think it is. This is a further merit of this theory. Accordingly, it seems that this value of a future-like-ours theory of the wrongness of killing shares strengths of both sanctity-of-life and personhood accounts while avoiding weaknesses of both. In addition, it meshes with a central intuition concerning what makes killing wrong.

The claim that the primary wrong-making feature of a killing is the loss to the victim of the value of its future has obvious consequences for the ethics of abortion. The future of a standard fetus includes a set of experiences, projects, activities, and such which are identical with the futures of adult human beings and are identical with the futures of young children. Since the reason that is sufficient to explain why it is wrong to kill human beings after the time of birth is a reason that also applies to fetuses, it follows that abortion is prima facie seriously morally wrong.

This argument does not rely on the invalid inference that, since it is wrong to kill persons, it is wrong to kill potential persons also. The category that is morally central to this analysis is the category of having a valuable future like ours; it is not the category of personhood. The argument to the conclusion that abortion is prima facie seriously morally wrong proceeded independently of the notion of person or potential person or any equivalent. Someone may wish to start with this analysis in terms of the value of a human future, conclude that abortion is, except perhaps in rare circumstances, seriously morally wrong, infer that fetuses have the right to life, and then call fetuses "persons" as a result of their having the right to life. Clearly, in this case, the category of person is being used to state the *conclusion* of the analysis rather than to generate the *argument* of the analysis.

The structure of this anti-abortion argument can be both illuminated and defended by comparing it to what appears to be the best argument for the wrongness of the wanton infliction of pain on animals. This latter argument is based on the assumption that it is prima facie wrong to inflict pain on me (or you, reader). What is the natural property associated with the infliction of pain which makes such infliction wrong? The obvious answer seems to be that the infliction of pain causes suffering and that suffering is a misfortune. The suffering caused by the infliction of pain is what makes the wanton infliction of pain on me wrong. The wanton infliction of pain on other adult humans causes suffering. The wanton infliction of pain on animals causes suffering. Since causing suffering is what makes the wanton infliction of pain wrong and since the wanton infliction of pain on animals causes suffering, it follows that the wanton infliction of pain on animals is wrong.

This argument for the wrongness of the wanton infliction of pain on animals shares a number of structural features with the argument for the serious prima facie wrongness of abortion. Both arguments start with an obvious assumption concerning what it is wrong to do to me (or you, reader). Both then look for the characteristic or the consequence of the wrong action which makes the action wrong. Both recognize that the wrong-making feature of these immoral actions is a property of actions sometimes directed at individuals other than postnatal human beings. If the structure of the argument for the wrongness of the wanton infliction of pain on animals is sound, then the structure of the argument for the prima facie serious wrongness of abortion is also sound, for the structure of the two arguments is the same. The structure common to both is the key to the explanation of how the wrongness of abortion can be demonstrated without recourse to the category of person. In neither argument is that category crucial.

This defense of an argument for the wrongness of abortion in terms of a structurally similar argument for the wrongness of the wanton infliction of pain on animals succeeds only if the account regarding animals is the correct account. Is it? In the first place, it seems plausible. In the second place, its major competition is Kant's account. Kant believed that we do not have direct duties to animals at all, because they are not persons. Hence, Kant had to explain and justify the wrongness of inflicting pain on animals on the grounds that "he who is hard in his dealings with animals becomes hard also in his dealing with men."[1] The problem with Kant's account is that there seems to be no reason for accepting this latter claim unless Kant's account is rejected. If the alternative to Kant's account is accepted, then it is easy to understand why someone who is indifferent to inflicting pain on animals is also indifferent to inflicting pain on humans, for one is indifferent to what makes inflicting pain wrong in both cases. But, if Kant's account is accepted, there is no intelligible reason why one who is hard in his dealings with animals (or crabgrass or stones) should also be hard in his dealings with men. After all, men are persons: animals are no more persons than crabgrass or stones. Persons are Kant's crucial moral category. Why, in short, should a Kantian accept the basic claim in Kant's argument?

Hence, Kant's argument for the wrongness of inflicting pain on animals rests on a claim that, in a world of Kantian moral agents, is demonstrably false. Therefore, the alternative analysis, being more plausible anyway, should be accepted. Since this alternative analysis has the same structure of the anti-abortion argument being defended here, we have further support for the argument for the immorality of abortion being defended in this essay.

Of course, this value of a future-like-ours argument, if sound, shows only that abortion is prima facie wrong, not that it is wrong in any and all circumstances. Since the loss of the future to a standard fetus, if killed, is, however, at least as great a loss as the loss of the future to a standard adult human being who is killed, abortion, like ordinary killing, could be justified only by the most compelling reasons. The loss of one's life is almost the greatest misfortune that can happen to one. Presumably abortion could be justified in some circumstances, only if the loss consequent on failing to abort would be at least as great. Accordingly, morally permissible abortions will be rare indeed unless, perhaps, they occur so early in pregnancy that a fetus is not yet definitely an individual. Hence, this argument should be taken as showing that abortion is presumptively very seriously wrong, where the presumption is very strong—as strong as the presumption that killing another adult human being is wrong.

## III

How complete an account of the wrongness of killing does the value of a future-like-ours account have to be in order that the wrongness of abortion is a consequence? This account does not have to be an account of the necessary conditions for the wrongness of killing. Some persons in nursing homes may lack valuable human futures, yet it may be wrong to kill them for other reasons. Furthermore, this account does not obviously have to be the sole reason killing is wrong where the victim did have a valuable future. This analysis claims only that, for any killing where the victim did have a valuable future like ours, having that future by itself is sufficient to create the strong presumption that the killing is seriously wrong.

One way to overturn the value of a future-like-ours argument would be to find some account of the wrongness of killing which is at least as intelligible and which has different implications for the ethics of abortion. Two rival accounts possess at least some degree of plausibility. One account is based on the obvious fact that people value the experience of living and wish for that valuable experience to continue. Therefore, it might be said, what makes killing wrong is the discontinuation of that experience for the victim. Let us call this the *discontinuation account.* Another rival account is based upon the obvious fact that people strongly desire to continue to live. This suggests that what makes killing us so wrong is that it interferes with the fulfillment of a strong and fundamental desire, the fulfillment of which is necessary for the fulfillment of any other desires we might have. Let us call this the *desire account.*[2]

Consider first the desire account as a rival account of the ethics of killing which would provide the basis for rejecting the anti-abortion position. Such an account will have to be stronger than the value of a future-like-ours account of the wrongness of abortion if it is to do the job expected of it. To entail the wrongness of abortion, the value of a future-like-ours account has only to provide a sufficient, but not a necessary, condition for the wrongness of killing. The desire account, on the other hand, must provide us also with a necessary condition for the wrongness of killing in order to generate a pro-choice conclusion on abortion. The reason for this is that presumably the argument from the desire account moves from the claim that what makes killing wrong is interference with a very strong desire to the claim that abortion is not wrong because the fetus lacks a strong desire to live. Obviously, this inference fails if someone's having the desire to live is not a necessary condition of its being wrong to kill that individual.

One problem with the desire account is that we do regard it as seriously wrong to kill persons who have little desire to live or who have no desire to live or, indeed, have a desire not to live. We believe it is seriously wrong to kill the unconscious, the sleeping, those who are tired of life, and those who are suicidal. The value-of-a-human-future account renders standard morality intelligible in these cases; these cases appear to be incompatible with the desire account.

The desire account is subject to a deeper difficulty. We desire life, because we value the goods of this life. The goodness of life is not secondary to our desire for it. If this were not so, the pain of one's own premature death could be done away with merely by an appropriate alteration in the configuration of one's desires. This is absurd. Hence, it would seem that it is the loss of the goods of one's future, not the interference with the fulfillment of a strong desire to live, which accounts ultimately for the wrongness of killing.

It is worth noting that, if the desire account is modified so that it does not provide a necessary, but only a sufficient, condition for the wrongness of killing, the desire account is compatible with the value of a future-like-ours account. The combined accounts will yield an anti-abortion ethic. This suggests that one can retain what is intuitively plausible about the desire account without a challenge to the basic argument of this paper.

It is also worth noting that, if future desires have moral force in a modified desire account of the wrongness of killing, one can find support for an anti-abortion ethic even in the absence of a value of a future-like-ours account. If one decides that a morally relevant property, the possession of which is sufficient to make it wrong to kill some individual, is the desire at some future time to live—one might decide to justify one's refusal to kill suicidal teenagers on these grounds, for example—then, since typical fetuses will have the desire in the future to live, it is wrong to kill typical fetuses. Accordingly, it does not seem that a desire account of the wrongness of killing can provide a justification of a pro-choice ethic of abortion which is nearly as adequate as the value of a human-future justification of an anti-abortion ethic.

The discontinuation account looks more promising as an account of the wrongness of killing. It seems just as intelligible as the value of a future-like-ours account, but it does not justify an anti-abortion position. Obviously, if it is the continuation of one's activities, experiences, and projects, the loss of which makes killing wrong, then it is not wrong to kill fetuses for that reason, for fetuses do not have experiences, activities, and projects to be continued or discontinued. Accordingly, the discontinuation account does not have the anti-abortion consequences that the value of a future-like-ours account has. Yet it seems as intelligible as the value of a future-like-ours account, for when we think of what would be wrong with our being killed, it does seem as if it is the discontinuation

of what makes our lives worthwhile which makes killing us wrong.

Is the discontinuation account just as good an account as the value of a future-like-ours account? The discontinuation account will not be adequate at all, if it does not refer to the *value* of the experience that may be discontinued. One does not want the discontinuation account to make it wrong to kill a patient who begs for death and who is in severe pain that cannot be relieved short of killing. (I leave open the question of whether it is wrong for other reasons.) Accordingly, the discontinuation account must be more than a bare discontinuation account. It must make some reference to the positive value of the patient's experiences. But, by the same token, the value of a future-like-ours account cannot be a bare future account either. Just having a future surely does not itself rule out killing the above patient. This account must make some reference to the value of the patient's future experiences and projects also. Hence, both accounts involve the value of experiences, projects, and activities. So far we still have symmetry between the accounts.

The symmetry fades, however, when we focus on the time period of the value of the experiences, etc., which has moral consequences. Although both accounts leave open the possibility that the patient in our example may be killed, this possibility is left open only in virtue of the utterly bleak future for the patient. It makes no difference whether the patient's immediate past contains intolerable pain, or consists in being in a coma (which we can imagine is a situation of indifference), or consists in a life of value. If the patient's future is a future of value, we want our account to make it wrong to kill the patient. If the patient's future is intolerable, whatever his or her immediate past, we want our account to allow killing the patient. Obviously, then, it is the value of that patient's future which is doing the work in rendering the morality of killing the patient intelligible.

This being the case, it seems clear that whether one has immediate past experiences or not does not work in the explanation of what makes killing wrong. The addition the discontinuation account makes to the value of a human future account is otiose. Its addition to the value-of-a-future account plays no role at all in rendering intelligible the wrongness of killing.

Therefore, it can be discarded with the discontinuation account of which it is a part.

IV

The analysis of the previous section suggests that alternative general accounts of the wrongness of killing are either inadequate or unsuccessful in getting around the anti-abortion consequences of the value of a future-like-ours argument. A different strategy for avoiding these anti-abortion consequences involves limiting the scope of the value of a future argument. More precisely, the strategy involves arguing that fetuses lack a property that is essential for the value-of-a-future argument (or for any anti-abortion argument) to apply to them.

One move of this sort is based upon the claim that a necessary condition of one's future being valuable is that one values it. Value implies a valuer. Given this, one might argue that, since fetuses cannot value their futures, their futures are not valuable to them. Hence, it does not seriously wrong them deliberately to end their lives.

This move fails, however, because of some ambiguities. Let us assume that something cannot be of value unless it is valued by someone. This does not entail that my life is of no value unless it is valued by me. I may think, in a period of despair, that my future is of no worth whatsoever, but I may be wrong because others rightly see value—even great value—in it. Furthermore, my future can be valuable to me even if I do not value it. This is the case when a young person attempts suicide, but is rescued and goes on to significant human achievements. Such young people's futures are ultimately valuable to them, even though such futures do not seem to be valuable to them at the moment of attempted suicide. A fetus's future can be valuable to it in the same way. Accordingly, this attempt to limit the anti-abortion argument fails.

Another similar attempt to reject the anti-abortion position is based on Tooley's claim that an entity cannot possess the right to life unless it has the capacity to desire its continued existence. It follows that, since fetuses lack the conceptual capacity to desire to continue to live, they lack the right to life. Accordingly, Tooley concludes that abortion cannot be seriously prima facie wrong (*op. cit.*, pp. 46/7). . . .

One might attempt to defend Tooley's basic claim on the grounds that, because a fetus cannot apprehend continued life as a benefit, its continued life cannot be a benefit or cannot be something it has a right to or cannot be something that is in its interest. This might be defended in terms of the general proposition that, if an individual is literally incapable of caring about or taking an interest in some $X$, then one does not have a right to $X$ or $X$ is not a benefit or $X$ is not something that is in one's interest.[3]

Each member of this family of claims seems to be open to objections. . . . As Tooley himself has pointed out, persons who have been indoctrinated, or drugged, or rendered temporarily unconscious may be literally incapable of caring about or taking an interest in something that is in their interest or is something to which they have a right, or is something that benefits them. Hence, the Tooley claim that would restrict the scope of the value of a future-like-ours argument is undermined by counterexamples.[4]

Finally, Paul Bassen[5] has argued that, even though the prospects of an embryo might seem to be a basis for the wrongness of abortion, an embryo cannot be a victim and therefore cannot be wronged. An embryo cannot be a victim, he says, because it lacks sentience. His central argument for this seems to be that, even though plants and the permanently unconscious are alive, they clearly cannot be victims. What is the explanation of this? Bassen claims that the explanation is that their lives consist of mere metabolism and mere metabolism is not enough to ground victimizability. Mentation is required.

The problem with this attempt to establish the absence of victimizability is that both plants and the permanently unconscious clearly lack what Bassen calls "prospects" or what I have called "a future life like ours." Hence, it is surely open to one to argue that the real reason we believe plants and the permanently unconscious cannot be victims is that killing them cannot deprive them of a future life like ours; the real reason is not their absence of present mentation. . . .

V

In this essay, it has been argued that the correct ethic of the wrongness of killing can be extended to fetal life and used to show that there is a strong presumption that any abortion is morally impermissible. If the ethic of killing adopted here entails, however, that contraception is also seriously immoral, then there would appear to be a difficulty with the analysis of this essay.

But this analysis does not entail that contraception is wrong. Of course, contraception prevents the actualization of a possible future of value. Hence, it follows from the claim that futures of value should be maximized that contraception is prima facie immoral. This obligation to maximize does not exist, however; furthermore, nothing in the ethics of killing in this paper entails that it does. The ethics of killing in this essay would entail that contraception is wrong only if something were denied a human future of value by contraception. Nothing at all is denied such a future by contraception, however.

Candidates for a subject of harm by contraception fall into four categories: (1) some sperm or other, (2) some ovum or other, (3) a sperm and an ovum separately, and (4) a sperm and an ovum together. Assigning the harm to some sperm is utterly arbitrary, for no reason can be given for making a sperm the subject of harm rather than an ovum. Assigning the harm to some ovum is utterly arbitrary, for no reason can be given for making an ovum the subject of harm rather than a sperm. One might attempt to avoid these problems by insisting that contraception deprives both the sperm and the ovum separately of a valuable future like ours. On this alternative, too many futures are lost. Contraception was supposed to be wrong, because it deprived us of one future of value, not two. One might attempt to avoid this problem by holding that contraception deprives the combination of sperm and ovum of a valuable future like ours. But here the definite article misleads. At the time of contraception, there are hundreds of millions of sperm, one (released) ovum and millions of possible combinations of all of these. There is no actual combination at all. Is the subject of the loss to be a merely possible combination? Which one? This alternative does not yield an actual subject of harm either. Accordingly, the immorality of contraception is not entailed by the loss of a future-like-ours argument simply because there is no nonarbitrarily identifiable subject of the loss in the case of contraception.

## VI

The purpose of this essay has been to set out an argument for the serious presumptive wrongness of abortion subject to the assumption that the moral permissibility of abortion stands or falls on the moral status of the fetus. Since a fetus possesses a property, the possession of which in adult human beings is sufficient to make killing an adult human being wrong, abortion is wrong. This way of dealing with the problem of abortion seems superior to other approaches to the ethics of abortion, because it rests on an ethics of killing which is close to self-evident, because the crucial morally relevant property clearly applies to fetuses, and because the argument avoids the usual equivocations on "human life," "human being," or "person." The argument rests neither on religious claims nor on Papal dogma. It is not subject to the objection of "speciesism." Its soundness is compatible with the moral permissibility of euthanasia and contraception. It deals with our intuitions concerning young children.

Finally, this analysis can be viewed as resolving a standard problem—indeed, *the* standard problem—concerning the ethics of abortion. Clearly, it is wrong to kill adult human beings. Clearly, it is not wrong to end the life of some arbitrarily chosen single human cell. Fetuses seem to be like arbitrarily chosen human cells in some respects and like adult humans in other respects. The problem of the ethics of abortion is the problem of determining the fetal property that settles this moral controversy. The thesis of this essay is that the problem of the ethics of abortion, so understood, is solvable.

## NOTES

1. "Duties to Animals and Spirits," in *Lectures on Ethics*, Louis Infeld, trans. (New York: Harper, 1963), p. 239.

2. Presumably a preference utilitarian would press such an objection. Tooley once suggested that his account has such a theoretical underpinning. See his "Abortion and Infanticide," *Philosophy and Public Affairs* 2 (1972), pp. 44–45.

3. Donald VanDeVeer seems to think this self-evident. See his "Whither Baby Doe?" in *Matters of Life and Death*, p. 233.

4. See Tooley again in "Abortion and Infanticide," pp. 47–49.

5. "Present Sakes and Future Prospects: The Status of Early Abortion," *Philosophy and Public Affairs*, XI, 4 (1982): 322–326.

# *GONZALES v. CARHART*

## United States Supreme Court, 2007

JUSTICE KENNEDY delivered the opinion of the Court.

These cases require us to consider the validity of the Partial-Birth Abortion Ban Act of 2003 (Act), a federal statute regulating abortion procedures.

• • •

### I

#### A

The Act proscribes a particular manner of ending fetal life, so it is necessary here, as it was in *Stenberg* [*v. Carhart*, 530 U.S. 914 (2000)] to discuss abortion procedures in some detail. . . .

Abortion methods vary depending to some extent on the preferences of the physician and, of course, on the term of the pregnancy and the resulting stage of the unborn child's development. Between 85 and 90 percent of the approximately 1.3 million abortions performed each year in the United States take place in the first three months of pregnancy, which is to say in the first trimester. . . . The Act does not regulate these procedures.

Of the remaining abortions that take place each year, most occur in the second trimester. The surgical

Excerpted from 550 U.S. 124 (2007). Some notes and references omitted.

procedure referred to as "dilation and evacuation" or "D & E" is the usual abortion method in this trimester. Although individual techniques for performing D & E differ, the general steps are the same. . . .

• • • •

After sufficient dilation the surgical operation can commence. The woman is placed under general anesthesia or conscious sedation. The doctor, often guided by ultrasound, inserts grasping forceps through the woman's cervix and into the uterus to grab the fetus. The doctor grips a fetal part with the forceps and pulls it back through the cervix and vagina, continuing to pull even after meeting resistance from the cervix. The friction causes the fetus to tear apart. For example, a leg might be ripped off the fetus as it is pulled through the cervix and out of the woman. The process of evacuating the fetus piece by piece continues until it has been completely removed. A doctor may make 10 to 15 passes with the forceps to evacuate the fetus in its entirety, though sometimes removal is completed with fewer passes. Once the fetus has been evacuated, the placenta and any remaining fetal material are suctioned or scraped out of the uterus. The doctor examines the different parts to ensure the entire fetal body has been removed. . . .

Some doctors, especially later in the second trimester, may kill the fetus a day or two before performing the surgical evacuation. They inject digoxin or potassium chloride into the fetus, the umbilical cord, or the amniotic fluid. Fetal demise may cause contractions and make greater dilation possible. Once dead, moreover, the fetus' body will soften, and its removal will be easier. Other doctors refrain from injecting chemical agents, believing it adds risk with little or no medical benefit. . . .

The abortion procedure that was the impetus for the numerous bans on "partial-birth abortion," including the Act, is a variation of [the] standard D & E. . . . For discussion purposes this D & E variation will be referred to as intact D & E. The main difference between the two procedures is that in intact D & E a doctor extracts the fetus intact or largely intact. . . . There are no comprehensive statistics indicating what percentage of all D & Es are performed in this manner. . . .

In an intact D & E procedure the doctor extracts the fetus in a way conducive to pulling out its entire body, instead of ripping it apart. . . .

Intact D & E gained public notoriety when, in 1992, Dr. Martin Haskell gave a presentation describing his method of performing the operation. In the usual intact D & E the fetus' head lodges in the cervix, and dilation is insufficient to allow it to pass. Haskell explained the next step as follows:

"At this point, the right-handed surgeon slides the fingers of the left [hand] along the back of the fetus and 'hooks' the shoulders of the fetus with the index and ring fingers (palm down).

"While maintaining this tension, lifting the cervix and applying traction to the shoulders with the fingers of the left hand, the surgeon takes a pair of blunt curved Metzenbaum scissors in the right hand. He carefully advances the tip, curved down, along the spine and under his middle finger until he feels it contact the base of the skull under the tip of his middle finger.

"[T]he surgeon then forces the scissors into the base of the skull or into the foramen magnum. Having safely entered the skull, he spreads the scissors to enlarge the opening.

"The surgeon removes the scissors and introduces a suction catheter into this hole and evacuates the skull contents. With the catheter still in place, he applies traction to the fetus, removing it completely from the patient." H.R. Rep. No. 108–58, p. 3 (2003).

This is an abortion doctor's clinical description. Here is another description from a nurse who witnessed the same method performed on a 26½-week fetus and who testified before the Senate Judiciary Committee:

"'Dr. Haskell went in with forceps and grabbed the baby's legs and pulled them down into the birth canal. Then he delivered the baby's body and the arms—everything but the head. The doctor kept the head right inside the uterus. . . .

"'The baby's little fingers were clasping and unclasping, and his little feet were kicking. Then the doctor stuck the scissors in the back of his head, and the baby's arms jerked out, like a startle reaction, like a flinch, like a baby does when he thinks he is going to fall.

"'The doctor opened up the scissors, stuck a high-powered suction tube into the opening, and sucked the baby's brains out. Now the baby went completely limp. . . .

"'He cut the umbilical cord and delivered the placenta. He threw the baby in a pan, along with the placenta and the instruments he had just used.'" *Ibid.*

Dr. Haskell's approach is not the only method of killing the fetus once its head lodges in the cervix, and "the process has evolved" since his presentation. Another doctor, for example, squeezes the skull after it has been pierced "so that enough brain tissue exudes to allow the head to pass through." Still other physicians reach into the cervix with their forceps and crush the fetus' skull. Others continue to pull the fetus out of the woman until it disarticulates at the neck, in effect decapitating it. These doctors then grasp the head with forceps, crush it, and remove it. . . .

D & E and intact D & E are not the only second-trimester abortion methods. Doctors also may abort a fetus through medical induction. The doctor medicates the woman to induce labor, and contractions occur to deliver the fetus. Induction, which unlike D & E should occur in a hospital, can last as little as 6 hours but can take longer than 48. It accounts for about five percent of second-trimester abortions before 20 weeks of gestation and 15 percent of those after 20 weeks. Doctors turn to two other methods of second-trimester abortion, hysterotomy and hysterectomy, only in emergency situations because they carry increased risk of complications. In a hysterotomy, as in a caesarean section, the doctor removes the fetus by making an incision through the abdomen and uterine wall to gain access to the uterine cavity. A hysterectomy requires the removal of the entire uterus. These two procedures represent about .07% of second-trimester abortions.

B

After Dr. Haskell's procedure received public attention, with ensuing and increasing public concern, bans on "partial birth abortion" proliferated. By the time of the *Stenberg* decision, about 30 States had enacted bans designed to prohibit the procedure. In 1996, Congress also acted to ban partial-birth abortion. President Clinton vetoed the congressional legislation, and the Senate failed to override the veto. Congress approved another bill banning the procedure in 1997, but President Clinton again vetoed it. In 2003, after this Court's decision in *Stenberg*, Congress passed the Act at issue here. On November 5, 2003, President Bush signed the Act into law. It was to take effect the following day.

The Act responded to *Stenberg* in two ways. First, Congress made factual findings. Congress determined that this Court in *Stenberg* "was required to accept the very questionable findings issued by the district court judge," but that Congress was "not bound to accept the same factual findings". Congress found, among other things, that "[a] moral, medical, and ethical consensus exists that the practice of performing a partial-birth abortion . . . is a gruesome and inhumane procedure that is never medically necessary and should be prohibited."

Second, and more relevant here, the Act's language differs from that of the Nebraska statute struck down in *Stenberg*. The operative provisions of the Act provide in relevant part:

"(a) Any physician who, in or affecting interstate or foreign commerce, knowingly performs a partial-birth abortion and thereby kills a human fetus shall be fined under this title or imprisoned not more than 2 years, or both. This subsection does not apply to a partial-birth abortion that is necessary to save the life of a mother whose life is endangered by a physical disorder, physical illness, or physical injury, including a life-endangering physical condition caused by or arising from the pregnancy itself. This subsection takes effect 1 day after the enactment.

"(b) As used in this section—

"(1) the term 'partial-birth abortion' means an abortion in which the person performing the abortion—

"(A) deliberately and intentionally vaginally delivers a living fetus until, in the case of a head-first presentation, the entire fetal head is outside the body of the mother, or, in the case of breech presentation, any part of the fetal trunk past the navel is outside the body of the mother, for the purpose of performing an overt act that the person knows will kill the partially delivered living fetus; and

"(B) performs the overt act, other than completion of delivery, that kills the partially delivered living fetus; and

"(2) the term 'physician' means a doctor of medicine or osteopathy legally authorized to practice medicine and surgery by the State in which the doctor performs such activity, or any other individual legally authorized by the State to perform abortions: *Provided, however,* That any individual who is not a physician or not otherwise legally authorized by the State to perform abortions, but who nevertheless directly performs a partial-birth abortion, shall be subject to the provisions of this section. . . .

"(d)(1) A defendant accused of an offense under this section may seek a hearing before the State Medical Board on whether the physician's conduct was necessary to save the life of the mother whose life was endangered by a physical disorder, physical illness, or physical injury, including a life-endangering physical condition caused by or arising from the pregnancy itself.

"(2) The findings on that issue are admissible on that issue at the trial of the defendant. Upon a motion of the defendant, the court shall delay the beginning of the trial for not more than 30 days to permit such a hearing to take place.

"(e) A woman upon whom a partial-birth abortion is performed may not be prosecuted under this section, for a conspiracy to violate this section, or for an offense under section 2, 3, or 4 of this title based on a violation of this section." 18 U.S.C. § 1531 (2000 ed., Supp. IV). . . .

•  •  •  •

II

•  •  •  •

*Casey* involved a challenge to *Roe v. Wade*, 410 U.S. 113 (1973). . . .

We assume the following principles for the purposes of this opinion. Before viability, a State "may not prohibit any woman from making the ultimate decision to terminate her pregnancy." 505 U.S., at 879 (plurality opinion). It also may not impose upon this right an undue burden, which exists if a regulation's "purpose or effect is to place a substantial obstacle in the path of a woman seeking an abortion before the fetus attains viability." *Id.*, at 878. On the other hand, "[r]egulations which do no more than create a structural mechanism by which the State, or the parent or guardian of a minor, may express profound respect for the life of the unborn are permitted, if they are not a substantial obstacle to the woman's exercise of the right to choose." *Id.*, at 877. *Casey*, in short, struck a balance. The balance was central to its holding. We now apply its standard to the cases at bar.

• • • •

## IV

Under the principles accepted as controlling here, the Act, as we have interpreted it, would be unconstitutional "if its purpose or effect is to place a substantial obstacle in the path of a woman seeking an abortion before the fetus attains viability." *Casey*, 505 U.S., at 878 (plurality opinion). The abortions affected by the Act's regulations take place both previability and postviability; so the quoted language and the undue burden analysis it relies upon are applicable. The question is whether the Act, measured by its text in this facial attack, imposes a substantial obstacle to late-term, but previability, abortions. The Act does not on its face impose a substantial obstacle, and we reject this further facial challenge to its validity.

### A

The Act's purposes are set forth in recitals preceding its operative provisions. A description of the prohibited abortion procedure demonstrates the rationale for the congressional enactment. The Act proscribes a method of abortion in which a fetus is killed just inches before completion of the birth process. Congress stated as follows: "Implicitly approving such a brutal and inhumane procedure by choosing not to prohibit it will further coarsen society to the humanity of not only newborns, but all vulnerable and innocent human life, making it increasingly difficult to protect such life." Congressional Findings (14)(N), in notes following 18 U.S.C. § 1531 (2000 ed., Supp. IV), p. 769. The Act expresses respect for the dignity of human life.

---

Editor's note: Portions of the opinion have been omitted here. The court concludes that the Act is not constitutionally void for vagueness and that the statutory text of the Act specifying restrictions on second trimester abortions does not impose an undue burden because it only applies to intact D & E, and does not prohibit a D & E procedure where the fetus is removed "in parts."

Congress was concerned, furthermore, with the effects on the medical community and on its reputation caused by the practice of partial-birth abortion. The findings in the Act explain:

"Partial-birth abortion . . . confuses the medical, legal, and ethical duties of physicians to preserve and promote life, as the physician acts directly against the physical life of a child, whom he or she had just delivered, all but the head, out of the womb, in order to end that life." Congressional Findings (14)(J), *ibid.*

There can be no doubt the government "has an interest in protecting the integrity and ethics of the medical profession." *Washington v. Glucksberg*, 521 U.S. 702, 731(1997). Under our precedents it is clear the State has a significant role to play in regulating the medical profession.

*Casey* reaffirmed these governmental objectives. The government may use its voice and its regulatory authority to show its profound respect for the life within the woman. A central premise of the opinion was that the Court's precedents after *Roe* had "undervalue[d] the State's interest in potential life." The plurality opinion indicated "[t]he fact that a law which serves a valid purpose, one not designed to strike at the right itself, has the incidental effect of making it more difficult or more expensive to procure an abortion cannot be enough to invalidate it." This was not an idle assertion. The three premises of *Casey* must coexist. The third premise, that the State, from the inception of the pregnancy, maintains its own regulatory interest in protecting the life of the fetus that may become a child, cannot be set at naught by interpreting *Casey's* requirement of a health exception so it becomes tantamount to allowing a doctor to choose the abortion method he or she might prefer. Where it has a rational basis to act, and it does not impose an undue burden, the State may use its regulatory power to bar certain procedures and substitute others, all in furtherance of its legitimate interests in regulating the medical profession in order to promote respect for life, including life of the unborn.

The Act's ban on abortions that involve partial delivery of a living fetus furthers the Government's objectives. No one would dispute that, for many, D & E is a procedure itself laden with the power to devalue human life. Congress could nonetheless conclude that the type of abortion proscribed by the Act requires specific regulation because it implicates additional ethical and moral concerns that justify a special prohibition. Congress determined that the abortion methods it proscribed had a "disturbing similarity to the killing of a newborn infant," Congressional Findings (14)(L), in notes following 18 U.S.C. § 1531 (2000 ed., Supp. IV), p. 769, and thus it was concerned with "draw[ing] a bright line that clearly distinguishes abortion and infanticide." Congressional Findings (14)(G), *ibid.* The Court has in the past confirmed the validity of drawing boundaries to prevent certain practices that extinguish life and are close to actions that are condemned. *Glucksberg* found reasonable the State's "fear that permitting assisted suicide will start it down the path to voluntary and perhaps even involuntary euthanasia." 521 U.S., at 732–735.

Respect for human life finds an ultimate expression in the bond of love the mother has for her child. The Act recognizes this reality as well. Whether to have an abortion requires a difficult and painful moral decision. While we find no reliable data to measure the phenomenon, it seems unexceptionable to conclude some women come to regret their choice to abort the infant life they once created and sustained. Severe depression and loss of esteem can follow.

In a decision so fraught with emotional consequence some doctors may prefer not to disclose precise details of the means that will be used, confining themselves to the required statement of risks the procedure entails. From one standpoint this ought not to be surprising. Any number of patients facing imminent surgical procedures would prefer not to hear all details, lest the usual anxiety preceding invasive medical procedures become the more intense. This is likely the case with the abortion procedures here in issue.

It is, however, precisely this lack of information concerning the way in which the fetus will be killed that is of legitimate concern to the State. The State has an interest in ensuring so grave a choice is well informed. It is self-evident that a mother who comes to regret her choice to abort must struggle with grief more anguished and sorrow more profound when she learns, only after the event, what she once did not know: that she allowed a doctor to pierce the skull and vacuum the fast-developing brain of her unborn child, a child assuming the human form.

It is a reasonable inference that a necessary effect of the regulation and the knowledge it conveys will be to encourage some women to carry the infant to full term, thus reducing the absolute number of late-term abortions. The medical profession, furthermore, may find different and less shocking methods to abort the fetus in the second trimester, thereby accommodating legislative demand. The State's interest in respect for life is advanced by the dialogue that better informs the political and legal systems, the medical profession, expectant mothers, and society as a whole of the consequences that follow from a decision to elect a late-term abortion.

It is objected that the standard D & E is in some respects as brutal, if not more, than the intact D & E, so that the legislation accomplishes little. What we have already said, however, shows ample justification for the regulation. Partial-birth abortion, as defined by the Act, differs from a standard D & E because the former occurs when the fetus is partially outside the mother to the point of one of the Act's anatomical landmarks. It was reasonable for Congress to think that partial-birth abortion, more than standard D & E, "undermines the public's perception of the appropriate role of a physician during the delivery process, and perverts a process during which life is brought into the world." Congressional Findings (14)(K), in notes following 18 U.S.C. § 1531 (2000 ed., Supp. IV), p. 769. There would be a flaw in this Court's logic, and an irony in its jurisprudence, were we first to conclude a ban on both D & E and intact D & E was overbroad and then to say it is irrational to ban only intact D & E because that does not proscribe both procedures. In sum, we reject the contention that the congressional purpose of the Act was "to place a substantial obstacle in the path of a woman seeking an abortion." 505 U.S., at 878, 112 S.Ct. 2791 (plurality opinion).

B

The Act's furtherance of legitimate government interests bears upon, but does not resolve, the next question: whether the Act has the effect of imposing an unconstitutional burden on the abortion right because it does not allow use of the barred procedure where "necessary, in appropriate medical judgment, for [the] preservation of the . . . health of the mother." *Ayotte,* 546 U.S., at 327–328 (quoting *Casey*). The prohibition in the Act would be unconstitutional, under precedents we here assume to be controlling, if it "subject[ed] [women] to significant health risks." *Ayotte* at 328; see also *Casey* at 880 (opinion of the Court). In *Ayotte* the parties agreed a health exception to the challenged parental-involvement statute was necessary "to avert serious and often irreversible damage to [a pregnant minor's] health." 546 U.S., at 328. Here, by contrast, whether the Act creates significant health risks for women has been a contested factual question. The evidence presented in the trial courts and before Congress demonstrates both sides have medical support for their position.

• • • •

The question becomes whether the Act can stand when this medical uncertainty persists. . . .

Medical uncertainty does not foreclose the exercise of legislative power in the abortion context any more than it does in other contexts. The medical uncertainty over whether the Act's prohibition creates significant health risks provides a sufficient basis to conclude in this facial attack that the Act does not impose an undue burden.

The conclusion that the Act does not impose an undue burden is supported by other considerations. Alternatives are available to the prohibited procedure. As we have noted, the Act does not proscribe D & E. . . . In addition the Act's prohibition only applies to the delivery of "a living fetus." If the intact D & E procedure is truly necessary in some circumstances, it appears likely an injection that kills the fetus is an alternative under the Act that allows the doctor to perform the procedure. . . .

In reaching the conclusion the Act does not require a health exception we reject certain arguments made by the parties on both sides of these cases. On the one hand, the Attorney General urges us to uphold the Act on the basis of the congressional findings alone. Although we review congressional factfinding under a deferential standard, we do not in the circumstances here place dispositive weight on Congress' findings. The Court retains an independent constitutional duty to review factual findings where constitutional rights are at stake. . . .

As respondents have noted, and the District Courts recognized, some recitations in the Act are factually incorrect. Whether or not accurate at the time, some of the important findings have been superseded. . . . Congress determined no medical schools provide instruction on the prohibited procedure. The testimony in the District Courts, however, demonstrated intact D & E is taught at medical schools. Congress also found there existed a medical consensus that the prohibited procedure is never medically necessary. The evidence

presented in the District Courts contradicts that conclusion. Uncritical deference to Congress' factual findings in these cases is inappropriate.

On the other hand, relying on the Court's opinion in *Stenberg*, respondents contend that an abortion regulation must contain a health exception "if 'substantial medical authority supports the proposition that banning a particular procedure could endanger women's health.'" Brief for Respondents in No. 05-380, p. 19 (quoting 530 U.S., at 938, 120 S.Ct. 2597); see also Brief for Respondent Planned Parenthood et al. in No. 05-1382, at 12 (same). As illustrated by respondents' arguments and the decisions of the Courts of Appeals, *Stenberg* has been interpreted to leave no margin of error for legislatures to act in the face of medical uncertainty.

A zero tolerance policy would strike down legitimate abortion regulations, like the present one, if some part of the medical community were disinclined to follow the proscription. This is too exacting a standard to impose on the legislative power, exercised in this instance under the Commerce Clause, to regulate the medical profession. Considerations of marginal safety, including the balance of risks, are within the legislative competence when the regulation is rational and in pursuit of legitimate ends. When standard medical options are available, mere convenience does not suffice to displace them; and if some procedures have different risks than others, it does not follow that the State is altogether barred from imposing reasonable regulations. The Act is not invalid on its face where there is uncertainty over whether the barred procedure is ever necessary to preserve a woman's health, given the availability of other abortion procedures that are considered to be safe alternatives.

• • •

*It is so ordered.*

JUSTICE GINSBURG, WITH WHOM JUSTICE STEVENS, JUSTICE SOUTER, AND JUSTICE BREYER JOIN, DISSENTING.

• • • •

Today's decision is alarming. It refuses to take *Casey* and *Stenberg* seriously. It tolerates, indeed applauds, federal intervention to ban nationwide a procedure found necessary and proper in certain cases by the American College of Obstetricians and Gynecologists (ACOG). It blurs the line, firmly drawn in *Casey*, between previability and postviability abortions. And, for the first time since *Roe*, the Court blesses a prohibition with no exception safeguarding a woman's health.

I dissent from the Court's disposition. Retreating from prior rulings that abortion restrictions cannot be imposed absent an exception safeguarding a woman's health, the Court upholds an Act that surely would not survive under the close scrutiny that previously attended state-decreed limitations on a woman's reproductive choices.

• • • •

## II

### A

The Court offers flimsy and transparent justifications for upholding a nationwide ban on intact D & E *sans* any exception to safeguard a women's health. Today's ruling, the Court declares, advances "a premise central to [*Casey's*] conclusion" i.e., the Government's "legitimate and substantial interest in preserving and promoting fetal life." But the Act scarcely furthers that interest: The law saves not a single fetus from destruction, for it targets only a *method* of performing abortion. And surely the statute was not designed to protect the lives or health of pregnant women. In short, the Court upholds a law that, while doing nothing to "preserv[e] . . . fetal life," bars a woman from choosing intact D & E although her doctor "reasonably believes [that procedure] will best protect [her]." *Stenberg*, 530 U.S., at 946 (STEVENS, J., concurring).

As another reason for upholding the ban, the Court emphasizes that the Act does not proscribe the nonintact D & E procedure. But why not, one might ask. Nonintact D & E could equally be characterized as "brutal," involving as it does "tear[ing] [a fetus] apart" and "ripp[ing] off" its limbs. "[T]he notion that either of these two equally gruesome procedures . . . is more akin to infanticide than the other, or that the State furthers any legitimate interest by banning one but not the other, is simply irrational." *Stenberg*, 530 U.S., at 946–947 (STEVENS, J., concurring).

Delivery of an intact, albeit nonviable, fetus warrants special condemnation, the Court maintains, because a fetus that is not dismembered resembles an infant. But so, too, does a fetus delivered intact after it is terminated by injection a day or two before the surgical evacuation, or a fetus delivered through medical induction or caesarean. Yet, the availability of those procedures—along with D & E by dismemberment—the Court says, saves the ban on intact D & E from a declaration of unconstitutionality. Never mind that the procedures deemed acceptable might put a woman's health at greater risk.

Ultimately, the Court admits that "moral concerns" are at work, concerns that could yield prohibitions on any abortion. Notably, the concerns expressed are untethered to any ground genuinely serving the Government's interest in preserving life. By allowing such concerns to carry the day and case, overriding fundamental rights, the Court dishonors our precedent. . . .

Revealing in this regard, the Court invokes an antiabortion shibboleth for which it concededly has no reliable evidence: Women who have abortions come to regret their choices, and consequently suffer from "[s]evere depression and loss of esteem." Because of women's fragile emotional state and because of the "bond of love the mother has for her child," the Court worries, doctors may withhold information about the nature of the intact D & E procedure. The solution the Court approves, then, is *not* to require doctors to inform women, accurately and adequately, of the different procedures and their attendant risks. Instead, the Court deprives women of the right to make an autonomous choice, even at the expense of their safety.

This way of thinking reflects ancient notions about women's place in the family and under the Constitution—ideas that have long since been discredited. . . .

Though today's majority may regard women's feelings on the matter as "self-evident," this Court has repeatedly confirmed that "[t]he destiny of the woman must be shaped . . . on her own conception of her spiritual imperatives and her place in society." *Casey*, 505 U.S., at 852.

### B

In cases on a "woman's liberty to determine whether to [continue] her pregnancy," this Court has identified viability as a critical consideration. See

*Casey*, 505 U.S., at 869–870 (plurality opinion). "[T]here is no line [more workable] than viability," the Court explained in *Casey*, for viability is "the time at which there is a realistic possibility of maintaining and nourishing a life outside the womb, so that the independent existence of the second life can in reason and all fairness be the object of state protection that now overrides the rights of the woman. . . . In some broad sense it might be said that a woman who fails to act before viability has consented to the State's intervention on behalf of the developing child." *Id.*, at 870.

Today, the Court blurs that line, maintaining that "[t]he Act [legitimately] appl[ies] both previability and postviability because . . . a fetus is a living organism while within the womb, whether or not it is viable outside the womb." Instead of drawing the line at viability, the Court refers to Congress' purpose to differentiate "abortion and infanticide" based not on whether a fetus can survive outside the womb, but on where a fetus is anatomically located when a particular medical procedure is performed.

One wonders how long a line that saves no fetus from destruction will hold in face of the Court's "moral concerns." The Court's hostility to the right *Roe* and *Casey* secured is not concealed. Throughout, the opinion refers to obstetrician-gynecologists and surgeons who perform abortions not by the titles of their medical specialties, but by the pejorative label "abortion doctor." A fetus is described as an "unborn child," and as a "baby," second-trimester, previability abortions are referred to as "late-term,"; and the reasoned medical judgments of highly trained doctors are dismissed as "preferences" motivated by "mere convenience." Instead of the heightened scrutiny we have previously applied, the Court determines that a "rational" ground is enough to uphold the Act. And, most troubling, *Casey's* principles, confirming the continuing vitality of "the essential holding of *Roe*," are merely "assume[d]" for the moment, rather than "retained" or "reaffirmed."

## III

### A

• • • •

Without attempting to distinguish *Stenberg* and earlier decisions, the majority asserts that the Act

survives review because respondents have not shown that the ban on intact D & E would be unconstitutional "in a large fraction of relevant cases." But *Casey* makes clear that, in determining whether any restriction poses an undue burden on a "large fraction" of women, the relevant class is *not* "all women," nor "all pregnant women," nor even all women "seeking abortions." 505 U.S., at 895. Rather, a provision restricting access to abortion, "must be judged by reference to those [women] for whom it is an actual rather than an irrelevant restriction," *ibid.* Thus the absence of a health exception burdens *all* women for whom it is relevant—women who, in the judgment of their doctors, require an intact D & E because other procedures would place their health at risk. It makes no sense to conclude that this facial challenge fails because respondents have not shown that a health exception is necessary for a large fraction of second-trimester abortions, including those for which a health exception is unnecessary: The very purpose of a health *exception* is to protect women in *exceptional* cases.

• • • •

## IV

• • • •

Though today's opinion does not go so far as to discard *Roe* or *Casey*, the Court, differently composed than it was when we last considered a restrictive abortion regulation, is hardly faithful to our earlier invocations of "the rule of law" and the "principles of *stare decisis*." Congress imposed a ban despite our clear prior holdings that the State cannot proscribe an abortion procedure when its use is necessary to protect a woman's health. Although Congress' findings could not withstand the crucible of trial, the Court defers to the legislative override of our Constitution-based rulings. A decision so at odds with our jurisprudence should not have staying power.

In sum, the notion that the Partial-Birth Abortion Ban Act furthers any legitimate governmental interest is, quite simply, irrational. The Court's defense of the statute provides no saving explanation. In candor, the Act, and the Court's defense of it, cannot be understood as anything other than an effort to chip away at a right declared again and again by this Court—and with increasing comprehension of its centrality to women's lives. When "a statute burdens constitutional rights and all that can be said on its behalf is that it is the vehicle that legislators have chosen for expressing their hostility to those rights, the burden is undue." *Stenberg*, 530 U.S., at 952 (GINSBURG, J., concurring).

. . .

For the reasons stated, I dissent from the Court's disposition and would affirm the judgments before us for review.

# JUDITH JARVIS THOMSON

# A Defense of Abortion[1]

Judith Jarvis Thomson is professor of philosophy at the Massachusetts Institute of Technology, where she works in both ethics and metaphysics. Her book *Realm of Rights* (Harvard) is a comprehensive theory of human and social rights.

Most opposition to abortion relies on the premise that the fetus is a human being, a person, from the moment of conception. The premise is argued for, but, as I think, not well. Take, for example, the most common argument. We are asked to notice that the development of a human being from conception through birth into childhood is continuous; then it is said that to draw a line, to choose a point in this development and say "before this point the thing is not a person, after this point it is a person" is to make an arbitrary choice, a choice for which in the nature of things no good reason can be given. It is concluded that the fetus is, or anyway that we had better say it is, a person from the moment of conception. But this conclusion does not follow. Similar things might be said about the development of an acorn into an oak tree, and it does not follow that acorns are oak trees, or that we had better say they are. Arguments of this form are

sometimes called "slippery slope arguments"—the phrase is perhaps self-explanatory—and it is dismaying that opponents of abortion rely on them so heavily and uncritically.

I am inclined to agree, however, that the prospects for "drawing a line" in the development of the fetus look dim. I am inclined to think also that we shall probably have to agree that the fetus has already become a human person well before birth. Indeed, it comes as a surprise when one first learns how early in its life it begins to acquire human characteristics. By the tenth week, for example, it already has a face, arms and legs, fingers and toes; it has internal organs, and brain activity is detectable.[2] On the other hand, I think that the premise is false, that the fetus is not a person from the moment of conception. A newly fertilized ovum, a newly implanted clump of cells, is no more a person than an acorn is an oak tree. But I shall not discuss any of this. For it seems to me to be of great interest to ask what happens if, for the sake of argument, we allow the premise. How, precisely, are we supposed to get from there to the conclusion that abortion is morally impermissible? Opponents of abortion commonly spend most of their time establishing that the fetus is a person, and hardly any time explaining the step from there to the impermissibility of abortion. Perhaps they think the step too simple and obvious to require much comment. Or perhaps instead they are simply being economical in argument. Many of those who defend abortion rely on the premise that the fetus is not a person, but only a bit of tissue that will become a person at birth; and why pay out more arguments than you have to? Whatever the explanation, I suggest that the step they take is neither easy nor obvious, that it calls for closer examination than it is commonly given, and that when we do give it this closer examination we shall feel inclined to reject it.

I propose, then, that we grant that the fetus is a person from the moment of conception. How does the argument go from here? Something like this, I take it. Every person has a right to life. So the fetus has a right to life. No doubt the mother has a right to decide what shall happen in and to her body; everyone would grant that. But surely a person's right to life is stronger and more stringent than the mother's right to decide what happens in and to her body, and so outweighs it. So the fetus may not be killed; an abortion may not be performed.

It sounds plausible. But now let me ask you to imagine this. You wake up in the morning and find yourself back to back in bed with an unconscious violinist. A famous unconscious violinist. He has been found to have a fatal kidney ailment, and the Society of Music Lovers has canvassed all the available medical records and found that you alone have the right blood type to help. They have therefore kidnapped you, and last night the violinist's circulatory system was plugged into yours, so that your kidneys can be used to extract poisons from his blood as well as your own. The director of the hospital now tells you, "Look, we're sorry the Society of Music Lovers did this to you—we would never have permitted it if we had known. But still, they did it, and the violinist now is plugged into you. To unplug you would be to kill him. But never mind, it's only for nine months. By then he will have recovered from his ailment, and can safely be unplugged from you." Is it morally incumbent on you to accede to this situation? No doubt it would be very nice of you if you did, a great kindness. But do you *have* to accede to it? What if it were not nine months, but nine years? Or longer still? What if the director of the hospital says, "Tough luck, I agree, but you've now got to stay in bed, with the violinist plugged into you, for the rest of your life. Because remember this. All persons have a right to life, and violinists are persons. Granted you have a right to decide what happens in and to your body, but a person's right to life outweighs your right to decide what happens in and to your body. So you cannot ever be unplugged from him." I imagine you would regard this as outrageous, which suggests that something really is wrong with that plausible-sounding argument I mentioned a moment ago.

In this case, of course, you were kidnapped; you didn't volunteer for the operation that plugged the violinist into your kidneys. Can those who oppose abortion on the ground I mentioned make an exception for a pregnancy due to rape? Certainly. They can say that persons have a right to life only if they didn't come into existence because of rape; or they can say that all persons have a right to life, but that some have less of a right to life than others, in particular, that those who came into existence because of rape have less. But these statements have a rather unpleasant sound. Surely the question of whether you have a right to life at all, or how much of it you have, shouldn't turn on the question of whether or not you are the product of a rape. And in fact the people who oppose abortion on the ground I mentioned do not make this distinction, and hence do not make an exception in case of rape.

Nor do they make an exception for a case in which the mother has to spend the nine months of her pregnancy in bed. They would agree that would be a great pity, and hard on the mother; but all the same, all persons have a right to life, the fetus is a person, and so on. I suspect, in fact, that they would not make an exception for a case in which, miraculously enough, the pregnancy went on for nine years, or even the rest of the mother's life.

Some won't even make an exception for a case in which continuation of the pregnancy is likely to shorten the mother's life; they regard abortion as impermissible even to save the mother's life. Such cases are nowadays very rare, and many opponents of abortion do not accept this extreme view. All the same, it is a good place to begin: a number of points of interest come out in respect to it.

1. Let us call the view that abortion is impermissible even to save the mother's life "the extreme view."

I want to suggest first that it does not issue from the argument I mentioned earlier without the addition of some fairly powerful premises. Suppose a woman has become pregnant, and now learns that she has a cardiac condition such that she will die if she carries the baby to term. What may be done for her? The fetus, being a person, has a right to life, but as the mother is a person too, so has she a right to life. Presumably they have an equal right to life. How is it supposed to come out that an abortion may not be performed? If mother and child have an equal right to life, shouldn't we perhaps flip a coin? Or should we add to the mother's right to life her right to decide what happens in and to her body, which everybody seems to be ready to grant—the sum of her rights now outweighing the fetus's right to life?

The most familiar argument here is the following. We are told that performing the abortion would be directly killing[3] the child, whereas doing nothing would not be killing the mother, but only letting her die. Moreover, in killing the child, one would be killing an innocent person, for the child has committed no crime, and is not aiming at his mother's death. And then there are a variety of ways in which this might be continued. (a) But as directly killing an innocent person is always and absolutely impermissible, an abortion may not be performed. Or, (b) as directly killing an innocent person is murder, and murder is always and absolutely impermissible, an abortion may not be performed.[4] Or, (c) as one's duty to refrain from directly killing an innocent person is more stringent than one's duty to keep a person from dying, an abortion may not be performed. Or, (d) if one's only options are directly killing an innocent person or letting a person die, one must prefer letting the person die, and thus an abortion may not be performed.[5]

Some people seem to have thought that these are not further premises which must be added if the conclusion is to be reached, but that they follow from the very fact that an innocent person has a right to life.[6] But this seems to me to be a mistake, and perhaps the simplest way to show this is to bring out that while we must certainly grant that innocent persons have a right to life, the theses in (a) through (d) are all false. Take (b), for example. If directly killing an innocent person is murder, and thus is impermissible, then the mother's directly killing the innocent person inside her is murder, and thus is impermissible. But it cannot

seriously be thought to be murder if the mother performs an abortion on herself to save her life. It cannot seriously be said that she *must* refrain, that she *must* sit passively by and wait for her death. Let us look again at the case of you and the violinist. There you are, in bed with the violinist, and the director of the hospital says to you, "It's all most distressing, and I deeply sympathize, but you see this is putting an additional strain on your kidneys, and you'll be dead within the month. But you *have* to stay where you are all the same. Because unplugging you would be directly killing an innocent violinist, and that's murder, and that's impermissible." If anything in the world is true, it is that you do not commit murder, you do not do what is impermissible, if you reach around to your back and unplug yourself from that violinist to save your life.

The main focus of attention in writings on abortion has been on what a third party may or may not do in answer to a request from a woman for an abortion. This is in a way understandable. Things being as they are, there isn't much a woman can safely do to abort herself. So the question asked is what a third party may do, and what the mother may do, if it is mentioned at all, is deduced, almost as an afterthought, from what it is concluded that third parties may do. But it seems to me that to treat the matter in this way is to refuse to grant to the mother that very status of person which is so firmly insisted on for the fetus. For we cannot simply read off what a person may do from what a third party may do. Suppose you find yourself trapped in a tiny house with a growing child. I mean a very tiny house, and a rapidly growing child—you are already up against the wall of the house and in a few minutes you'll be crushed to death. The child on the other hand won't be crushed to death; if nothing is done to stop him from growing he'll be hurt, but in the end he'll simply burst open the house and walk out a free man. Now I could well understand it if a bystander were to say, "There's nothing we can do for you. We cannot choose between your life and his, we cannot be the ones to decide who is to live, we cannot intervene." But it cannot be concluded that you too can do nothing, that you cannot attack it to save your life. However innocent the child may be, you do not have to wait passively while it crushes you to death. Perhaps a pregnant woman is vaguely felt to have the status of house, to which we don't allow the right of self-defense. But if the woman houses the child, it should be remembered that she is a person who houses it.

I should perhaps stop to say explicitly that I am not claiming that people have a right to do anything whatever to save their lives. I think, rather, that there are drastic limits to the right of self-defense. If someone threatens you with death unless you torture someone else to death, I think you have not the right, even to save your life, to do so. But the case under consideration here is very different. In our case there are only two people involved, one whose life is threatened, and one who threatens it. Both are innocent: the one who is threatened is not threatened because of any fault, the one who threatens does not threaten because of any fault. For this reason we may feel that we bystanders cannot intervene. But the person threatened can.

In sum, a woman surely can defend her life against the threat to it posed by the unborn child, even if doing so involves its death. And this shows not merely that the theses in (a) through (d) are false; it shows also that the extreme view of abortion is false, and so we need not canvass any other possible ways of arriving at it from the argument I mentioned at the outset.

2. The extreme view could of course be weakened to say that while abortion is permissible to save the mother's life, it may not be performed by a third party, but only by the mother herself. But this cannot be right either. For what we have to keep in mind is that the mother and the unborn child are not like two tenants in a small house which has, by an unfortunate mistake, been rented to both: the mother *owns* the house. The fact that she does adds to the offensiveness of deducing that the mother can do nothing from the supposition that third parties can do nothing. But it does more than this: it casts a bright light on the supposition that third parties can do nothing. Certainly it lets us see that a third party who says "I cannot choose between you" is fooling himself if he thinks this is impartiality. If Jones has found and fastened on a certain coat, which he needs to keep him from freezing, but which Smith also needs to keep him from freezing, then it is not impartiality that says "I cannot choose between you" when Smith owns the coat. Women have said again and again "This body is *my* body!" and they have reason to feel angry, reason to feel that it has been like shouting into the wind. Smith, after

all, is hardly likely to bless us if we say to him, "Of course it's your coat, anybody would grant that it is. But no one may choose between you and Jones who is to have it."

We should really ask what it is that says "no one may choose" in the face of the fact that the body that houses the child is the mother's body. It may be simply a failure to appreciate this fact. But it may be something more interesting, namely, the sense that one has a right to refuse to lay hands on people, even where it would be just and fair to do so, even where justice seems to require that somebody do so. Thus justice might call for somebody to get Smith's coat back from Jones, and yet you have a right to refuse to be the one to lay hands on Jones, a right to refuse to do physical violence to him. This, I think, must be granted. But then what should be said is not "no one may choose," but only "*I* cannot choose," and indeed not even this, but "*I* will not *act*," leaving it open that somebody else can or should, and in particular that anyone in a position of authority, with the job of securing people's rights, both can and should. So this is no difficulty. I have not been arguing that any given third party must accede to the mother's request that he perform an abortion to save her life, but only that he may.

I suppose that in some views of human life the mother's body is only on loan to her, the loan not being one which gives her any prior claim to it. One who held this view might well think it impartiality to say "I cannot choose." But I shall simply ignore this possibility. My own view is that if a human being has any just, prior claim to anything at all, he has a just, prior claim to his own body. And perhaps this needn't be argued for here anyway, since, as I mentioned, the arguments against abortion we are looking at do grant that the woman has a right to decide what happens in and to her body.

But although they do grant it, I have tried to show that they do not take seriously what is done in granting it. I suggest the same thing will reappear even more clearly when we turn away from cases in which the mother's life is at stake, and attend, as I propose we now do, to the vastly more common cases in which a woman wants an abortion for some less weighty reason than preserving her own life.

3. Where the mother's life is not at stake, the argument I mentioned at the outset seems to have a much

stronger pull. "Everyone has a right to life, so the unborn person has a right to life." And isn't the child's right to life weightier than anything other than the mother's own right to life, which she might put forward as ground for an abortion?

This argument treats the right to life as if it were unproblematic. It is not, and this seems to me to be precisely the source of the mistake.

For we should now, at long last, ask what it comes to, to have a right to life. In some views having a right to life includes having a right to be given at least the bare minimum one needs for continued life. But suppose that what in fact *is* the bare minimum a man needs for continued life is something he has no right at all to be given. If I am sick unto death, and the only thing that will save my life is the touch of Henry Fonda's cool hand on my fevered brow, then all the same, I have no right to be given the touch of Henry Fonda's cool hand on my fevered brow. It would be frightfully nice of him to fly in from the West Coast to provide it. It would be less nice, though no doubt well meant, if my friends flew out to the West Coast and carried Henry Fonda back with them. But I have no right at all against anybody that he should do this for me. Or again, to return to the story I told earlier, the fact that for continued life that violinist needs the continued use of your kidneys does not establish that he has a right to be given the continued use of your kidneys. He certainly has no right against you that *you* should give him continued use of your kidneys. For nobody has any right to use your kidneys unless you give him such a right; and nobody has the right against you that you shall give him this right—if you do allow him to go on using your kidneys, this is a kindness on your part, and not something he can claim from you as his due. Nor has he any right against anybody else that they should give him continued use of your kidneys. Certainly he had no right against the Society of Music Lovers that *they* should plug him into you in the first place. And if you now start to unplug yourself, having learned that you will otherwise have to spend nine years in bed with him, there is nobody in the world who must try to prevent you, in order to see to it that he is given something he has a right to be given.

Some people are rather stricter about the right to life. In their view, it does not include the right to be given anything, but amounts to, and only to, the right not to be killed by anybody. But here a related difficulty arises. If everybody is to refrain from killing that violinist, then everybody must refrain from doing a great many different sorts of things. Everybody must refrain from slitting his throat, everybody must refrain from shooting him—and everybody must refrain from unplugging you from him. But does he have a right against everybody that they shall refrain from unplugging you from him? To refrain from doing this is to allow him to continue to use your kidneys. It could be argued that he has a right against us that we should allow him to continue to use your kidneys. That is, while he had no right against us that we should give him the use of your kidneys, it might be argued that he anyway has a right against us that we shall not now intervene and deprive him of the use of your kidneys. I shall come back to third-party interventions later. But certainly the violinist has no right against you that *you* shall allow him to continue to use your kidneys. As I said, if you do allow him to use them, it is a kindness on your part, and not something you owe him.

The difficulty I point to here is not peculiar to the right to life. It reappears in connection with all the other natural rights; and it is something which an adequate account of rights must deal with. For present purposes it is enough just to draw attention to it. But I would stress that I am not arguing that people do not have a right to life—quite to the contrary, it seems to me that the primary control we must place on the acceptability of an account of rights is that it should turn out in that account to be a truth that all persons have a right to life. I am arguing only that having a right to life does not guarantee having either a right to be given the use of or a right to be allowed continued use of another person's body—even if one needs it for life itself. So the right to life will not serve the opponents of abortion in the very simple and clear way in which they seem to have thought it would.

4. There is another way to bring out the difficulty. In the most ordinary sort of case, to deprive someone of what he has a right to is to treat him unjustly. Suppose a boy and his small brother are jointly given a box of chocolates for Christmas. If the older boy takes the box and refuses to give his brother any of the chocolates, he is unjust to him, for the brother has been given a right to half of them. But suppose that, having learned that otherwise it means nine years in bed with that violinist, you unplug yourself from him.

You surely are not being unjust to him for you gave him no right to use your kidneys, and no one else can have given him any such right. But we have to notice that in unplugging yourself, you are killing him; and violinists, like everybody else, have a right to life, and thus in the view we were considering just now, the right not to be killed. So here you do what he supposedly has a right you shall not do, but you do not act unjustly to him in doing it.

The emendation which may be made at this point is this: the right to life consists not in the right not to be killed, but rather in the right not to be killed unjustly. This runs a risk of circularity, but never mind: it would enable us to square the fact that the violinist has a right to life with the fact that you do not act unjustly toward him in unplugging yourself, thereby killing him. For if you do not kill him unjustly, you do not violate his right to life, and so it is no wonder you do him no injustice.

But if this emendation is accepted, the gap in the argument against abortion stares us plainly in the face: It is by no means enough to show that the fetus is a person, and to remind us that all persons have a right to life—we need to be shown also that killing the fetus violates its right to life, i.e., that abortion is unjust killing. And is it?

I suppose we may take it as a datum that in a case of pregnancy due to rape the mother has not given the unborn person a right to the use of her body for food and shelter. Indeed, in what pregnancy could it be supposed that the mother has given the unborn person such a right? It is not as if there were unborn persons drifting about the world, to whom a woman who wants a child says "I invite you in."

But it might be argued that there are other ways one can have acquired a right to the use of another person's body than by having been invited to use it by that person. Suppose a woman voluntarily indulges in intercourse, knowing of the chance it will issue in pregnancy, and then she does become pregnant; is she not in part responsible for the presence, in fact the very existence, of the unborn person inside her? No doubt she did not invite it in. But doesn't her partial responsibility for its being there itself give it a right to the use of her body?[7] If so, then her aborting it would be more like the boy's taking away the chocolates, and less like your unplugging yourself from the violinist—doing so would be depriving it of what it

does have a right to, and thus would be doing it an injustice.

And then, too, it might be asked whether or not she can kill it even to save her own life: If she voluntarily called it into existence, how can she now kill it, even in self-defense?

The first thing to be said about this is that it is something new. Opponents of abortion have been so concerned to make out the independence of the fetus, in order to establish that it has a right to life, just as its mother does, that they have tended to overlook the possible support they might gain from making out that the fetus is *dependent* on the mother, in order to establish that she has a special kind of responsibility for it, a responsibility that gives it rights against her which are not possessed by any independent person—such as an ailing violinist who is a stranger to her.

On the other hand, this argument would give the unborn person a right to its mother's body only if her pregnancy resulted from a voluntary act, undertaken in full knowledge of the chance a pregnancy might result from it. It would leave out entirely the unborn person whose existence is due to rape. Pending the availability of some further argument, then, we would be left with the conclusion that unborn persons whose existence is due to rape have no right to the use of their mothers' bodies, and thus that aborting them is not depriving them of anything they have a right to and hence is not unjust killing.

And we should also notice that it is not at all plain that this argument really does go even as far as it purports to. For there are cases and cases, and the details make a difference. If the room is stuffy, and I therefore open a window to air it, and a burglar climbs in, it would be absurd to say, "Ah, now he can stay, she's given him a right to the use of her house—for she is partially responsible for his presence there, having voluntarily done what enabled him to get in, in full knowledge that there are such things as burglars, and that burglars burgle." It would be still more absurd to say this if I had had bars installed outside my windows, precisely to prevent burglars from getting in, and a burglar got in only because of a defect in the bars. It remains equally absurd if we imagine it is not a burglar who climbs in, but an innocent person who blunders or falls in. Again, suppose it were like this: people-seeds drift about in the air like pollen, and if you open your windows, one may drift in and take root in your carpets or upholstery. You don't want children, so you fix up your windows with fine mesh screens, the very best you can buy. As can happen, however, and on very, very rare occasions does happen, one of the screens is defective; and a seed drifts in and takes root. Does the person-plant who now develops have a right to the use of your house? Surely not—despite the fact that you voluntarily opened your windows, you knowingly kept carpets and upholstered furniture, and you knew that screens were sometimes defective. Someone may argue that you are responsible for its rooting, that it does have a right to your house, because after all you *could* have lived out your life with bare floors and furniture, or with sealed windows and doors. But this won't do—for by the same token anyone can avoid a pregnancy due to rape by having a hysterectomy, or anyway by never leaving home without a (reliable!) army.

It seems to me that the argument we were looking at can establish at most that there are *some* cases in which the unborn person has a right to the use of its mother's body, and therefore *some* cases in which abortion is unjust killing. There is room for much discussion and argument as to precisely which, if any. But I think we should sidestep this issue and leave it open, for at any rate the argument certainly does not establish that all abortion is unjust killing.

5. There is room for yet another argument here, however. We surely must all grant that there may be cases in which it would be morally indecent to detach a person from your body at the cost of his life. Suppose you learn that what the violinist needs is not nine years of your life, but only one hour. All you need do to save his life is to spend one hour in that bed with him. Suppose also that letting him use your kidneys for that one hour would not affect your health in the slightest. Admittedly you were kidnapped. Admittedly you did not give anyone permission to plug him into you. Nevertheless it seems to me plain you *ought* to allow him to use your kidneys for that hour—it would be indecent to refuse.

Again, suppose pregnancy lasted only an hour, and constituted no threat to life or health. And suppose that a woman becomes pregnant as a result of rape. Admittedly she did not voluntarily do anything to bring about the existence of a child. Admittedly she did nothing at all which would give the unborn person a right to the use of her body. All the same it might well be said, as in the newly emended violinist story, that she *ought* to allow it to remain for that hour—that it would be indecent in her to refuse.

Now some people are inclined to use the term "right" in such a way that it follows from the fact that you ought to allow a person to use your body for the hour he needs, that he has a right to use your body for the hour he needs, even though he has not been given that right by any person or act. They may say that it follows also that if you refuse, you act unjustly toward him. This use of the term is perhaps so common that it cannot be called wrong; nevertheless it seems to me to be an unfortunate loosening of what we would do better to keep a tight rein on. Suppose that box of chocolates I mentioned earlier had not been given to both boys jointly, but was given only to the older boy. There he sits, stolidly eating his way through the box, his small brother watching enviously. Here we are likely to say "You ought not to be so mean. You ought to give your brother some of those chocolates." My own view is that it just does not follow from the truth of this that the brother has any right to any of the chocolates. If the boy refuses to give his brother any, he is greedy, stingy, callous—but not unjust. I suppose that the people I have in mind will say it does follow that the brother has a right to some of the chocolates, and thus that the boy does act unjustly if he refuses to give his brother any. But the effect of saying this is to obscure what we should keep distinct, namely the difference between the boy's refusal in this case and the boy's refusal in the earlier case, in which the box was given to both boys jointly, and in which the small brother thus had what was from any point of view clear title to half.

A further objection to so using the term "right" that from the fact that A ought to do a thing for B, it follows that B has a right against A that A do it for him, is that it is going to make the question of whether or not a man has a right to a thing turn on how easy it is to provide him with it; and this seems not merely unfortunate, but morally unacceptable. Take the case of Henry Fonda again. I said earlier that I had no right to the touch of his cool hand on my fevered brow, even though I needed it to save my life. I said it would be frightfully nice of him to fly in from the West Coast to provide me with it, but that I had no right against him that he should do so. But suppose he isn't on the West Coast. Suppose he has only to walk across the room, place a hand briefly on my brow—and lo, my life is saved. Then surely he ought to do it, it would be indecent to refuse. Is it to be said "Ah well, it follows that in this case she has a right to the touch of his hand on her brow, and so it would be an injustice in him to refuse"? So that I have a right to it when it is easy for him to provide it, though no right when it's hard? It's rather a shocking idea that anyone's right should fade away and disappear as it gets harder and harder to accord them to him.

So my own view is that even though you ought to let the violinist use your kidneys for the one hour he needs, we should not conclude that he has a right to do so—we would say that if you refuse, you are, like the boy who owns all the chocolates and will give none away, self-centered and callous, indecent in fact, but not unjust. And similarly, that even supposing a case in which a woman pregnant due to rape ought to allow the unborn person to use her body for the hour he needs, we should not conclude that he has a right to do so; we should conclude that she is self-centered, callous, indecent, but not unjust, if she refuses. The complaints are no less grave; they are just different. However, there is no need to insist on this point. If anyone does wish to deduce "he has a right" from "you ought," then all the same he must surely grant that there are cases in which it is not morally required of you that you allow that violinist to use your kidneys, and in which he does not have a right to use them, and in which you do not do him an injustice if you refuse. And so also for mother and unborn child. Except in such cases as the unborn person has a right to demand it—and we were leaving open the possibility that there may be such cases—nobody is morally *required* to make large sacrifices, of health, of all other interests and concerns, of all other duties and commitments, for nine years, or even for nine months, in order to keep another person alive.

6. We have in fact to distinguish between two kinds of Samaritan: the Good Samaritan and what we might call the Minimally Decent Samaritan. The story of the Good Samaritan, you will remember, goes like this:

A certain man went down from Jerusalem to Jericho, and fell among thieves, which stripped him of his raiment, and wounded him, and departed, leaving him half dead.

And by chance there came down a certain priest that way; and when he saw him, he passed by on the other side.

And likewise a Levite, when he was at the place, came and looked on him, and passed by on the other side.

But a certain Samaritan, as he journeyed, came where he was; and when he saw him he had compassion on him.

And went to him, and bound up his wounds, pouring in oil and wine, and set him on his own beast, and brought him to an inn, and took care of him.

And on the morrow, when he departed, he took out two pence, and gave them to the host, and said unto him, "Take care of him; and whatsoever thou spendest more, when I come again, I will repay thee."

(Luke 10:30–35)

The Good Samaritan went out of his way, at some cost to himself, to help one in need of it. We are not told what the options were, that is, whether or not the priest and the Levite could have helped by doing less than the Good Samaritan did, but assuming they could have, then the fact they did nothing at all shows they were not even Minimally Decent Samaritans, not because they were not Samaritans, but because they were not even minimally decent.

These things are a matter of degree, of course, but there is a difference, and it comes out perhaps most clearly in the story of Kitty Genovese, who, as you will remember, was murdered while thirty-eight people watched or listened, and did nothing at all to help her. A Good Samaritan would have rushed out to give direct assistance against the murderer. Or perhaps we had better allow that it would have been a Splendid Samaritan who did this, on the ground that it would have involved a risk of death for himself. But the thirty-eight not only did not do this, they did not even trouble to pick up a phone to call the police. Minimally Decent Samaritanism would call for doing at least that, and their not having done it was monstrous.

After telling the story of the Good Samaritan, Jesus said, "Go, and do thou likewise." Perhaps he meant that we are morally required to act as the Good Samaritan did. Perhaps he was urging people to do more than is morally required of them. At all events it seems plain that it was not morally required of any of the thirty-eight that he rush out to give direct assistance at the risk of his own life, and that it is not morally required of anyone that he give long stretches of his life—nine years or nine months—to sustaining the life of a person who has no special right (we were leaving open the possibility of this) to demand it.

Indeed, with one rather striking class of exceptions, no one in any country in the world is *legally* required to do anywhere near as much as this for anyone else. The class of exceptions is obvious. My main concern here is not the state of the law in respect to abortion, but it is worth drawing attention to the fact that in no state in this country is any man compelled by law to be even a Minimally Decent Samaritan to any person; there is no law under which charges could be brought against the thirty-eight who stood by while Kitty Genovese died. By contrast, in most states in this country women are compelled by law to be not merely Minimally Decent Samaritans, but Good Samaritans to unborn persons inside them. This doesn't by itself settle anything one way or the other, because it may well be argued that there should be laws in this country—as there are in many European countries—compelling at least Minimally Decent Samaritanism.[8] But it does show that there is a gross injustice in the existing state of the law. And it shows also that the groups currently working against liberalization of abortion laws, in fact working toward having it declared unconstitutional for a state to permit abortion, had better start working for the adoption of Good Samaritan laws generally, or earn the charge that they are acting in bad faith.

I should think, myself, that Minimally Decent Samaritan laws would be one thing, Good Samaritan laws quite another, and in fact highly improper. But we are not here concerned with the law. What we should ask is not whether anybody should be compelled by law to be a Good Samaritan, but whether we must accede to a situation in which somebody is being compelled—by nature, perhaps—to be a Good Samaritan. We have, in other words, to look now at third-party interventions. I have been arguing that no person is morally required to make large sacrifices to sustain the life of another who has no right to demand them, and this even where the sacrifices do not include life itself; we are not morally required to be Good Samaritans or anyway Very Good Samaritans to one another. But what if a man cannot extricate himself from such a situation? What if he appeals to us to extricate him? It seems to me plain that there are cases in which we can, cases in which a Good Samaritan would extricate him. There you are, you were kidnapped, and nine years in bed with that violinist lie ahead of you. You have your own life to lead. You are sorry, but you simply cannot

see giving up so much of your life to the sustaining of his. You cannot extricate yourself, and ask us to do so. I should have thought that—in light of his having no right to the use of your body—it was obvious that we do not have to accede to your being forced to give up so much. We can do what you ask. There is no injustice to the violinist in our doing so.

7. Following the lead of the opponents of abortion, I have throughout been speaking of the fetus merely as a person, and what I have been asking is whether or not the argument we began with, which proceeds only from the fetus's being a person, really does establish its conclusion. I have argued that it does not.

But of course there are arguments and arguments, and it may be said that I have simply fastened on the wrong one. It may be said that what is important is not merely the fact that the fetus is a person, but that it is a person for whom the woman has a special kind of responsibility issuing from the fact that she is its mother. And it might be argued that all my analogies are therefore irrelevant—for you do not have that special kind of responsibility for that violinist, Henry Fonda does not have that special kind of responsibility for me. And our attention might be drawn to the fact that men and women both *are* compelled by law to provide support for their children.

I have in effect dealt (briefly) with this argument in section 4 above; but a (still briefer) recapitulation now may be in order. Surely we do not have any such "special responsibility" for a person unless we have assumed it, explicitly or implicitly. If a set of parents do not try to prevent pregnancy, do not obtain an abortion, and then at the time of birth of the child do not put it out for adoption, but rather take it home with them, then they have assumed responsibility for it, they have given it rights, and they cannot *now* withdraw support from it at the cost of its life because they now find it difficult to go on providing for it. But if they have taken all reasonable precautions against having a child, they do not simply by virtue of their biological relationship to the child who comes into existence have a special responsibility for it. They may wish to assume responsibility for it, or they may not wish to. And I am suggesting that if assuming responsibility for it would require large sacrifices, then they may refuse. A Good Samaritan would not refuse—or anyway, a Splendid Samaritan, if the sacrifices that had to be made were enormous. But then so would a Good

Samaritan assume responsibility for that violinist; so would Henry Fonda, if he is a Good Samaritan, fly in from the West Coast and assume responsibility for me.

8. My argument will be found unsatisfactory on two counts by many of those who want to regard abortion as morally permissible. First, while I do argue that abortion is not impermissible, I do not argue that it is always permissible. There may well be cases in which carrying the child to term requires only Minimally Decent Samaritanism of the mother, and this is a standard we must not fall below. I am inclined to think it a merit of my account precisely that it does *not* give a general yes or a general no. It allows for and supports our sense that, for example, a sick and desperately frightened fourteen-year-old schoolgirl, pregnant due to rape, may *of course* choose abortion, and that any law which rules this out is an insane law. And it also allows for and supports our sense that in other cases resort to abortion is even positively indecent. It would be indecent in the woman to request an abortion, and indecent in a doctor to perform it, if she is in her seventh month and wants the abortion just to avoid the nuisance of postponing a trip abroad. The very fact that the arguments I have been drawing attention to treat all cases of abortion, or even all cases of abortion in which the mother's life is not at stake, as morally on a par ought to have made them suspect at the outset.

Secondly, while I am arguing for the permissibility of abortion in some cases, I am not arguing for the right to secure the death of the unborn child. It is easy to confuse these two things in that up to a certain point in the life of the fetus it is not able to survive outside the mother's body; hence removing it from her body guarantees its death. But they are importantly different. I have argued that you are not morally required to spend nine months in bed, sustaining the life of that violinist; but to say this is by no means to say that if, when you unplug yourself, there is a miracle and he survives, you then have a right to turn around and slit his throat. You may detach yourself even if this costs him his life; you have no right to be guaranteed his death, by some other means, if unplugging yourself does not kill him. There are some people who will feel dissatisfied by this feature of my argument. A woman may be utterly devastated by the thought of a child, a bit of herself, put out for adoption and never seen or heard of again. She may therefore want not merely that the child be detached from her, but more, that it

die. Some opponents of abortion are inclined to regard this as beneath contempt—thereby showing insensitivity to what is surely a powerful source of despair. All the same, I agree that the desire for the child's death is not one which anybody may gratify, should it turn out to be possible to detach the child alive.

At this place, however, it should be remembered that we have only been pretending throughout that the fetus is a human being from the moment of conception. A very early abortion is surely not the killing of a person, and so is not dealt with by anything I have said here.

## NOTES

1. I am very much indebted to James Thomson for discussion, criticism, and many helpful suggestions.

2. Daniel Callahan, *Abortion: Law, Choice and Morality* (New York, 1970), p. 373. This book gives a fascinating survey of the available information on abortion. The Jewish tradition is surveyed in David M. Feldman, *Birth Control in Jewish Law* (New York, 1968), Part 5; the Catholic tradition in John T. Noonan, Jr., "An Almost Absolute Value in History," in *The Morality of Abortion*, ed. John T. Noonan, Jr. (Cambridge, Mass., 1970).

3. The term "direct" in the arguments I refer to is a technical one. Roughly, what is meant by "direct killing" is either killing as an end in itself, or killing as a means to some end, for example, the end of saving someone else's life. See note 6, below, for an example of its use.

4. Cf. *Encyclical Letter of Pope Pius XI on Christian Marriage*, St. Paul Editions (Boston, n.d.), p. 32: "however much we may pity the mother whose health and even life is gravely imperiled in the performance of the duty allotted to her by nature, nevertheless what could ever be a sufficient reason for excusing in any way the direct murder of the innocent? This is precisely what we are dealing with here." Noonan (*The Morality of Abortion*, p. 43) reads this as follows: "What cause can ever avail to excuse in any way the direct killing of the innocent? For it is a question of that."

5. The thesis in (d) is in an interesting way weaker than those in (a), (b), and they rule out abortion even in cases in which both mother and child will die if the abortion is not performed. By contrast, one who held the view expressed in (d) could consistently say that one needn't prefer letting two persons die to killing one.

6. Cf. the following passage from Pius XII, *Address to the Italian Catholic Society of Midwives*: "The baby in the maternal breast has the right to life immediately from God.—Hence there is no man, no human authority, no science, no medical eugenic, social, economic or moral 'indication' which can establish or grant a valid juridical ground for a direct deliberate disposition of an innocent human life, that is a disposition which looks to its destruction either as an end or as a means to another end perhaps in itself not illicit.—The baby, still not born, is a man in the same degree and for the same reason as the mother" (quoted in Noonan, *The Morality of Abortion*, p. 45).

7. The need for a discussion of this argument was brought home to me by members of the Society for Ethical and Legal Philosophy, to whom this paper was originally presented.

8. For a discussion of the difficulties involved, and a survey of the European experience with such laws, see *The Good Samaritan and the Law*, ed. James M. Ratcliffe (New York, 1966).

# BARUCH BRODY

# The Morality of Abortion

Baruch Brody is Leon Jaworski Professor of Biomedical Ethics, director of the
Center for Medical Ethics and Health Policy at the Baylor College of Medicine,
Andrew Mellow Professor of Humanities in the Department of Philosophy at Rice
University, and director of the Ethics Program at Methodist Hospital. Brody is a
prolific writer in many areas of bioethics. Representative works include *Abortion
and the Sanctity of Human Life* (MIT), *Life and Death Decision-Making* (Oxford), and
*Taking Issue: Pluralism and Casuistry in Bioethics* (Georgetown).

## THE WOMAN'S RIGHT TO HER BODY

It is a common claim that a woman ought to be in
control of what happens to her body to the greatest
extent possible, that she ought to be able to use her

From *Abortion and the Sanctity of Human Life: A Philosophical
View* (Cambridge, MA: MIT Press, 1975), pp. 26–30, 37–39, and
"Fetal Humanity and the Theory of Essentialism," in *Philosophy
and Sex*, Robert Baker and Frederick Elliston, eds. (Buffalo, NY:
Prometheus Books, 1975), pp. 348–352. (Some parts of these essays
were later revised by Professor Brody.)

body in ways that she wants to and refrain from using
it in ways that she does not want to. This right is particularly pressed where certain uses of her body have
deep and lasting effects upon the character of her life,
personal, social, and economic. Therefore, it is argued,
a woman should be free either to carry her fetus to
term, thereby using her body to support it, or to abort
the fetus, thereby not using her body for that purpose.

In some contexts in which this argument is advanced,
it is clear that it is not addressed to the issue of the

morality of abortion at all. Rather, it is made in opposition to laws against abortion on the ground that the choice to abort or not is a moral decision that should belong only to the mother. But that specific direction of the argument is irrelevant to our present purposes; I will consider it [later] when I deal with the issues raised by laws prohibiting abortions. For the moment, I am concerned solely with the use of this principle as a putative ground tending to show the permissibility of abortion, with the claim that because it is the woman's body that carries the fetus and upon which the fetus depends, she has certain rights to abort the fetus that no one else may have.

We may begin by remarking that it is obviously correct that, as carrier of the fetus, the mother has it within her power to choose whether or not to abort the fetus. And, as an autonomous and responsible agent, she must make this choice. But let us notice that this in no way entails either that whatever choice she makes is morally right or that no one else has the right to evaluate the decision that she makes.

• • •

At first glance, it would seem that this argument cannot be used by anyone who supposes, as we do for the moment, that there is a point in fetal development from which time on the fetus is a human being. After all, people do not have the right to do anything whatsoever that may be necessary for them to retain control over the uses of their bodies. In particular, it would seem wrong for them to kill another human being in order to do so.

In a recent article,[1] Professor Judith Thomson has, in effect, argued that this simple view is mistaken. How does Professor Thomson defend her claim that the mother has a right to abort the fetus, even if it is a human being, whether or not her life is threatened and whether or not she has consented to the act of intercourse in which the fetus is conceived? At one point,[2] discussing just the case in which the mother's life is threatened, she makes the following suggestion:

In [abortion], there are only two people involved, one whose life is threatened and one who threatens it. Both are innocent: the one who is threatened is not threatened because of any fault, the one who threatens does not threaten because of any fault. For this reason, we may feel that we bystanders cannot intervene. But the person threatened can.

But surely this description is equally applicable to the following case: A and B are adrift on a lifeboat, B has

a disease that he can survive, but A, if he contracts it, will die, and the only way that A can avoid that is by killing B and pushing him overboard. Surely, A has no right to do this. So there must be some special reason why the mother has, if she does, the right to abort the fetus.

There is, to be sure, an important difference between our lifeboat case and abortion, one that leads us to the heart of Professor Thomson's argument. In the case that we envisaged, both A and B have equal rights to be in the lifeboat, but the mother's body is hers and not the fetus's and she has first rights to its use. The primacy of these rights allows an abortion whether or not her life is threatened. Professor Thomson summarizes this argument in the following way:[3]

I am arguing only that having a right to life does not guarantee having either a right to be given the use of, or a right to be allowed continued use of, another person's body—even if one needs it for life itself.

One part of this claim is clearly correct. I have no duty to X to save X's life by giving him the use of my body (or my life savings, or the only home I have, and so on), and X has no right, even to save his life, to any of those things. Thus, the fetus conceived in the laboratory that will perish unless it is implanted into a woman's body has in fact no right to any woman's body. But this portion of the claim is irrelevant to the abortion issue, for in abortion of the fetus that is a human being the mother must kill X to get back the sole use of her body, and that is an entirely different matter.

This point can also be put as follows: . . . we must distinguish the taking of X's life from the saving of X's life, even if we assume that one has a duty not to do the former and to do the latter. Now that latter duty, if it exists at all, is much weaker than the first duty; many circumstances may relieve us from the latter duty that will not relieve us from the former one. Thus, I am certainly relieved from my duty to save X's life by the fact that fulfilling it means the loss of my life savings. It may be noble for me to save X's life at the cost of everything I have, but I certainly have no duty to do that. And the same observation may be made about cases in which I can save X's life by giving him the use of my body for an extended period of time. However, I am not relieved of my duty not to take X's life by the fact that fulfilling it means the loss of everything I have and not even by the fact that fulfilling it means the loss of my life. . . .

At one point in her paper, Professor Thomson does consider this objection. She has previously imagined the following case: a famous violinist, who is dying from a kidney ailment, has been, without your consent, plugged into you for a period of time so that his body can use your kidneys:

> Some people are rather stricter about the right to life. In their view, it does not include the right to be given anything, but amounts to, and only to, the right not to be killed by anybody. But here a related difficulty arises. If everybody is to refrain from killing that violinist, then everybody must refrain from doing a great many different sorts of things . . . everybody must refrain from unplugging you from him. But does he have a right against everybody that they shall refrain from unplugging you from him? To refrain from doing this is to allow him to continue to use your kidneys . . . certainly the violinist has no right against you that you shall allow him to continue to use your kidneys.

Applying this argument to the case of abortion, we can see that Professor Thomson's argument would run as follows:

a. Assume that the fetus's right to life includes the right not to be killed by the woman carrying him.
b. But to refrain from killing the fetus is to allow him the continued use of the woman's body.
c. So our first assumption entails that the fetus's right to life includes the right to the continued use of the woman's body.
d. But we all grant that the fetus does not have the right to the continued use of the woman's body.
e. Therefore, the fetus's right to life cannot include the right not to be killed by the woman in question.

And it is also now clear what is wrong with this argument. When we granted that the fetus has no right to the continued use of the woman's body, all that we meant was that he does not have this right merely because the continued use saves his life. But, of course, there may be other reasons why he has this right. One would be that the only way to take the use of the woman's body away from the fetus is by killing him, and that is something that neither she nor we have the right to do. So, I submit, the way in which Assumption d is true is irrelevant, and cannot be used by Professor Thomson, for Assumption d is true only in cases where the saving of the life of the fetus is at stake and not in cases where the taking of his life is at stake.

I conclude therefore that Professor Thomson has not established the truth of her claims about abortion, primarily because she has not sufficiently attended to the distinction between our duty to save X's life and our duty not to take it. Once one attends to that distinction, it would seem that the mother, in order to regain control over her body, has no right to abort the fetus from the point at which it becomes a human being.

It may also be useful to say a few words about the larger and less rigorous context of the argument that the woman has a right to her own body. It is surely true that one way in which women have been oppressed is by their being denied authority over their own bodies. But it seems to me that, as the struggle is carried on for meaningful amelioration of such oppression, it ought not to be carried so far that it violates the steady responsibilities all people have to one another. Parents may not desert their children, one class may not oppress another, one race or nation may not exploit another. For parents, powerful groups in society, races or nations in ascendancy, there are penalties for refraining from these wrong actions, but those penalties can in no way be taken as the justification for such wrong actions. Similarly, if the fetus is a human being, the penalty of carrying it cannot, I believe, be used as the justification for destroying it.

• • •

## THE MODEL PENAL CODE CASES

All of the arguments that we have looked at so far are attempts to show that there is something special about abortion that justifies its being treated differently from other cases of the taking of human life. We shall now consider claims that are confined to certain special cases of abortion: the case in which the mother has been raped, the case in which bearing the child would be harmful to her health, and the case in which having the child may cause a problem for the rest of her family (the latter case is a particular case of the societal argument). In addressing these issues, we shall see whether there is any point to the permissibility of abortions in some of the cases covered by the Model Penal Code[4] proposals.

When the expectant mother has conceived after being raped, there are two different sorts of considerations that might support the claim that she has the right to take the life of the fetus. They are the following: (A) the woman in question has already suffered immensely from the act of rape and the physical and/or psychological aftereffects of that act. It would be particularly unjust, the argument runs, for her to have to live through an unwanted pregnancy owing to that act of rape. Therefore, even if we are at a stage at which the fetus is a human being, the mother has the right to abort it; (B) the fetus in question has no right to be in that woman. It was put there as a result of an act of aggression upon her by the rapist, and its continued presence is an act of aggression against the mother. She has a right to repel that aggression by aborting the fetus.

The first argument is very compelling. We can all agree that a terrible injustice has been committed on the woman who is raped. The question that we have to consider, however, is whether it follows that it is morally permissible for her to abort the fetus. We must make that consideration reflecting that, however unjust the act of rape, it was not the fetus who committed or commissioned it. The injustice of the act, then, should in no way impinge upon the rights of the fetus, for it is innocent. What remains is the initial misfortune of the mother (and the injustice of her having to pass through the pregnancy, and, further, to assume responsibility of at least giving the child over for adoption or assuming the burden of its care). However unfortunate that circumstance, however unjust, the misfortune and the injustice are not sufficient cause to justify the taking of the life of an innocent human being as a means of mitigation.

It is at this point that Argument B comes in, for its whole point is that the fetus, by its mere presence in the mother, is committing an act of aggression against her, one over and above the one committed by the rapist, and one that the mother has a right to repel by abortion. But . . . (1) the fetus is certainly innocent (in the sense of not responsible) for any act of aggression against the mother and . . . (2) the mere presence of the fetus in the mother, no matter how unfortunate for her, does not constitute an act of aggression by the fetus against the mother. Argument B fails then at just that point at which Argument A needs its support, and we can therefore conclude that the fact that pregnancy is the result of rape does not give the mother the right to abort the fetus.

We turn next to the case in which the continued existence of the fetus would threaten the mental and/or physical health but not necessarily the life of the mother. Again, . . . the fact that the fetus's continued existence poses a threat to the life of the mother does not justify her aborting it.[*] It would seem to be true, a fortiori, that the fact that the fetus's continued existence poses a threat to the mental and/or physical health of the mother does not justify her aborting it either.

We come finally to those cases in which the continuation of the pregnancy would cause serious problems for the rest of the family. There are a variety of cases that we have to consider here together. Perhaps the health of the mother will be affected in such a way that she cannot function effectively as a wife and mother during, or even after, the pregnancy. Or perhaps the expenses incurred as a result of the pregnancy would be utterly beyond the financial resources of the family. The important point is that the continuation of the pregnancy raises a serious problem for other innocent people involved besides the mother and the fetus, and it may be argued that the mother has the right to abort the fetus to avoid that problem.

By now, the difficulties with this argument should be apparent. We have seen earlier that the mere fact that the continued existence of the fetus threatens to harm the mother does not, by itself, justify the aborting of the fetus. Why should anything be changed by the fact that the threatened harm will accrue to the other members of the family and not to the mother? Of course, it would be different if the fetus were committing an act of aggression against the other members of the family. But, once more, this is certainly not the case.

---

[*]*Editor's note*: Professor Brody provided a lengthy argument to this effect in a chapter not here excerpted. His summary of that argument is as follows: "Is it permissible, as an act of killing a pursuer, to abort the fetus in order to save the mother? The first thing that we should note is that Pope Pius's objection to aborting the fetus as a permissible act of killing a pursuer is mistaken. His objection is that the fetus shows no knowledge or intention in his attempt to take the life of the mother, that the fetus is, in a word, innocent. But that only means that the condition of guilt is not satisfied, and we have seen that its satisfaction is not necessary."

"Is, then, the aborting of the fetus, when necessary to save the life of the mother, a permissible act of killing a pursuer? It is true that in such cases the fetus is a danger to the mother. But it is also clear that the condition of attempt is not satisfied. The fetus has neither the beliefs nor the intention to which we have referred. Furthermore, there is on the part of the fetus no action that threatens the life of the mother. So not even the condition of action is satisfied. It seems to follow, therefore, that aborting the fetus could not be a permissible act of killing a pursuer."

We conclude, therefore, that none of these special circumstances justifies an abortion from that point at which the fetus is a human being.

• • •

## FETAL HUMANITY AND BRAIN FUNCTION

The question which we must now consider is the question of fetal humanity. Some have argued that the fetus is a human being with a right to life (or, for convenience, just a human being) from the moment of conception. Others have argued that the fetus only becomes a human being at the moment of birth. Many positions in between these two extremes have also been suggested. How are we to decide which is correct?

The analysis which we will propose here rests upon certain metaphysical assumptions which I have defended elsewhere. These assumptions are: (a) the question is when has the fetus acquired all the properties essential (necessary) for being a human being, for when it has, it is a human being; (b) these properties are such that the loss of any one of them means that the human being in question has gone out of existence and not merely stopped being a human being; (c) human beings go out of existence when they die. It follows from these assumptions that the fetus becomes a human being when it acquires all those characteristics which are such that the loss of any one of them would result in the fetus's being dead. We must, therefore, turn to the analysis of death.

• • •

We will first consider the question of what properties are essential to being human if we suppose that death and the passing out of existence occur only if there has been an irreparable cessation of brain function (keeping in mind that that condition itself, as we have noted, is a matter of medical judgment). We shall then consider the same question on the supposition that [Paul] Ramsey's more complicated theory of death (the modified traditional view) is correct.

According to what is called the brain-death theory, as long as there has not been an irreparable cessation of brain function the person in question continues to exist, no matter what else has happened to him. If so, it seems to follow that there is only one property—leaving aside those entailed by this one property—that is essential to humanity, namely, the possession of a brain that has not suffered an irreparable cessation of function.

Several consequences follow immediately from this conclusion. We can see that a variety of often advanced claims about the essence of humanity are false. For example, the claim that movement, or perhaps just the ability to move, is essential for being human is false. A human being who has stopped moving, and even one who has lost the ability to move, has not therefore stopped existing. Being able to move, and a fortiori moving, are not essential properties of human beings and therefore are not essential to being human. Similarly, the claim that being perceivable by other human beings is essential for being human is also false. A human being who has stopped being perceivable by other humans (for example, someone isolated on the other side of the moon, out of reach even of radio communication) has not stopped existing. Being perceivable by other human beings is not an essential property of human beings and is not essential to being human. And the same point can be made about the claims that viability is essential for being human, that independent existence is essential for being human, and that actual interaction with other human beings is essential for being human. The loss of any of these properties would not mean that the human being in question had gone out of existence, so none of them can be essential to that human being and none of them can be essential for being human.

Let us now look at the following argument: (1) A functioning brain (or at least, a brain that, if not functioning, is susceptible of function) is a property that every human being must have because it is essential for being human. (2) By the time an entity acquires that property, it has all the other properties that are essential for being human. Therefore, when the fetus acquires that property it becomes a human being. It is clear that the property in question is, according to the brain-death theory, one that is had essentially by all human beings. The question that we have to consider is whether the second premise is true. It might appear that its truth does follow from the brain-death theory. After all, we did see that the theory entails that only one property (together with those entailed by it) is essential for being human. Nevertheless, rather than relying solely on my earlier argument, I shall adopt an alternative approach to strengthen the conviction that this second premise is true: I shall note the important ways in which the fetus resembles and differs from an ordinary human being by the time it definitely has a functioning brain (about the end of the sixth week of development). It shall then be evident, in light of our theory of essentialism, that none of these differences involves the lack of some property in the fetus that is essential for its being human.

Structurally, there are few features of the human being that are not fully present by the end of the sixth week. Not only are the familiar external features and all the internal organs present, but the contours of the body are nicely rounded. More important, the body is functioning. Not only is the brain functioning, but the heart is beating sturdily (the fetus by this time has its own completely developed vascular system), the stomach is producing digestive juices, the liver is manufacturing blood cells, the kidney is extracting uric acid from the blood, and the nerves and muscles are operating in concert, so that reflex reactions can begin.

What are the properties that a fetus acquires after the sixth week of its development? Certain structures do appear later. These include the fingernails (which appear in the third month), the completed vocal chords (which also appear then), taste buds and salivary glands (again, in the third month), and hair and eyelashes (in the fifth month). In addition, certain functions begin later than the sixth week. The fetus begins to urinate (in the third month), to move spontaneously (in the third month), to respond to external stimuli (at least in the fifth month), and to breathe (in the sixth month). Moreover, there is a constant growth in size. And finally, at the time of birth the fetus ceases to receive its oxygen and food through the placenta and starts receiving them through the mouth and nose.

I will not examine each of these properties (structures and functions) to show that they are not essential for being human. The procedure would be essentially the one used previously to show that various essentialist claims are in error. We might, therefore, conclude, on the supposition that the brain-death theory is correct, that the fetus becomes a human being about the end of the sixth week after its development.

There is, however, one complication that should be noted here. There are, after all, progressive stages in the physical development and in the functioning of the brain. For example, the fetal brain (and nervous system) does not develop sufficiently to support spontaneous motion until some time in the third month after conception. There is, of course, no doubt that that stage of development is sufficient for the fetus to be human. No one would be likely to maintain that a spontaneously moving human being has died; and similarly, a spontaneously moving fetus would seem to have become human. One might, however, want to claim that the fetus does not become a human being until the point of spontaneous movement. So then, on the supposition that the brain-death theory of death is correct, one ought to conclude that the fetus becomes a human being at some time between the sixth and twelfth week after its conception.

But what if we reject the brain-death theory, and replace it with its equally plausible contender, Ramsey's theory of death? According to that theory—which we can call the brain, heart, and lung theory of death—the human being does not die, does not go out of existence, until such time as the brain, heart, and lungs have irreparably ceased functioning naturally. What are the essential features of being human according to this theory?

Actually, the adoption of Ramsey's theory requires no major modifications. According to that theory, what is essential to being human, what each human being must retain if he is to continue to exist, is the possession of a functioning (actually or potentially) heart, lung, or brain. It is only when a human being possesses none of these that he dies and goes out of existence; and the fetus comes into humanity, so to speak, when he acquires one of these.

On Ramsey's theory, the argument would now run as follows: (1) The property of having a functioning brain, heart, or lungs (or at least organs of the kind that, if not functioning, are susceptible of function) is one that every human being must have because it is essential for being human. (2) By the time that an entity acquires that property it has all the other properties that are essential for being human. Therefore, when the fetus acquires that property it becomes a human being. There remains, once more, the problem of the second premise. Since the fetal heart starts operating rather early, it is not clear that the second premise is correct. Many systems are not yet operating, and many structures are not yet present. Still, following our theory of essentialism, we should conclude that the fetus becomes a human being when it acquires a functioning heart (the first of the organs to function in the fetus).

There is, however, a further complication here, and it is analogous to the one encountered if we adopt the brain-death theory: When may we properly say that the fetal heart begins to function? At two weeks, when occasional contractions of the primitive fetal heart are present? In the fourth to fifth week, when the heart, although incomplete, is beating regularly and pumping blood cells through a closed vascular system, and when the tracings obtained by an ECG exhibit the classical elements of an adult tracing? Or after the end of the seventh week, when the fetal heart is functionally complete and "normal"?

We have not reached a precise conclusion in our study of the question of when the fetus becomes a human being. We do know that it does so some time between the end of the second week and the end of the third month. But it surely is not a human being at the moment of conception and it surely is one by the end of the third month. Though we have not come to a final answer to our question, we have narrowed the range of acceptable answers considerably.

[In summary] we have argued that the fetus becomes a human being with a right to life some time between the second and twelfth week after conception. We have also argued that abortions are morally impermissible after that point except in rather unusual circumstances. What is crucial to note is that neither of these arguments appeal to any theological considerations. We conclude, therefore, that there is a human-rights basis for moral opposition to abortions.

## NOTES

1. J. Thomson, "A Defense of Abortion," *Philosophy and Public Affairs*, Vol. 1 (1971), pp. 47–66.

2. Ibid., p. 53.

3. Ibid., p. 56.

4. On the Model Penal Code provisions, see American Law Institute, *Model Penal Code:* Tentative Draft No. 9 (1959).

# Chapter 5
## End of Life

*Introduction*

In recent decades patients have demanded, and physicians have given, greater deference to patients' wishes regarding how they will die. Respect for a patient's autonomy has grown to encompass a patient's decisions about life-sustaining treatment and whether to hasten death. But what are the precise boundaries of the legitimate practice of medicine when patients request help in ending their lives? There is no consensus among health care professionals, the public, or in public policy about this matter. Many physicians feel strongly that, under appropriate circumstances, assistance in hastening death is a legitimate form of addressing a patient's needs, but other physicians are equally strongly opposed to this idea. The bioethics community is similarly divided. The moral problems underlying this profound disagreement are addressed in the present chapter.

### KEY TERMS AND DISTINCTIONS

Physicians and nurses have long worried that if they withdraw treatment and a patient dies, they will be accused of killing the patient. A parallel concern exists that patients who refuse life-sustaining treatment or hasten death are killing themselves and that health professionals assist in the suicide if they comply with refusals or satisfy requests to refuse treatment. A related concern is that physicians who help patients "actively" hasten the time of their deaths are involved either in physician-assisted suicide or euthanasia. What do these key moral notions refer to and what is their moral import?

#### THE DISTINCTION BETWEEN KILLING AND LETTING DIE

Those who reject physician assistance in hastening death often distinguish between overseeing a refusal of treatment and assisting in a suicide. They ground this distinction in the difference between "letting die" and "killing." This distinction is applied to distinguish practices considered permissible from practices that are always impermissible. Withdrawals or withholdings of treatment have generally been classified in the "letting die" category—depending on the nature of the illness and the intent of the physician. In its ordinary language meaning, *killing* represents a family of ideas whose central condition is direct causation of another's death, whereas *letting die* represents another family of ideas whose central condition is intentional avoidance of intervention so that a death is caused by a disease, injury, or some other "natural" cause.

This distinction between killing and letting die is controversial. A person can be killed by intentionally letting him or her die of a "natural" condition of disease when the death should have been prevented by a physician. If a physician removes a respirator from a patient who needs it and wants to continue to use it, the action is wrong, even though the physician has only removed artificial life support and let nature take its course. Absent the patient's authorization, such "letting die" is morally unacceptable and looks like a case of killing. Is this circumstance properly characterized as a killing, a letting die, or both? Can an act be both? What are we to say about a circumstance in which a physician prescribes a lethal medication at a patient's request, which the patient then voluntarily ingests? Is this a killing, a letting die, or something else altogether?

Of course, physicians could use a so-called active means to bring about death, and many would argue that it is the use of an "active" means that accounts for the language of "killing." But there are also problems inherent in the idea that we can determine appropriate and inappropriate conduct by considering whether or not an active means to death was involved. This is notably true in the case of laws (such as the laws of Oregon, Washington and Montana) that allow physicians to prescribe lethal medication to a patient, but do not allow physicians to administer what they prescribe. This does not look like a case of killing, but it also does not look like a case of letting die. It has been termed "physician aid in dying," but that doesn't answer the killing/letting die distinction, nor tell us whether it is morally permissible.

### EUTHANASIA

Killing, especially by an active means, is often said to be "euthanasia," but this term needs careful definition. *Euthanasia* is the act or practice of ending a person's life in order to release the person from an incurable disease, intolerable suffering, or undignified death. The term is used to refer both to painlessly causing death—an "active" means to death—and to failing to prevent death from natural causes for merciful reasons—a "passive" means to death. Accordingly, two main types of euthanasia are commonly distinguished: *active* euthanasia and *passive* euthanasia. If a person requests the termination of his or her life, the action is called *voluntary euthanasia*. (See the introduction to Dan Brock's essay in this chapter.) If the person is not mentally competent to make an informed request, the action is called *nonvoluntary euthanasia*. Both forms should be distinguished from *involuntary euthanasia*, in which a person capable of making an informed request has not done so. Involuntary euthanasia has been universally condemned and is not under discussion in this chapter. Articles in this chapter that are concerned with euthanasia are exclusively concerned with voluntary active euthanasia (or VAE).

### PHYSICIAN-ASSISTED SUICIDE AND PHYSICIAN AID IN DYING

The term "euthanasia" is today less central to discussions of the problems discussed in this chapter than are the terms "physician-assisted suicide" and "physician aid in dying." In the last few years, there has been a shift in terminology, and a move towards the use of physician aid in dying. This shift is reflected in public policy: Oregon and Washington adopted the terminology "physician aid in dying" to describe the practice that allows physicians to support patients' decisions on dying if carefully articulated criteria about the terminal nature of illness are satisfied. Oregon's landmark legislation establishing the legal right to physician aid in dying is included in this chapter.

Physician aid in dying can be difficult to distinguish from both treatment withdrawals and aggressive physician assistance to control pain. Patients who refuse a treatment often intend to end their suffering, not because they seek death as an end in itself. In some cases, physicians heavily sedate dying patients and the drugs have the unintended though foreseen effect of causing death. Is this circumstance more appropriately described as suicide or physician aid in dying?

It is critically important to be clear about the meanings of all of the central terms in this chapter in order to avoid biased discussion of the issues. As Alan Meisel points out in his article, terms like "active euthanasia," "physician-assisted suicide," and "mercy killing" have deeply negative connotations that may unfairly influence readers prior to hearing arguments on both sides of an issue.

## LANDMARK LEGISLATION AND LEGAL CASES

Particular acts of assisting patients in hastening death may be humane, compassionate, and in a patient's best interest. But a social policy that authorizes such acts in medicine, it is often argued, would weaken existing moral restraints that we cannot replace, threatening practices that provide a basis of trust between patients and health care professionals. Should we, then, *legalize* physician involvement in hastening death? If so, what are the limits of the ways in which physicians may be involved? Moral and legal questions in this area are often difficult to separate.

Several issues about killing, letting die, and physician-assisted death have been discussed under the general heading of the "right to die." The notion of a right to die, in particular, points to a liberty right. It derives historically in the United States from a series of landmark "right-to-die" cases dating from *In re Quinlan* (1976). In *Quinlan*, the New Jersey Supreme Court held that it is permissible for a guardian to direct a physician and hospital to discontinue all extraordinary measures. The court asserted that the patient's rights and autonomous judgment are to prevail over the physician's judgment in decisions at the end of life.

The main ethical and legal issue became whether all medical treatments, depending on the circumstances, can be construed as optional. It soon became widely agreed that a passive letting die at a patient's or family's request is acceptable, but an active hastening of death or killing is not. The accepted rule became that there is a right to refuse treatment, but no right to request (or perform) an intentionally hastened death. However, withdrawal or withholding of treatment will hasten death only for persons whose lives are being sustained by such treatment. Many other individuals face a protracted period of dying even when respirators and other life-preserving technology are not being utilized.

Legal and related moral arguments about how these matters should be treated in law are discussed in two articles in this chapter, one by Yale Kamisar and the other by Alan Meisel. Both look carefully at early and late precedent right-to-die cases. Kamisar points out that more than one right is under discussion, so that a patient might have a right against intrusion and a right to privacy, but not a right to assisted suicide. Likewise, one might have a moral right, but not a constitutional right to something—for example, a (moral) right to pain relief, but not a (constitutional) right to lethal drugs, etc. After carefully assessing the status of rights in the precedent legal cases, Kamisar argues that the Supreme Court has not, should not, and likely will not reach a finding of a right to physician-assisted suicide. By contrast, Meisel argues that almost the entire superstructure of the law rests on a body of untenable moral distinctions, such as those between passively and actively hastening death, intending death and merely foreseeing that death will occur, causing death and merely intentionally allowing death, and so on. Meisel tries to show that all major legal arguments advanced by the courts are "fundamentally unsound," using "stock arguments" that are spurious. Most notably, he finds that the courts' persistent reliance on the distinction between a right to passively hasten death and a right to actively hasten death is untenable. At his hands, there truly is a right to die—passively and actively—and it is rooted in rights of self-determination.

The so-called right-to-die movement—a diverse collection of social groups and institutions—has exerted pressure to reform current laws so that physicians are allowed more leeway in facilitating the wishes of patients. A major right-to-die initiative was accepted by the majority of citizens in the state of Oregon. A ballot measure (Measure 16) was first approved by voters in that state in November 1994. It allowed physicians to prescribe lethal drugs for those terminally ill patients who wish to escape unbearable suffering. Under the provisions of Measure 16, officially titled the Oregon Death with Dignity Act, which is excerpted in this chapter, a physician is authorized to comply with the request of a terminally ill, mentally competent patient for a prescription for a lethal dose of medication, which the patient can ingest if the dying process becomes intolerable. Eligibility is limited to patients who have received a diagnosis from their attending physician that they have a terminal illness that will cause their death within six months. Patients must manifest a durable, verifiable desire for assistance, and there are various procedural safeguards to ensure that the patient's request is informed and truly voluntary. The patient must ingest the prescribed drug; the physician may not administer it.

This Oregon legislation was upheld as a result of two 1997 U.S. Supreme Court decisions: *Vacco v. Quill* and *Washington v. Glucksberg*, both reprinted in this chapter. The Supreme Court reviewed two decisions in circuit courts that had endorsed a constitutional right to limited physician-assisted suicide (or a right to die). The decisions of these lower courts were reversed by the Supreme Court, which found that there are no *constitutional* rights to physician-hastened dying, but that each state may set its own policy on patients' rights. By returning the issue to the states, the Supreme Court effectively recognized the legal validity of statutes that allow physician-hastened death as well as those that disallow it.

Chief Justice Rehnquist maintains in these opinions that a doctor may provide "aggressive palliative care" that "hastens a patient's death" if the doctor's intent is "only to ease his patient's pain." This doctor is presumably distinguished from the doctor who has the intention of assisting in a suicide because, according to Rehnquist, doctors involved in physician-assisted suicide "must, necessarily and indubitably, intend primarily that the patient be made dead." The Chief Justice appears to be using intention to distinguish between killing and letting die, while assuming that the former is unwarranted and the latter permissible.

This approach has generated controversy. The doctor who prescribes a fatal medication with the intention of giving the patient the choice of using or not using it need have no ill intention; the physician may even try to convince the patient not to use the medication. The doctor's intention may be a benevolent one of easing the patient's anxiety about a loss of control over the dying process, while giving the patient an option he or she has requested. This raises the question of whether the physician's intention is an important consideration at all in assessing the morality of the physician's action.

Despite Rehnquist's stated reservations about physician-assisted suicide, the U.S. Supreme Court decision had the effect of clearing the way for a right to physician-assisted death to be enacted by individual states, which then occurred in Oregon in 1997. The Oregon law appears to reflect the new frontier of issues about whether society should expand autonomy rights to control the moment of death. The cutting edge of the right-to-die movement seems, from this perspective, to have shifted from *refusal* of treatment to *request* for aid.

However, the Oregon law is itself morally controversial. In November 2001, then-U.S. Attorney General John Ashcroft attempted to trump the Oregon law by issuing a rule asserting that "assisting suicide is not a 'legitimate medical purpose'" under the U.S. Code of Federal Regulations. The cited regulation requires all prescriptions for controlled substances to "be issued for a legitimate medical purpose by an individual practitioner acting in the usual course of professional practice." The Attorney General sought to make the prescribing of lethal substances a violation of the Controlled Substances Act, allowing him to revoke the license of any physician who would prescribe the very drugs used in Oregon. The state of Oregon, in turn, sued the U.S. government. The state challenged Ashcroft's authority to limit the practice of medicine under Oregon law. The case—known as *Gonzales v. Oregon*—was eventually decided in 2006 by the U.S. Supreme Court and is included in this chapter. The Supreme Court determined that the Attorney General has no authority to prevent states from authorizing physicians to prescribe lethal medications in the practice of medicine. The Attorney General claimed that intentionally prescribing fatal drugs is not part of acceptable medical practice, which is fundamentally "a healing or curative art." The Court acknowledged that this is one proper understanding of "medicine's boundaries," but the Court also allowed a broader understanding and asserted that the Attorney General could not dictate to physicians the nature of medicine.

The implications of the *Gonzales* case for the near future in bioethics are discussed in the article by Ronald Lindsay, Tom Beauchamp, and Rebecca Dick. One result of the Supreme Court's series of decisions (the cases in this chapter) is that physician assistance in hastening death remains a legal option in Oregon. Oregon and all states are therefore legally allowed to determine what a physician may do in the way of helping to hasten death. In 2008, Washington State voters approved a law based on the Oregon model. Washington thus became the second U.S. state to legalize physician aid in dying. Reflecting a shift in popular opinion in the state, the measure was approved by a 58 percent voting majority; a similar attempt to pass such a law failed in the state in 1991 by a 54 percent majority.[1] Washington State Department of Health statistics indicate that from 2009 to 2011, 255 terminally ill adults chose to use the procedures under the law to hasten their deaths.[2] In 2009, Montana became the third state to permit physician aid in dying, but through judicial decision rather than by statute.[3] Of course, a legal right does not entail a moral right, and the question of a moral right to physician-hastened death is clearly the central bioethical issue.

While not a case involving an individual requesting physician aid in dying, the 2005 death of Terri Schiavo is worth mentioning because it raised important questions about the limits of legal intervention at the end of life and highlighted the role of the courts in end-of-life decision making. Ms. Schiavo was left in a persistent vegetative state after suffering a heart attack, and over the successive months and years a controversy ensued over whether care should be continued or withdrawn, and who should speak on her behalf in making the decision. After multiple court rulings, including appeals to the U.S. Supreme Court, interventions by the U.S. Congress and the President of the United States himself, all appeals were exhausted, support was withdrawn, and Ms. Schiavo died.[4]

## MORAL ISSUES ABOUT PHYSICIAN-ASSISTED DEATH

Many who are opposed to the legalization of killing or any form of intentional hastening of death appeal neither to the law nor to the intrinsic moral wrongness of helping someone hasten his or her death. Rather, they appeal to the social consequences that would result from a public policy that supports physician-assisted dying. They argue that assistance in hastening death could not be effectively regulated and would have serious adverse consequences for many, including for those who do not desire such assistance. They believe that the practice inevitably would be expanded to include euthanasia (including nonvoluntary euthanasia), that the quality of palliative care for all patients would deteriorate, that patients would be manipulated or coerced into requesting assistance in hastening death, that patients whose judgment was impaired would be allowed to request such assistance, and that members of allegedly vulnerable groups (the elderly, women, members of racial and ethnic minorities, etc.) would be adversely affected in disproportionate numbers.

A prominent argument in this discussion is the *slippery slope argument*. It proceeds as follows: Although particular acts of active killing are sometimes morally justified, the social consequences of sanctioning practices of killing would run serious risks of abuse and misuse and, on balance, would cause more harm than benefit. The argument is not that these negative consequences will occur immediately, but that they will grow incrementally over time. Although society might start by carefully restricting the number of patients who qualify for assistance in suicide or aid in dying, these restrictions would be revised and expanded over time, with an ever-increasing risk of unjustified killing. Unscrupulous persons would learn how to abuse the system, just as they learn how to be tax evaders. Slippery slope and other consequence-oriented arguments are discussed in this chapter by several authors, including Brock, Felicia Cohn and Joanne Lynn, Kamisar, and Meisel.

Supporters of a public policy that permits physician-hastened death argue that there is a certain range of cases in which respect for the rights of patients obligates society to respect their decisions. Brock supports this position. Clearly competent patients have a legal and moral right to refuse treatment that brings about their deaths. Why, then, should there not be a similar right to arrange for death by an active means? Proponents of assisted death, such as Brock, point to circumstances in which a condition has become overwhelmingly burdensome for a patient, pain management for the patient is inadequate, and only a physician seems capable of bringing relief. Brock argues that the "central ethical argument" for VAE is that it promotes patient autonomy and well-being in circumstances in which persons have a strong need to be in control of their lives. Brock does not balk at the thesis that euthanasia involves intentionally killing the innocent, but he argues that such killing is justified under specifiable circumstances. Brock views the argument against euthanasia at the policy level as stronger than the argument against it at the level of individual cases, but he maintains that the objections are unpersuasive at both levels.

In the next reading in this section, Cohn and Lynn rebut the types of arguments (as they see it) that are relied upon by writers of Brock's persuasion. They consider a wide variety of arguments advanced in defense of physician-assisted means to death and try to show that every major argument fails. They argue that the legalization of physician-assisted suicide would pose serious and predictable social harms, especially to the elderly, the frail, the disabled, and the poor, who are already vulnerable to the effects of inadequate health care. Among their basic convictions is that supporters of allowing physician-hastened deaths underestimate how much medicine has to offer to persons who are dying. They believe that a correct approach to pain relief and end-of-life care would eliminate the need for physician-hastened death. Accordingly, they think that the main faults in the current system are in the area of poor palliative and end-of-life care, not in the area of a lack of patient choices about how to die. The best public policy, they suggest, is one that would improve end-of-life care—especially a policy that would promote excellence in palliative care—and not a policy that confers a right to physician-assisted suicide.

In the final article in this section of the chapter, H. Tristram Engelhardt denies that anyone holding any of the persuasions thus far discussed can or will prevail in controversies over physician-hastened death. He thinks that this controversy must be situated in the culture wars that run deeply across all societies that allow open discussion of these issues. Although figures in bioethics may present themselves as having the imprint of morality ("a canonical moral vision") in their views on physician-hastened death, in fact those views are contestable at every important level. Bioethicists therefore need to take moral diversity more seriously than they have in the past and allow "moral difference to have its place" in society and in the negotiation of public policies.

If dire consequences or systemic failures of care will flow from the legal legitimation of hastened death, then it would appear that such practices should be legally prohibited, as Kamisar and Cohn and Lynn recommend. However, Brock and Meisel insist that we need to establish what the evidence is that dire consequences will occur in a system with a strong right to die. In particular, is there a sufficient reason to think that we cannot provide safeguards and maintain control over a public policy of assisted death?

## ALTERNATIVES TO PHYSICIAN-ASSISTED DEATH

The final two articles in this chapter discuss alternatives to physician-hastened death that either increase the range of patient autonomy or offer better end-of-life care. In the first, Bernard Gert, Charles M. Culver, and K. Danner Clouser argue that no patient should feel constrained by the health care or long-term care systems to stay alive, because every patient can refuse hydration and nutrition, which will ultimately cause death—a form of so-called *passive* euthanasia. All patients therefore already have the right to control their own destinies, and there is no need to rush to physician-assisted suicide or voluntary *active* euthanasia. These authors maintain that key questions turn on whether a competent patient has rationally refused treatment. What makes a circumstance one of letting a competent person die is the patient's refusal of treatment, not some omission by the physician. Therefore, the distinction between killing and letting die should be retained, but should be based on the difference between patients' *requests* and patients' *refusals*: Dying by self-determined refusal of nutrition (often said to be starvation) is, on this analysis, a case of letting die, not of killing, despite the fact that the physician cares for the patient during, and oversees, the dying process. In this theory, the administration of a lethal dose by the physician would be a case of killing.

In the final article in this chapter, Dan Brock discusses four options that might be presented to patients so that they can choose how they will die. He argues that both terminal sedation and voluntarily stopping eating and drinking would allow physicians to be responsive to the suffering of certain types of patients, but he argues that these strategies are ethically and clinically closer to physician-assisted suicide and VAE than has generally been appreciated. He proposes safeguards for a system in which patients can choose to die as they wish and maintains that explicit public policy allowing these alternatives (rather than leaving them hidden, as is now often the case) would reassure many patients who fear a bad death in their future. Unlike Gert and colleagues, he considers physician-assisted suicide as one among the four viable options for patients, the other three being improved palliative care, terminal sedation, and refusal of hydration and nutrition.

Virtually all parties to these controversies believe that improved pain management has made circumstances at least bearable for many patients, reducing the need for physician-hastened death and increasing the need for adequate medical facilities, training, and hospice programs. Nonetheless, as Brock points out, some patients cannot be satisfactorily relieved by medical means because they experience intolerable suffering. If physicians can benefit patients of this description by means of physician-hastened death, should they be restricted by law or morals from doing so? This question is at the center of the contemporary discussion and likely will be for many years into the future.

J. P. K.

A. C. M.

T. L. B.

## NOTES

1. Robert Steinbrook, "Physician-Assisted Death—From Oregon to Washington State," *New England Journal of Medicine* 359 (2008), 2513–15.

2. Washington State Department of Health, 2011 Death with Dignity Act Report, available at http://www.doh.wa.gov/dwda/, accessed May 10, 2012.

3. *Baxter v. State of Montana,* 224 P.3d 1211 (Mont. 2009).

4. Timothy Quill, "Terri Schiavo—A Tragedy Compounded," *New England Journal of Medicine* 352 (2005), 1630–33.

*Alternatives to Physician-Assisted Death*

# BERNARD GERT, CHARLES M. CULVER, AND K. DANNER CLOUSER

## An Alternative to Physician-Assisted Suicide

The late Bernard Gert was Stone Professor of Intellectual and Moral Philosophy, Emeritus, at Dartmouth College, adjunct professor of psychiatry at Dartmouth Medical School, and research professor in the Department of Social Medicine at the University of North Carolina, Chapel Hill. He is the author of *Morality: Its Nature and Justification* (Oxford) and *Common Morality: Deciding What to Do* (Oxford), which focus on general ethical theory. He is also coauthor with Edward M. Berger, George F. Cahill Jr., K. Danner Clouser, Charles M. Culver, John B. Moeschler, and George H. S. Singer of *Morality and the New Genetics: A Guide for Students and Health Care Providers* (Jones and Bartlett), and *Bioethics: A Return to Fundamentals* (Oxford) with Charles M. Culver and K. Danner Clouser.

From Margaret Battin, Rosamond Rhodes, and Anita Silvers, eds., *Physician Assisted Suicide: Expanding the Debate*, Psychology Press, 1998, Ch. 12. Used with permission of the publisher.

Charles M. Culver is a physician and professor of medical education at Barry University. He is a psychiatrist who has coauthored with Bernard Gert and K. Danner Clouser *Bioethics: A Return to Fundamentals* (Oxford). Dr. Culver is also the coauthor with Bernard Gert of *Philosophy in Medicine: Conceptual and Ethical Problems in Medicine and Psychiatry* (Oxford) and editor of *Ethics at the Bedside* (Dartmouth).

The late K. Danner Clouser was a university professor of humanities at the Penn State College of Medicine from 1968 until his retirement in 1996. His publications include (with Bernard Gert and Charles M. Culver) *Bioethics: A Return to Fundamentals* (Oxford) and *Teaching Bioethics: Strategies, Problems, and Resources* (Hastings Center). His work was examined in a book entitled *Building Bioethics: Conversations with Clouser and Friends on Medical Ethics* (Kluwer).

Two tasks are necessary in order to determine whether physician-assisted suicide should be legalized. The first is to clarify the meaning of the phrase "physician-assisted suicide" (PAS) so that one can be precise about what procedures are correctly specified by the phrase. The second task is to inquire into the moral acceptability of doctors' carrying out those procedures that are appropriately labeled as PAS. It is essential to settle the conceptual task before deciding about PAS's moral acceptability. Once conceptual matters are clarified and the moral acceptability of PAS is determined, disagreements about the social consequences of legalizing PAS continue to make it an issue on which reasonable people can take either side. However, we shall show that awareness of an alternative to PAS, namely, the refusal of food and fluids, significantly weakens the arguments in favor of legalizing PAS.

It may seem odd to claim that there is a problem in clarifying what is meant by PAS. The prototypical example of PAS, and the way it is almost always practiced, is for a doctor to provide a lethal quantity of sedating medication to a patient who subsequently ingests it and dies. Everyone agrees that the doctor who carries out such an action has engaged in PAS. The conceptual problem arises not with the prototypical example but with the conceptual analyses that some philosophers and some courts have made in commenting on whether PAS is morally justified, or is legally sanctioned or forbidden. One philosopher, for example, has claimed that there is no morally significant difference between killing a patient (voluntary, active euthanasia; VAE) and helping a patient commit suicide (PAS).[1] One circuit court has argued that performing PAS is exactly the same as withdrawing life support and rendering palliative care as a patient dies.[2] Thus PAS has been identified both as the same as killing a patient (VAE) and the same as allowing a patient to die (voluntary, passive euthanasia; VPE). We believe that the three alternatives, 1) PAS, 2) killing a patient (VAE), and 3) allowing a patient to die (VPE), are quite distinct from one another conceptually and morally.

## ACTIVE AND PASSIVE EUTHANASIA

To understand how PAS, VAE, and VPE differ, it is useful to begin with the distinction between VAE and VPE. A distinction between these two has traditionally been made and accepted both by clinicians and by philosophers. VAE is killing and, even if requested by a competent patient, is illegal and has been historically prohibited by the American Medical Association. VPE is "allowing to die" and, if requested by a competent patient, it is legally permitted and morally acceptable.

None of the standard attempts to describe the conceptual distinction between VAE and VPE have gained wide acceptance. These attempts have involved the following concepts and issues: 1) acts versus omissions, 2) stopping treatment (withdrawing) versus not starting treatment (withholding), 3) ordinary care versus extraordinary care, and 4) whether the patient's death is due to an underlying malady. However none of these four ways of making the distinction has any clear moral significance and all are inadequate because they all fail to appreciate the moral significance of the *kind of decision* the patient makes, in particular whether it is a request or a refusal.[3] It is this failure that leads to the mistaken conclusion that there is no morally significant distinction between VAE and VPE.

First, a terminological matter needs to be clarified. It is perfectly standard English to use the term "request" when talking about a refusal. Thus one can say that a patient requests that a treatment (such as ventilation) be stopped. The patient is, in fact, refusing continued use of the respirator. Unfortunately, this perfectly correct and common way of talking obscures the crucial moral distinction between patients' refusals and requests. When combined with the use of the terms "choice" and "decision," which also can be applied to both requests and refusals, the language fosters the false conclusion that all patient decisions or choices, whether refusals or requests, generate the same moral obligation for physicians.

This confusion is compounded because the most common use of the terms "decision" and "choice" with regard to a patient involves neither refusals nor requests, but rather the patient's picking one of the options that her physician has presented to her during the process of informed consent. However, when dealing with patients who want to die, this most common use of "decision" or "choice" is not relevant. Rather a patient is either 1) refusing life-sustaining treatment (VPE), or 2) requesting that the physician kill her (VAE), or 3) requesting that the physician provide the medical means for the patient to kill herself (PAS). Thus talking of a patient's decision or choice to die can be extremely ambiguous. Furthermore, refusals of treatment and requests for treatment, whether or not death is a foreseeable result, have very different moral and legal implications.[4]

• • •

## REFUSAL OF TREATMENT AND THE DUTIES OF A PHYSICIAN

Overruling a competent informed patient's rational refusal of treatment, including life preserving treatment, always involves depriving the patient of freedom, and usually involves causing him pain. No impartial rational person would publicly allow these kinds of paternalistic actions and so they are morally unacceptable. Since it is morally unacceptable to overrule the rational refusal of a competent informed patient, it cannot be the duty of a physician to do so. Theoretically, the situation does not change when lack of treatment will result in the patient's death, but as a practical matter, it does make a difference. Death is such a serious harm that it is never irrational to choose any other harm in order to prevent death. Even though it is sometimes rational to choose death over other harms, choosing death may be, and often is, irrational. Further, people are usually ambivalent about choosing death, often changing their minds several times, but death is permanent, and once it occurs, no further change of mind is possible.

The seriousness of death requires physicians to make certain that patients realize that death will result from failure to receive the life sustaining treatment. It also requires physicians to make sure a patient's desire to die is not due to suffering that can be relieved by palliative care. The physician also must make certain that a patient's desire to die, and hence his request to die, is not primarily the result of a treatable depression and, more generally, that a patient's unavoidable suffering is sufficient to make it rational for him to prefer death to continuing to live. When patients have terminal diseases, however, it is generally the case that when they want to die, it is rational for them to choose death. Further, although there is often some ambivalence, in our experience, their desire to die usually remains their dominant desire. When an informed competent patient makes a rational decision to stop life-prolonging treatment, a physician cannot have a duty to overrule his refusal of treatment, even though normally a physician has a duty to prevent death.

We have shown that physicians cannot have a duty to preserve the lives of their competent patients when those patients want to die and their desires are informed and rational. When prolonging a person's life requires unjustifiably depriving him of freedom, it is morally unacceptable to do so. We have thus established that physicians do not and cannot have a duty to prolong the lives of their patients when their patients have a rational desire to die. We are not suggesting that whenever a patient with a terminal disease makes any tentative suggestion that treatment be stopped, the physician should, with no question, immediately do so. It is part of the duty of a physician to make sure both that the refusal is rational and that it is the informed, considered, and noncoerced preference of the patient. When, however, it is clear that a patient really does want to die and the refusal is rational, then it is morally unacceptable for the physician to administer life prolonging treatment.

## KILLING VERSUS ALLOWING TO DIE

Having shown that a physician does not have a duty to prolong the lives of patients who rationally prefer to die, the next issue to be settled is whether not treating such patients counts as killing them. If it does count as killing them, then the conclusions of the previous section may have to be revised. In the previous section not treating was taken as simply not prolonging the life of a competent patient when he rationally refuses treatment. However, not treating is sometimes correctly regarded as killing. If a physician turns off the respirator of a competent patient who does not want to die, with the result that the patient dies, the physician has killed him. The same is true if the physician discontinues antibiotics, or food and fluids. It may even count as killing if the physician refuses to start any of these treatments for his patient when the patient wants the treatment started and there is no medical reason for not starting it. Just as parents whose children die because of not being fed can be regarded as having killed their children, physicians who have a duty to provide life-saving treatment for their patients can be regarded as killing them if they do not provide that treatment. However, we have shown that a physician does not have a duty to provide life-saving treatment when a competent patient rationally refuses such treatment. Not treating counts as killing only when there is a duty to treat; in the absence of such a duty, not treating does not count as killing.[5]

If the patient refuses treatment and there is no duty to treat, then it does not make any moral difference whether the physician stops treating by an act, e.g., turning off the respirator, or an omission, e.g., not giving antibiotics. It also makes no moral difference whether the physician stops some treatment that has already started, e.g., turning off the respirator or discontinuing antibiotics, or simply does not start such treatment. . . .

## STOPPING FOOD AND FLUIDS

. . . Since the point of dying sooner is to avoid the pain and suffering of a terminal illness, stopping only food while continuing fluids is not a good method of dying because it takes a long time, often more than a month. However, when fluids are also stopped, dying is much quicker; usually unconsciousness occurs within a week and death less than a week later. Further, contrary to what is widely assumed, dying because of lack of food and fluids is not physically unpleasant or painful if there is even minimal nursing care.[6] When there is no medical treatment keeping the patient alive, stopping food and fluids may be the best way of allowing a patient to die. It is usually painless, it takes long enough for the patient to have the opportunity to change his mind, but is short enough that significant relief from pain and suffering is gained. However, because of the psychological difficulties involved in a longer dying process, some patients may still prefer PAS to discontinuing food and fluids.

## ANALYSIS OF KILLING

It may be thought that, if complying with a patient's refusal of treatment requires the physician to perform some identifiable act, e.g., turning off a respirator, which is the act that results in the patient's death, then regardless of what was said before, the doctor has killed the patient. This seems to have the support of the *Oxford English Dictionary* which says that to kill is simply to deprive of life. One may accept that a doctor is morally and legally required to turn off the respirator and thus is justified in killing her patient, but still maintain that she has killed him. Even those who accept the death penalty and hold that some prison official is morally and legally required to execute the prisoner do not deny that the official has killed the prisoner. Killing in self-defense is both morally and legally allowed, yet no one denies that it is killing. Similarly, one could agree that the doctor is doing nothing morally or legally unacceptable by turning off the respirator and even that the doctor is morally and legally required to do so, yet claim that in doing so the doctor is killing the patient.

If one accepts this analysis, then it might also seem plausible to say that an identifiable decision to omit a life-prolonging treatment, even if such an omission is morally and legally required, also counts as killing the patient. One could simply stipulate that doctors are sometimes morally and legally required to kill their patients, namely, when their action or omission is the result of a competent patient rationally refusing to start or to continue a life-prolonging treatment. Thus it would seem that the important point is that the doctor is morally and legally required to act as she does, not whether what she does is appropriately called killing. However, it is still significant whether such an action should be regarded as killing because having a too simple account of killing can cause numerous problems.

Many doctors do not want to regard themselves as killing their patients, even justifiably killing them. More importantly, all killing requires a justification or an excuse. If all the morally relevant features are the same, the justification or excuse that is not adequate for one way of killing will not be adequate for all other ways of killing either. Thus, if a justification is not publicly allowed for injecting a lethal dose of morphine, then it will not be publicly allowed for disconnecting the patient from the respirator. Since even advocates of VAE do not propose that doctors should ever be morally and legally required to kill their patients, even justifiably, doctors would not be required to comply with rational refusals of treatment by competent patients. It might even come to be thought justifiable to prohibit physicians from honoring the rational refusals of life-sustaining treatments of competent patients. Thus changing the way killing is understood (i.e., counting complying with a patient's rational refusal as killing him) would have unfortunate implications.

Those who favor legalizing VAE do not want to require doctors to kill their patients; they merely want to allow those doctors who are willing to kill, to do so. Similarly for PAS, no one has yet suggested that a doctor be required to comply with a patient's request for a lethal prescription. On the other hand, since doctors are morally and legally required to comply with a competent patient's rational refusal of life-sustaining treatment, complying with such a refusal has not been regarded as killing. Providing palliative care to a patient who refuses life-sustaining treatment is not morally controversial either. Killing a competent patient on his rational request or assisting him to commit suicide are morally controversial. No one claims that doctors are morally and legally

required to do either. Thus it is clear that complying with a competent patient's rational refusal of treatment is not normally regarded as killing, nor does providing palliative care to such a patient count as assisting suicide.

Part of the problem is that insufficient attention is paid to the way in which the term "kill" is actually used. Killing is not as simple a concept as it is often taken to be. Killing is causing death, but what counts as causing death or any other harm is a complex matter. If the harm that results from one's action, or omission, needs to be justified or excused, then one is regarded as having caused that harm. Of course, causing harm often can be completely justified or excused, so that one can cause a harm and be completely free of any unfavorable moral judgment. So killing, taken as causing death, may be completely justified, perhaps even morally required.

All acts that are done in order to bring about someone's death count as causing the person's death, or killing them, for all such intentional actions need justification. Also, if the act which results in death is the kind of act which is morally unacceptable such as deceiving, breaking a promise, cheating, breaking the law, or neglecting one's duty, knowingly performing the act or omission needs justification and so counts as killing. For example, if I lie to someone, telling him that a mushroom that I know to be intensely poisonous is safe to eat, then if he eats the mushroom and dies, I have caused his death. Or if a child dies because her parents did not feed her, they have killed her, because parents have a duty to feed their children. This analysis shows why it is important to make clear that doctors have no duty to treat, or even feed, patients who refuse treatment or food. However, if one does not intend, but only knows, that one's act will result in someone's death, and the act is the kind of act that is morally acceptable (such as giving a patient sufficient analgesia to control her severe pain), then even though this act results in the person's death, it may not count as causing his death.

When complying with the rational refusal of a competent patient, the doctor's intention is not to kill the patient, but rather to honor the patient's refusal even though she knows that the result will be that the patient dies. Even if the doctor agrees that it is best for the patient to die, her honoring that refusal does not count as intentionally causing his death. Of course, an individual doctor can want her patient to die, but her intention in these circumstances is not determined by whether she wants her patient to die. Rather, the intention is determined by what facts account for her deciding to act in one way rather than another. If she would cease treatment even if she did not want the patient to die and would not cease it if the patient had not refused such treatment, then her intention is not to kill the patient but to comply with the patient's refusal. Further, most doctors do not want to kill their patients, even if such actions were morally and legally justified, so clearly their intentions are simply to honor their patients' rational refusals. . . .

That our society does not regard death resulting from complying with a competent patient's rational refusal, even a refusal of food and fluids, as killing, is shown by the fact that almost all states have advance directives that explicitly require a physician to stop treatment, even food and fluids, if the patient has the appropriate advance directive. They also allow a presently competent patient to refuse treatment and food and fluids. None of these states allow a physician to kill a patient, under any circumstances. Most of these states do not even allow physicians to assist suicide, which strongly suggests that turning off a respirator is not regarded even as assisting suicide when doing so is required by the rational refusal of a competent patient.

Thus, complying with a competent patient's rational refusal of treatment is not killing or assisting suicide, and it may even be misleading to say that a physician is allowing the patient to die. To talk of a physician allowing the patient to die suggests that the physician has a choice, that it is up to her to decide whether or not to save the patient's life. When a competent patient has rationally refused treatment, however, a physician has no choice. It is morally and legally prohibited to overrule the patient's refusal. The physician allows her patient to die only in the sense that it is physically possible for her to save her patient and she does not. Complying with the rational refusal of life-saving treatment by a competent patient is not merely morally acceptable, it is morally required. Overruling such a refusal is itself a morally unacceptable deprivation of freedom. . . .

## IS THE REFUSAL OF LIFE-SUSTAINING TREATMENT SUICIDE?

If suicide is regarded simply as killing oneself, then the analysis of killing should apply to it in a fairly straightforward fashion. An action or an omission which is intended to result in the death of a patient and which does result in his death counts as killing. Therefore, one might argue that the refusal of treatment or of food and fluids that is intended by the patient to result in his own death and which does result in his death, should count as suicide. And if "assisting suicide" simply means doing those acts which help the person commit suicide, then physicians who provide palliative care to patients who are refusing life sustaining treatments are assisting suicide. Accepting this analysis would make providing palliative care to such patients a kind of assisted suicide.

However, it is not clear that the view that suicide is simply killing oneself should be accepted. Partly, this may be because "killing oneself" does not seem to need a justification or excuse as much as killing another person. This may be because our society, with some limitations, regards each person as allowed to do anything he wants to himself, as long as no one else is harmed. Indeed, it seems that any act which one does not intend but only knows will result in one's own death does not count as suicide. (It is only in an extended sense that someone who continues to smoke or drink or eat too much, when he knows that it may result in his death, could be said to be slowly committing suicide.) It also seems that our society does not count as suicide any death that results from omissions, at least omissions stemming from rational decisions to omit or to stop treatment. Rather only those positive acts that are done in order to bring about one's own death immediately count as suicide, since those acts so closely resemble the paradigms of killing. Patients who take some pills to bring about their own death are committing suicide, but those who have the respirator removed or who refuse food and fluids are usually not regarded as committing suicide.[7]

This more complex analysis of suicide explains why the law has never regarded providing palliative care to those who are refusing treatment as assisting suicide. Even those states which explicitly forbid assisting suicide do not prohibit providing palliative care to those who are refusing treatment or food and fluids. Of course those who support legalizing PAS favor the simpler account of suicide because they can then claim that some PAS is already allowed, and hence that it is simply inconsistent not to allow other quicker and less painful suicides. That our society does not count refusals of treatment as suicide and hence does not count palliative care for patients who refuse treatment as assisting suicide is not intended by us as an argument against legalizing PAS. However, it does show that one argument for legalizing PAS, namely, that PAS is already allowed in the provision of palliative care for those who are refusing life-prolonging treatment, is based on a misunderstanding of how our society regards providing such palliative care.

Our argument places PAS much closer to VPE than to VAE, and so allowing PAS, one could argue, need not lead to allowing VAE. It is compatible with our analyses so far that one can either be for or against legalizing PAS. However, we believe that recognition of the option of refusing treatment or food and fluids makes much stronger the major argument against legalizing PAS, namely, that doing so will not have sufficient benefits to compensate for the risks involved. But we are also aware that different people can rank and weigh these benefits and risks differently. . . .

IS KILLING PATIENTS EVER JUSTIFIED?

Stopping food and fluids is often the best way of allowing a patient to die, but it may be claimed that killing is sometimes better. Given present knowledge and technology, one can kill a patient or allow a patient to kill herself absolutely painlessly within a matter of minutes. If patients have a rational desire to die, why wait several days or weeks for them to die; why not kill them or let them kill themselves quickly and painlessly in a matter of minutes? We have provided no argument against allowing patients to kill themselves or even killing patients who want to die that applies to an ideal world where there are never any misunderstandings between people and everyone is completely moral and trustworthy. In such a world, if one could provide a patient with pills or inject the patient with appropriate drugs so that the patient dies painlessly and almost instantaneously, there would be no need to worry about the distinction between refusals and requests, or between killing, assisting suicide, and allowing to die. But in the real world, there are misunderstandings and not everyone is completely moral and trustworthy. In the real world no one even

proposes that PAS or VAE be allowed without elaborate procedural safeguards, which almost always require at least two weeks. So, on a practical level, legalizing PAS or VAE would not result in a quicker death than simply complying with a refusal of food and fluids.

On our account, VPE is complying with the rational refusal of life-saving treatment or food and fluids by a competent patient. Since there is no duty to overrule a rational refusal by a competent patient, complying with this refusal does not count as killing. Further, failing to comply with such a refusal is itself morally prohibited, for it is an unjustified deprivation of the patient's freedom. Also, in some newer codes of medical ethics, e.g., that of the American College of Physicians, respecting patients' refusals is now listed as a duty. Physicians are not merely morally allowed to practice VPE, they are morally required to do so. VAE is killing; it is complying with the rational request of a competent patient to be killed. Although PAS is not killing, it does involve active intervention by the physician that is more than merely stopping treatment. It is not simply complying with a patient's desire to be left alone; it is providing the patient with some substance that causes his death, when one has no duty to do so.

VAE is killing and so needs to be justified. This contrasts quite sharply with VPE, and even with PAS, which may not even need to be morally justified. When a patient refuses treatment or food and fluids, it is not the complying with a patient's refusal but rather the overruling of the refusal that needs to be justified. But, as noted earlier, physicians may cause pain to their patients and be completely justified, because they do so at their patients' request, or at least with their consent, and do it in order to prevent what the patient takes to be a greater harm, e.g., disability or death. VAE could be regarded as no different than any other instance of a doctor being morally justified in doing a morally unacceptable *kind of act* with regard to a patient at the patient's request, in order to prevent what the patient takes to be a greater harm. In VAE the patient takes death to be a lesser harm than suffering pain and requests that the moral rule prohibiting killing be violated with regard to himself.

If causing pain can be justified, why is killing not justified when all of the other morally relevant features are the same? The answer is that killing needs a stronger justification because of a special feature of death that distinguishes it from all of the other serious harms. The special feature is that, after death, the person killed no longer exists and so cannot protest that he did not want to be killed. All impartial rational persons would advocate that violations against causing pain be publicly allowed when the person toward whom the rule is being violated rationally prefers to suffer that pain rather than suffer some other harm, e.g., disability or death. It is uncertain how many impartial rational persons would advocate that killing be publicly allowed when the person being killed rationally prefers to be killed rather than to continue to suffer pain. This uncertainty stems from taking seriously the two features that are essential to morality, the public character of morality and the fallibility of persons.

Causing pain with valid consent can be publicly allowed without any significant anxiety being caused thereby. Patients can usually correct a mistake rather quickly by ordering a stop to the painful treatment. Also physicians have a constant incentive to be careful not to cause pain by mistake, for patients will complain if they did not really want the pain caused. Killing, even with valid consent, being publicly allowed may create significant anxiety. Patients may fear that they will be mistakenly killed and that they will have no opportunity to correct that mistake. That a patient will not be around to complain if they are mistakenly killed removes a strong safeguard against mistaken violations. But it is not merely mistakes about which a patient would not be able to complain. If a physician tries to take advantage of legalized killing and intentionally kills a patient, complaint would not be possible. Taking advantage of causing pain being publicly allowed does not pose similar problems.

Legalizing PAS might prevent some pain and suffering that could not be prevented by greater education concerning refusing food and fluids, but it would also be likely to create significant anxiety and some unwanted deaths. Impartial rational persons can therefore disagree on whether they would advocate legalizing PAS. Once it is recognized that withholding food and fluids 1) can be painless, 2) usually results in unconsciousness in one week and death in two weeks, and 3) allows for patients to change their minds, the need for PAS significantly diminishes.

Unlike others who argue against legalizing PAS, we do not claim that PAS is in itself morally unacceptable, only that it may create a serious risk of unwanted deaths. Since impartial rational persons can rank these risks as outweighing the benefits of legalization, legalizing PAS is controversial. If the goal is to allow a patient to choose her own time of dying and also dying to be accomplished relatively painlessly, there seems to be little need for PAS. If patient refusal of treatment, including refusal of food and fluids, were not sufficient for a relatively quick and painless death for the overwhelming number of terminally ill patients, then we would favor PAS, although we would still have serious objections to VAE. However, since VPE, especially when this includes refusing food and fluids, is available together with appropriate palliative care, it seems far more difficult to justify controversial methods like PAS. The harms prevented by PAS are no longer the long term suffering of patients who have no other way to die, they are only the one week of suffering that may be present while the patient is refusing food and fluids, and this suffering can be almost completely controlled by appropriate palliative care. This is an excellent example of why the presence of an alternative is a morally relevant feature.

Given the alternative of refusing food and fluids, very little additional harm seems to be prevented by PAS. The presence of an alternative is a morally relevant feature and makes it questionable whether it has sufficient benefits to justify the risks involved in legalizing it. There are good reasons for believing that the advantages of refusing food and fluids together with adequate palliative care make it preferable to legalizing PAS. This is especially true in a multicultural society where doctors and patients sometimes do not even speak the same language. There are a small number of cases in which refusal of food and fluids might be difficult, but it is necessary to weigh the benefit to this relatively small number of people against the harm that might be suffered by a great number of people by the legalizing of PAS. . . .

## SUMMARY

. . . We believe that the strongest argument against PAS is that, given the alternatives available, it does not provide sufficient benefit to individual patients to justify the societal risks. Patients already have the alternative of refusing treatment and food and fluids, and of receiving palliative care while they are refusing that treatment. If physicians were to educate patients about these matters and to make clear that they will support their choices and continue to care for them if they choose to refuse treatment, there might be little, if any, call for PAS. Because of the time involved, patients seem far less likely to be pressured into refusing treatment or food and fluids than they are to avail themselves of PAS. There would also be far fewer opportunities for abuse. PAS provides less incentive to be concerned with palliative care. And finally, given the bureaucratic safeguards that most regard as necessary with PAS, death can come as soon or sooner with refusal of treatment or refusal of food and fluids than it would with PAS.[8]

### A PRACTICAL PROPOSAL FOR STATE LEGISLATORS

In order to avoid the serious societal risks of legalizing physician-assisted suicide, while still providing a method for allowing seriously ill patients to determine the timing of their deaths, we think that states should consider passing legislation based on language such as the following. This language is completely consistent with the statement of the United States Supreme Court that, "Just as a State may prohibit assisting suicide while permitting patients to refuse unwanted lifesaving treatment, it may permit palliative care related to that refusal, which may have the foreseen but unintended 'double effect' of hastening the patient's death."

If a competent patient is terminally ill or suffering from a condition involving severe chronic pain or serious permanent disability, that patient's refusal of treatment, or refusal or food and fluids, shall not count as suicide, even though the patient knows that death will result from not starting or from stopping that treatment. All physicians and other healthcare workers shall be informed that they are legally prohibited from overruling any rational refusal of a competent patient, including refusal of food and fluids, even though it is known that death will result. All patients will be informed that they are allowed to refuse any treatment, or to refuse food and fluids, even though it is known that death will result, and that physicians and other healthcare workers are legally prohibited from overruling any such rational refusal by a competent patient.

Further, there shall be no prohibition placed upon any physician who provides pain relief in any form, in order to relieve the pain and suffering of the patient who has refused treatment, or food and fluids. In particular, providing pain medication shall not be considered as assisting suicide, and there shall be no liability for the physician who provides such pain medication for the purpose of relieving pain and suffering. The physician shall not provide such medication for the purpose of hastening the time of death, but is not prohibited from providing medication which is consistent with adequate pain relief even if he knows that such medication will hasten the time of death. Physicians are required to rigorously follow the accepted standards of medical practice in determining the competence of patients who refuse any treatment, or who refuse food and fluids, when they know that death will result from complying with that refusal.

## NOTES

1. Dan W. Brock, "Voluntary Active Euthanasia," *Hastings Center Report* 22 (2): 10–22 (1992).

2. *Quill v. Vacco*, the U.S. Court of Appeals for the Second Circuit.

3. See James L. Bernat, Bernard Gert, and R. Peter Mogielnicki, "Patient Refusal of Hydration and Nutrition: An Alternative to Physician Assisted Suicide or Voluntary Euthanasia," *Archives of Internal Medicine* 153: 2723–28 (December 27, 1993).

4. See Bernard Gert, James L. Bernat, and R. Peter Mogielnicki, "Distinguishing between Patients' Refusals and Requests," *The Hastings Center Report* 24 (4): 13–15 (July–August 1994).

5. See K. Danner Clouser, "Allowing or Causing: Another Look," *Annals of Internal Medicine* 87: 622–24 (1977).

6. See Kathleen M. Foley, M.D., "The Relationship of Pain and Symptom Management to Patient Requests for Physician-Assisted Suicide," *Journal of Pain and Symptom Management* 6 (5): 289–297 (July 1991).

7. This view is not held by all. Some, especially those with religious views, regard refusing treatment and especially refusing food and fluids when treatment, or food and fluids would sustain life for a long time, as committing suicide. But this is not the prevailing view, nor is it the view that governs the legal classification of the act. However, a terminally ill patient who intentionally goes into the woods in order to stop eating and drinking, does so, and thereby dies, would be regarded by most as having committed suicide. For a sensitive analysis of the difficulty of formulating a precise definition of "suicide," see Tom L. Beauchamp, "Suicide" in Tom Regan, ed., *Matters of Life and Death*, 2nd ed. (New York: Random House, 1986), pp. 77–89.

8. See K. Danner Clouser, "The Challenge for Future Debate on Euthanasia," *The Journal of Pain and Symptom Management* 6 (5): 306–311 (July 1991).

# When Self-Determination Runs Amok

Daniel Callahan

Daniel Callahan argues against any social policy allowing voluntary euthanasia and assisted suicide. He maintains that self-determination and mercy (the two values supporting them) may become separated. When this happens, assisted suicide for any reason and nonvoluntary euthanasia for the incompetent will become acceptable.

Callahan rejects Rachels' claim that the difference between killing and letting die is morally irrelevant. He holds that the difference is fundamental and that the decision to terminate a life requires a judgment about meaning and quality that physicians are not competent to make.

In general, Callahan warns us, we must not allow physicians to move beyond the bounds of promoting health, and exercise the power of deciding questions about human happiness and well-being. Permitting them to make such decisions will lead to widespread abuse and destroy the integrity of the medical profession.

The euthanasia debate is not just another moral debate, one in a long list of arguments in our pluralistic society. It is profoundly emblematic of three important turning points in Western thought. The first is that of the legitimate conditions under which one person can kill another. The acceptance of voluntary active euthanasia would morally sanction what can only be called "consenting adult killing." By the term I mean the killing of one person by another in the name of their mutual right to be killer and killed if they freely agree to play those roles. This turn flies in the face of a long-standing effort to limit the circumstances under which one person can take the life of another, from efforts to control the free flow of guns and arms, to abolish capital punishment, and to more tightly control warfare. Euthanasia would add a whole new category of killing to a society that already has too many excuses to indulge itself in that way.

The second turning point lies in the meaning and limits of self-determination. The acceptance of euthanasia would sanction a view of autonomy holding that individuals may, in the name of their own private, idiosyncratic view of the good life, call upon others, including such institutions as medicine, to help them pursue that life, even at the risk of harm to the common good. This works against the idea that the meaning and scope of our own right to lead our own lives must be conditioned by, and be compatible with, the good of the community, which is more than an aggregate of self-directing individuals.

The third turning point is to be found in the claim being made upon medicine: it should be prepared to make its skills available to individuals to help them achieve their private vision of the good life. This puts medicine in the business of promoting the individualistic pursuit of general human happiness and well-being. It would overturn the traditional belief that medicine should limit its domain to promoting and preserving human health, redirecting it instead to the relief of that suffering which stems from life itself, not merely from a sick body.

I believe that, at each of these three turning points, proponents of euthanasia push us in the wrong direction. Arguments in favor of euthanasia fall into four general categories, which I will take up in turn: (1) the moral claim of individual self-determination and well-being; (2) the moral irrelevance of the difference between killing and allowing to die; (3) the supposed paucity of evidence to show likely harmful consequences of legalized euthanasia; and (4) the compatibility of euthanasia and medical practice.

## Self-Determination

Central to most arguments for euthanasia is the principle of self-determination. People are presumed to have an interest in deciding for themselves, according to their own beliefs about what makes life good, how they will conduct their lives. That is an important value, but the question in the euthanasia context is, What does it mean and how far should it extend? If it were a question of suicide, where a person takes their own life without assistance from another, that principle might be pertinent, at least for debate. But euthanasia is not that limited a matter. The self-determination in that case can only be effected by the moral and physical assistance of another. Euthanasia is thus no longer a matter only of self-determination, but of a mutual, social decision between two people, the one to be killed and the other to do the killing.

How are we to make the moral move from my right of self-determination to some doctor's right to kill me—from *my* right to *his* right? Where does the doctor's moral warrant to kill come from? Ought doctors to be able to kill anyone they want as long as permission is given by competent persons? Is our right to life just like a piece of property, to be given away or alienated if the price (happiness, relief of suffering) is right? And then to be destroyed with our permission once alienated?

In answer to all those questions, I will say this: I have yet to hear a plausible argument why it should be permissible for us to put this kind of power in the hands of another, whether a doctor or anyone else. The idea that we can waive our right to life, and then give to another the power to take that life, requires a justification yet to be provided by anyone.

Slavery was long ago outlawed on the ground that one person should not have the right to own another, even with the other's permission. Why? Because it is a fundamental moral wrong for one person to give over his life and fate to another, whatever the good consequences, and no less a wrong for another person to have that kind of total, final power. Like slavery, dueling was long ago banned on similar grounds: even free, competent individuals should not have the power to kill each other, whatever their motives, whatever the circumstances. Consenting adult killing, like consenting adult slavery or degradation, is a strange route to human dignity.

There is another problem as well. If doctors, once sanctioned to carry out euthanasia, are to be themselves responsible moral agents—not simply hired hands with lethal injections at the ready—then they must have their own *independent* moral grounds to kill those who request such services. What do I mean? As those who favor euthanasia are quick to point out, some people want it because their life has become so burdensome it no longer seems worth living.

The doctor will have a difficulty at this point. The degree and intensity to which people suffer from their diseases and their dying, and whether they find life more of a burden than a benefit, has very little directly to do with the nature or extent of their actual physical condition. Three people can have the same condition, but only one will find the suffering unbearable. People suffer, but suffering is as much a function of the values of individuals as it is of the physical causes of that suffering. Inevitably in that circumstance, the doctor will in effect be treating the patient's values. To be responsible, the doctor would have to share those values. The doctor would have to decide, on her own, whether the patient's life was "no longer worth living."

But how could a doctor possibly know that or make such a judgment? Just because the patient said so? I raise this question because, while in Holland at the euthanasia conference reported by Maurice de Wachter . . . , the doctors present agreed that there is no objective way of measuring or judging the claims of patients that their suffering is unbearable. And if it is difficult to measure suffering, how much more difficult to determine the value of a patient's statement that her life is not worth living?

However one might want to answer such questions, the very need to ask them, to inquire into the physician's responsibility and grounds for medical and moral judgment, points out the social nature of the decision. Euthanasia is not a private matter of self-determination. It is an act that requires two people to make it possible, and a complicit society to make it acceptable.

## Killing and Allowing to Die

Against common opinion, the argument is sometimes made that there is no moral difference between stopping life-sustaining treatment and more active forms of killing, such as lethal injection. Instead I would contend that the notion that there is no morally significant difference between omission and commission is just wrong. Consider in its broad implications what the eradication of the distinction implies: that death from disease has been banished, leaving only the actions of physicians in terminating treatment as the cause of death. Biology, which used to bring about death, has apparently been displaced by human agency. Doctors have finally, I suppose, thus genuinely become gods, now doing what nature and the deities once did.

What is the mistake here? It lies in confusing causality and culpability, and in failing to note the way in which human societies have overlaid natural causes with moral rules and interpretations. Causality (by which I mean the direct physical causes of death) and culpability (by which I mean our attribution of moral responsibility to human actions) are confused under three circumstances.

They are confused, first, when the action of a physician in stopping treatment of a patient with an underlying lethal disease is construed as *causing* death. On the contrary, the physician's omission can only bring about death on the condition that the patient's disease will kill him in the absence of treatment. We may hold the physician morally responsible for the death, if we have morally judged such actions wrongful omissions. But it confuses reality and moral judgment to see an omitted action as having the same causal status as one that directly kills. A lethal injection will kill both a healthy person and a sick person. A physician's omitted treatment will have no effect on a healthy person. Turn off the machine on me, a healthy person, and nothing will happen. It will only, in contrast, bring the life of a sick person to an end because of an underlying fatal disease.

Causality and culpability are confused, second, when we fail to note that judgments of moral responsibility and culpability are human constructs. By that I mean that we human beings, after moral reflection, have decided to call some actions right or wrong, and to devise moral rules to deal with them. When physicians could do nothing to stop death, they were not held responsible for it. When, with medical progress, they began to have some power over death—but only its timing and circumstances, not its ultimate inevitability—moral rules were devised to set forth their obligations. Natural causes of death were not thereby banished. They were, instead, overlaid with a medical ethics designed to determine moral culpability in deploying medical power.

To confuse the judgments of this ethics with the physical causes of death—which is the connotation of the word kill—is to confuse nature and human action. People will, one way or another, die of some disease; death will have dominion over all of us. To say that a doctor "kills" a patient by allowing this to happen should only be understood as a moral judgment about the licitness of his omission, nothing more. We can, as a fashion of speech only, talk about a doctor *killing* a patient by omitting treatment he should have provided. It is a fashion of speech precisely because it is the underlying disease that brings death when treatment is omitted; that is its cause, not the physician's omission. It is a misuse of the word *killing* to use it when a doctor stops a treatment he believes will no longer benefit the patient—when, that is, he steps aside to allow an eventually inevitable death to occur now rather than later. The only deaths that human beings invented are those that come from direct killing—when, with a lethal injection, we both cause death and are morally responsible for it. In the case of omissions, we do not cause death even if we may be judged morally responsible for it.

This difference between causality and culpability also helps us see why a doctor who has omitted a treatment he should have provided has "killed" that patient while another doctor—performing precisely the same act of omission on another patient in different circumstances—does not kill her, but only allows her to die. The difference is that we have come, by moral convention and conviction, to classify unauthorized or illegitimate omissions as acts of "killing." We call them "killing" in the expanded sense of the term: a culpable action that permits the real cause of death, the underlying disease, to proceed to its lethal conclusion. By contrast, the doctor who, at the patient's request, omits or terminates unwanted treatment does not kill at all. Her underlying disease, not his action, is the physical cause of death; and we have agreed to consider actions of that kind to be morally licit. He thus can truly be said to have "allowed" her to die.

If we fail to maintain the distinction between killing and allowing to die, moreover, there are some disturbing possibilities. The first would be to confirm many physicians in their already too-powerful belief that, when patients die or when physicians stop treatment because of the futility of continuing it, they are somehow both morally and physically responsible for the deaths that follow. That notion needs to be abolished, not strengthened. It needlessly and wrongly burdens the physician, to whom should not be attributed the powers of the gods. The second possibility would be that, in every case where a doctor judges medical treatment no longer effective in prolonging life, a quick and direct killing of the patient would be seen as the next, most reasonable step, on grounds of both humaneness and economics. I do not see how that logic could easily be rejected.

## Calculating the Consequences

When concerns about the adverse social consequences of permitting euthanasia are raised, its advocates tend to dismiss them as unfounded and overly speculative. On the contrary, recent data about the Dutch experience suggests that such concerns are right on target. From my own discussions in Holland, and from the articles on that subject in this issue and elsewhere, I believe we can now fully see most of the *likely* consequences of legal euthanasia.

Three consequences seem almost certain, in this or any other country: the inevitability of some abuse of the law; the difficulty of precisely writing, and then enforcing, the law; and the inherent slipperiness of the moral reasons for legalizing euthanasia in the first place.

Why is abuse inevitable? One reason is that almost all laws on delicate, controversial matters are to some extent abused. This happens because not everyone will agree with the law as written and will bend it, or ignore it, if they can get away with it. From explicit admissions to me by Dutch proponents of euthanasia, and from the corroborating information provided by the Remmelink Report and the outside studies of Carlos Gomez and John Keown, I am convinced that

in the Netherlands there are a substantial number of cases of nonvoluntary euthanasia, that is, euthanasia undertaken without the explicit permission of the person being killed. The other reason abuse is inevitable is that the law is likely to have a low enforcement priority in the criminal justice system. Like other laws of similar status, unless there is an unrelenting and harsh willingness to pursue abuse, violations will ordinarily be tolerated. The worst thing to me about my experience in Holland was the casual, seemingly indifferent attitude toward abuse. I think that would happen everywhere.

Why would it be hard to precisely write, and then enforce, the law? The Dutch speak about the requirement of "unbearable" suffering, but admit that such a term is just about indefinable, a highly subjective matter admitting of no objective standards. A requirement for outside opinion is nice, but it is easy to find complaisant colleagues. A requirement that a medical condition be "terminal" will run aground on the notorious difficulties of knowing when an illness is actually terminal.

Apart from those technical problems there is a more profound worry. I see no way, even in principle, to write or enforce a meaningful law that can guarantee effective procedural safeguards. The reason is obvious yet almost always overlooked. The euthanasia transaction will ordinarily take place within the boundaries of the private and confidential doctor–patient relationship. No one can possibly know what takes place in that context unless the doctor chooses to reveal it. In Holland, less than 10 percent of the physicians report their acts of euthanasia and do so with almost complete legal impunity. There is no reason why the situation should be any better elsewhere. Doctors will have their own reasons for keeping euthanasia secret, and some patients will have no less a motive for wanting it concealed.

I would mention, finally, that the moral logic of the motives for euthanasia contain within them the ingredients of abuse. The two standard motives for euthanasia and assisted suicide are said to be our right of self-determination, and our claim upon the mercy of others, especially doctors, to relieve our suffering. These two motives are typically spliced together and presented as a single justification. Yet if they are considered independently—and there is no inherent reason why they must be linked—they reveal serious problems. It is said that a competent, adult person should have a right to euthanasia for the relief of suffering. But why must the person be suffering? Does not that stipulation already compromise the principle of self-determination? How can self-determination have any limits? Whatever the person's motives may be, why are they not sufficient?

Consider next the person who is suffering but not competent, who is perhaps demented or mentally retarded. The standard argument would deny euthanasia to that person. But why? If a person is suffering but not competent, then it would seem grossly unfair to deny relief solely on the grounds of incompetence. Are the incompetent less entitled to relief from suffering than the competent? Will it only be affluent, middle-class people, mentally fit and savvy about working the medical system, who can qualify? Do the incompetent suffer less because of their incompetence?

Considered from these angles, there are no good moral reasons to limit euthanasia once the principle of taking life for that purpose has been legitimated. If we really believe in self-determination, then any competent person should have a right to be killed by a doctor for any reason that suits him. If we believe in the relief of suffering, then it seems cruel and capricious to deny it to the incompetent. There is, in short, no reasonable or logical stopping point once the turn has been made down the road to euthanasia, which could soon turn into a convenient and commodious expressway.

## Euthanasia and Medical Practice

A fourth kind of argument one often hears both in the Netherlands and in this country is that euthanasia and assisted suicide are perfectly compatible with the aims of medicine. I would note at the very outset that a physician who participates in another person's suicide already abuses medicine. Apart from depression (the main statistical cause of suicide), people commit suicide because they find life empty, oppressive, or meaningless. Their judgment is a judgment about the value of continued life, not only about health (even if they are sick). Are doctors now to be given the right to make judgments about the kinds of life worth living and to give their blessing to suicide for those they judge wanting? What conceivable competence, technical or moral, could doctors claim to play such a role? Are we to medicalize suicide, turning judgments about its worth and value into one more clinical issue? Yes, those are rhetorical questions.

Yet they bring us to the core of the problem of euthanasia and medicine. The great temptation of modern medicine, not always resisted, is to move beyond the promotion and preservation of health into the boundless realm of general human happiness and well-being. The root problem of illness and mortality is both medical and philosophical or religious. "Why must I die?" can be asked as a technical, biological question or as a question about the meaning of life. When medicine tries to respond to the latter, which it is always under pressure to do, it moves beyond its proper role.

It is not medicine's place to lift from us the burden of that suffering which turns on the meaning we assign to the decay of the body and its eventual death. It is not medicine's place to determine when lives are not worth living or when the burden of life is too great to be borne. Doctors have no conceivable way of evaluating such claims on the part of patients, and they should have no right to act in response to them. Medicine should try to relieve human suffering, but only that suffering which is brought on by illness and dying as biological phenomena, not that suffering which comes from anguish or despair at the human condition.

Doctors ought to relieve those forms of suffering that medically accompany serious illness and the threat of death. They should relieve pain, do what they can to allay anxiety and uncertainty, and be a comforting presence. As sensitive human beings, doctors should be prepared to respond to patients who ask why they must die, or die in pain. But here the doctor and the patient are at the same level. The doctor may have no better an answer to those old questions than anyone else; and certainly no special insight from his training as a physician. It would be terrible for physicians to forget this, and to think that in a swift, lethal injection, medicine has found its own answer to the riddle of life. It would be a false answer, given by the wrong people. It would be no less a false answer for patients. They should neither ask medicine to put its own vocation at risk to serve their private interests, nor think that the answer to suffering is to be killed by another. The problem is precisely that, too often in human history, killing has seemed the quick, efficient way to put aside that which burdens us. It rarely helps, and too often simply adds to one evil still another. That is what I believe euthanasia would accomplish. It is self-determination run amok.

# DENNIS C. VACCO ATTORNEY GENERAL OF NEW YORK, ET AL. v. TIMOTHY E. QUILL ET AL.

## United States Supreme Court, 1997
### ON WRIT OF CERTIORARI TO THE UNITED STATES COURT OF APPEALS FOR THE SECOND CIRCUIT

CHIEF JUSTICE REHNQUIST delivered the opinion of the Court.

In New York, as in most States, it is a crime to aid another to commit or attempt suicide, but patients may refuse even lifesaving medical treatment. The question presented by this case is whether New York's prohibition on assisting suicide therefore violates the Equal Protection Clause of the Fourteenth Amendment. We hold that it does not. . . .

The Equal Protection Clause commands that no State shall "deny to any person within its jurisdiction the equal protection of the laws." This provision creates no substantive rights. . . . Instead, it embodies a general rule that States must treat like cases alike but may treat unlike cases accordingly. . . .

On their faces, neither New York's ban on assisting suicide nor its statutes permitting patients to refuse medical treatment treat anyone differently than anyone else or draw any distinction between persons. *Everyone*, regardless of physical condition, is entitled, if competent, to refuse unwanted lifesaving medical treatment; *no one* is permitted to assist a suicide. Generally speaking, laws that apply evenhandedly to all "unquestionably comply" with the Equal Protection Clause. . . .

The Court of Appeals, however, concluded that some terminally ill people—those who are on life-support systems—are treated differently than those who are not, in that the former may "hasten death" by ending treatment, but the latter may not "hasten

Excerpted from 521 U.S. 793 (1997). Some references and notes omitted.

death" through physician-assisted suicide. 80 F.3d, at 729. This conclusion depends on the submission that ending or refusing lifesaving medical treatment "is nothing more nor less than assisted suicide." *Id.* Unlike the Court of Appeals, we think the distinction between assisting suicide and withdrawing life-sustaining treatment, a distinction widely recognized and endorsed in the medical profession and in our legal traditions, is both important and logical; it is certainly rational. . . .

The distinction comports with fundamental legal principles of causation and intent. First, when a patient refuses life-sustaining medical treatment, he dies from an underlying fatal disease of pathology; but if a patient ingests lethal medication prescribed by a physician, he is killed by that medication. . . .

Furthermore, a physician who withdraws, or honors a patient's refusal to begin, life-sustaining medical treatment purposefully intends, or may so intend, only to respect his patient's wishes and "to cease doing useless and futile or degrading things to the patient when [the patient] no longer stands to benefit from them." Assisted Suicide in the United States, Hearing before the Subcommittee on the Constitution of the House Committee on the Judiciary, 104th Cong., 2d Sess., 368 (1996) (testimony of Dr. Leon R. Kass). The same is true when a doctor provides aggressive palliative care; in some cases, painkilling drugs may hasten a patient's death, but the physician's purpose and intent is, or may be, only to ease his patient's pain. A doctor who assists a suicide, however, "must, necessarily and indubitably, intend primarily that the patient be made dead." *Id.*, at 367.

Similarly, a patient who commits suicide with a doctor's aid necessarily has the specific intent to end his or her own life, while a patient who refuses or discontinues treatment might not. . . .

The law has long used actors' intent or purpose to distinguish between two acts that may have the same result. See, e.g., *United States v. Bailey*, 444 U.S., at 394, 403–406 (1980). . . . Put differently, the law distinguishes actions taken "because of" a given end from actions taken "in spite of" their unintended but foreseen consequences. *Feeney*, 442 U.S., at 279; *Compassion in Dying v. Washington*, 79 F.3d 790, 858. . . .

Given these general principles, it is not surprising that many courts, including New York courts, have carefully distinguished refusing life-sustaining treatment from suicide. See, e.g., *Fosmire v. Nicoleau*, 75 N.Y. 2d 218, 227, and n. 2, 551 N.E. 2d 77, 82, and n. 2 (1990) ("[M]erely declining medical . . . care is not considered a suicidal act").[1] In fact, the first state-court decision explicitly to authorize withdrawing lifesaving treatment noted the "real distinction between the self-infliction of deadly harm and a self-determination against artificial life support." *In re Quinlan*, 70 N.J. 10, 43, 52. . . .

Similarly, the overwhelming majority of state legislatures have drawn a clear line between assisting suicide and withdrawing or permitting the refusal of unwanted lifesaving medical treatment by prohibiting the former and permitting the latter. And "nearly all states expressly disapprove of suicide and assisted suicide either in statutes dealing with durable powers of attorney in health-care situations, or in 'living will' statutes." *Kevorkian*, 447 Mich., at 478–479, and nn. 53–54, 527 N.W 2d, at 731–732, and nn. 53–54. Thus, even as the States move to protect and promote patients' dignity at the end of life, they remain opposed to physician-assisted suicide. . . .

For all these reasons, we disagree with respondents' claim that the distinction between refusing lifesaving medical treatment and assisted suicide is "arbitrary" and "irrational." Brief for Respondents 44. Granted, in some cases, the line between the two may not be clear, but certainty is not required, even were it possible. Logic and contemporary practice support New York's judgment that the two acts are different, and New York may therefore, consistent with the Constitution, treat them differently. By permitting everyone to refuse unwanted medical treatment while prohibiting anyone from assisting a suicide, New York law follows a longstanding and rational distinction.

New York's reasons for recognizing and acting on this distinction—including prohibiting intentional killing and preserving life; preventing suicide; maintaining physicians' role as their patients' healers; protecting vulnerable people from indifference, prejudice, and psychological and financial pressure to end their lives; and avoiding a possible slide towards euthanasia—are discussed in greater detail in our opinion in *Glucksberg, ante*. These valid and important public interests easily satisfy the constitutional requirement that a legislative classification bear a rational relation to some legitimate end.

The judgment of the Court of Appeals is reversed.

*It is so ordered.*

## NOTE

1. Thus, the Second Circuit erred in reading New York law as creating a "right to hasten death"; instead, the authorities cited by the court recognize a right to refuse treatment, and nowhere equate the exercise of this right with suicide. *Schloendorff v. Society of New York Hospital*, 211 N.Y. 125, 129–130, 105 N.E. 92, 93 (1914), which contains Justice Cardozo's famous statement that "[e]very human being of adult years and sound mind has a right to determine what shall be done with his own body," was simply an informed-consent case. . . .

# WASHINGTON ET AL. v. HAROLD GLUCKSBERG ET AL.

## United States Supreme Court, 1997
ON WRIT OF CERTIORARI TO THE UNITED STATES
COURT OF APPEALS FOR THE NINTH CIRCUIT

CHIEF JUSTICE REHNQUIST delivered the opinion of the Court.

[T]he States are currently engaged in serious, thoughtful examinations of physician-assisted suicide and other similar issues. . . .

Attitudes toward suicide itself have changed . . . but our laws have consistently condemned, and continue to prohibit, assisting suicide. Despite changes in medical technology and notwithstanding an increased emphasis on the importance of end-of-life decision-making, we have not retreated from this prohibition. Against this backdrop of history, tradition, and practice, we now turn to respondents' constitutional claim.

II

The Due Process Clause guarantees more than fair process, and the liberty it protects includes more than the absence of physical restraint. . . . The Clause also provides heightened protection against government interference with certain fundamental rights and liberty interests. . . . We have . . . assumed, and strongly suggested, that the Due Process Clause protects the traditional right to refuse unwanted lifesaving medical treatment. *Cruzan*, 497 U.S., at 278–279. . . .

By extending constitutional protection to an asserted right or liberty interest, we, to a great extent, place the matter outside the arena of public debate and legislative action. . . .

Our established method of substantive-due-process analysis has two primary features: First, we have regularly observed that the Due Process Clause specially

Excerpted from 521 U.S. 702 (1997). Notes and some references omitted.

protects those fundamental rights and liberties which are, objectively, "deeply rooted in this Nation's history and tradition," *id.*, at 503 (plurality opinion); . . . Second, we have required in substantive-due-process cases a "careful description" of the asserted fundamental liberty interest. . . .

The Washington statute at issue in this case prohibits "aid[ing] another person to attempt suicide," Wash. Rev. Code § 9A.36.060(1) (1994), and, thus, the question before us is whether the "liberty" specially protected by the Due Process Clause includes a right to commit suicide which itself includes a right to assistance in doing so.

We now inquire whether this asserted right has any place in our Nation's traditions. Here, as discussed above . . . we are confronted with a consistent and almost universal tradition that has long rejected the asserted right. . . .

Respondents contend, however, that the liberty interest they assert *is* consistent with this Court's substantive-due-process line of cases, if not with this Nation's history and practice. Pointing to *Casey* and *Cruzan*, respondents read our jurisprudence in this area as reflecting a general tradition of "self-sovereignty," Brief of Respondents 12, and as teaching that the "liberty" protected by the Due Process Clause includes "basic and intimate exercises of personal autonomy," *id.*, at 10; see *Casey*, 505 U.S., at 847 ("It is a promise of the Constitution that there is a realm of personal liberty which the government may not enter"). According to respondents, our liberty jurisprudence, and the broad, individualistic principles it reflects, protects the "liberty of competent, terminally ill adults to make end-of-life

decisions free of undue government interference."
Brief for Respondents 10. . . .

[O]ur decisions lead us to conclude that the asserted "right" to assistance in committing suicide is
not a fundamental liberty interest protected by the
Due Process Clause. The Constitution also requires,
however, that Washington's assisted-suicide ban be
rationally related to legitimate government interests.
. . . This requirement is unquestionably met here. As
the court below recognized, 79 F.3d, at 816–817,[1]
Washington's assisted-suicide ban implicates a number of state interests.[2] . . .

First, Washington has an "unqualified interest in
the preservation of human life." *Cruzan*, 497 U.S., at
282. The State's prohibition on assisted suicide, like
all homicide laws, both reflects and advances its commitment to this interest. . . .

Next, the State has an interest in protecting vulnerable groups—including the poor, the elderly, and
disabled persons—from abuse, neglect, and mistakes. The Court of Appeals dismissed the State's
concern that disadvantaged persons might be pressured into physician-assisted suicide as "ludicrous
on its face." 79 F.3d, at 825. We have recognized,
however, the real risk of subtle coercion and undue
influence in end-of-life situations. *Cruzan*, 497 U.S.,
at 281. Similarly, the New York Task Force warned
that "[l]egalizing physician-assisted suicide would
pose profound risks to many individuals who are ill
and vulnerable. . . . The risk of harm is greatest for
the many individuals in our society whose autonomy
and well-being are already compromised by poverty,
lack of access to good medical care, advanced age,
or membership in a stigmatized social group." New
York Task Force 120. . . .

We need not weigh exactingly the relative
strengths of these various interests. They are
unquestionably important and legitimate, and
Washington's ban on assisted suicide is at least
reasonably related to their promotion and protection. We therefore hold that Wash. Rev. Code §
9A.36.060(1) (1994) does not violate the Fourteenth
Amendment, either on its face or "as applied to
competent, terminally ill adults who wish to hasten
their deaths by obtaining medication prescribed by
their doctors." 79 F.3d, at 838.

• • •

Throughout the Nation, Americans are engaged in
an earnest and profound debate about the morality,
legality, and practicality of physician-assisted suicide. Our holding permits this debate to continue, as
it should in a democratic society. The decision of the
en banc Court of Appeals is reversed, and the case is
remanded for further proceedings consistent with this
opinion.

*It is so ordered.*

JUSTICE STEVENS, concurring in the judgments.

A State, like Washington, that has authorized the
death penalty and thereby has concluded that the sanctity of human life does not require that it always be
preserved, must acknowledge that there are situations
in which an interest in hastening death is legitimate.
Indeed, not only is that interest sometimes legitimate,
I am also convinced that there are times when it is entitled to constitutional protection.

• • •

The state interests supporting a general rule banning the practice of physician-assisted suicide do not
have the same force in all cases. . . . That interest
not only justifies—it commands—maximum protection of every individual's interest in remaining alive,
which in turn commands the same protection for decisions about whether to commence or to terminate
life-support systems or to administer pain medication
that may hasten death. Properly viewed, however, this
interest is not a collective interest that should always
outweigh the interests of a person who because of
pain, incapacity, or sedation finds her life intolerable,
but rather, an aspect of individual freedom. . . .

Although as a general matter the State's interest
in the contributions each person may make to society
outweighs the person's interest in ending her life,
this interest does not have the same force for a terminally ill patient faced not with the choice of whether
to live, only of how to die. Allowing the individual,
rather than the State, to make judgments " 'about
the "quality" of life that a particular individual may
enjoy' " *ante*, at 25 (quoting *Cruzan*, 497 U.S., at
282), does not mean that the lives of terminally
ill, disabled people have less value than the lives
of those who are healthy, see *ante*, at 28. Rather, it

gives proper recognition to the individual's interest in choosing a final chapter that accords with her life story, rather than one that demeans her values and poisons memories of her. . . .

Similarly, the State's legitimate interests in preventing suicide, protecting the vulnerable from coercion and abuse, and preventing euthanasia are less significant in this context. I agree that the State has a compelling interest in preventing persons from committing suicide because of depression, or coercion by third parties. But the State's legitimate interest in preventing abuse does not apply to an individual who is not victimized by abuse, who is not suffering from depression, and who makes a rational and voluntary decision to seek assistance in dying. . . .

Relatedly, the State and *amici* express the concern that patients whose physical pain is inadequately treated will be more likely to request assisted suicide. Encouraging the development and ensuring the availability of adequate pain treatment is of utmost importance; palliative care, however, cannot alleviate all pain and suffering. . . . An individual adequately informed of the care alternatives thus might make a rational choice for assisted suicide. For such an individual, the State's interest in preventing potential abuse and mistake is only minimally implicated.

The final major interest asserted by the State is its interest in preserving the traditional integrity of the medical profession. The fear is that a rule permitting physicians to assist in suicide is inconsistent with the perception that they serve their patients solely as healers. But for some patients, it would be a physician's refusal to dispense medication to ease their suffering and make their death tolerable and dignified that would be inconsistent with the healing role. . . . For doctors who have long-standing relationships with their patients, who have given their patients advice on alternative treatments, who are attentive to their patient's individualized needs, and who are knowledgeable about pain symptom management and palliative care options, see Quill, Death and Dignity, A Case of Individualized Decision Making, 324 *New England J. of Med.* 691–694 (1991), heeding a patient's desire to assist in her suicide would not serve to harm the physician–patient relationship. Furthermore, because physicians are already involved in making decisions that hasten the death of terminally ill patients— through termination of life support, withholding of

medical treatment, and terminal sedation—there is in fact significant tension between the traditional view of the physician's role and the actual practice in a growing number of cases. . . .

I agree that the distinction between permitting death to ensue from an underlying fatal disease and causing it to occur by the administration of medication or other means provides a constitutionally sufficient basis for the State's classification. Unlike the Court, however, . . . I am not persuaded that in all cases there will in fact be a significant difference between the intent of the physicians, the patients or the families in the two situations.

There may be little distinction between the intent of a terminally ill patient who decides to remove her life-support and one who seeks the assistance of a doctor in ending her life; in both situations, the patient is seeking to hasten a certain, impending death. The doctor's intent might also be the same in prescribing lethal medication as it is in terminating life support. A doctor who fails to administer medical treatment to one who is dying from a disease could be doing so with an intent to harm or kill that patient. Conversely, a doctor who prescribes lethal medication does not necessarily intend the patient's death—rather that doctor may seek simply to ease the patient's suffering and to comply with her wishes. The illusory character of any differences in intent or causation is confirmed by the fact that the American Medical Association unequivocally endorses the practice of terminal sedation—the administration of sufficient dosages of pain-killing medication to terminally ill patients to protect them from excruciating pain even when it is clear that the time of death will be advanced. The purpose of terminal sedation is to ease the suffering of the patient and comply with her wishes, and the actual cause of death is the administration of heavy doses of lethal sedatives. This same intent and causation may exist when a doctor complies with a patient's request for lethal medication to hasten her death.

Thus, although the differences the majority notes in causation and intent between terminating life-support and assisting in suicide support the Court's rejection of the respondents' facial challenge, these distinctions may be inapplicable to particular terminally ill patients and their doctors. Our holding today in *Vacco v. Quill* that the Equal Protection Clause is not violated by New York's classification, just like our holding in

*Washington v. Glucksberg* that the Washington statute is not invalid on its face, does not foreclose the possibility that some applications of the New York statute may impose an intolerable intrusion on the patient's freedom.

There remains room for vigorous debate about the outcome of particular cases that are not necessarily resolved by the opinions announced today. How such cases may be decided will depend on their specific facts. In my judgment, however, it is clear that the so-called "unqualified interest in the preservation of human life," *Cruzan*, 497 U.S., at 282, *Glucksberg, ante*, at 24, is not itself sufficient to outweigh the interest in liberty that may justify the only possible means of preserving a dying patient's dignity and alleviating her intolerable suffering. . . .

JUSTICE O'CONNOR, concurring.*

. . . I join the Court's opinions because I agree that there is no generalized right to "commit suicide." But respondents urge us to address the narrower question whether a mentally competent person who is experiencing great suffering has a constitutionally cognizable interest in controlling the circumstances of his or her imminent death. I see no need to reach that question in the context of the facial challenges to the New York and Washington laws at issue here. . . . The parties and *amici* agree that in these States a patient who is suffering from a terminal illness and who is experiencing great pain has no legal barriers to obtaining medication, from qualified physicians, to alleviate that suffering, even to the point of causing unconsciousness and hastening death. . . . In this light, even assuming that we would recognize such an interest, I agree that the State's interests in protecting those who are not truly competent or facing imminent death, or those whose decisions to hasten death would not truly be voluntary, are sufficiently weighty to justify a prohibition against physician-assisted suicide. . . .

Every one of us at some point may be affected by our own or a family member's terminal illness. There is no reason to think the democratic process will not strike the proper balance between the interests of terminally ill, mentally competent individuals who would seek to end their suffering and the State's interests in protecting those who might seek to end life mistakenly or under pressure. As the Court recognizes, States are presently undertaking extensive and serious evaluation of physician-assisted suicide and other related issues. . . . In such circumstances, "the . . . challenging task of crafting appropriate procedures for safeguarding . . . liberty interests is entrusted to the 'laboratory' of the States . . . in the first instance." *Cruzan v. Director, Mo. Dept. of Health*, 497 U.S. 261, 292 (1990) (O'Connor, J., concurring) (citing *New State Ice Co. v. Liebmann*, 285 U.S. 262, 311 [1932]).

In sum, there is no need to address the question whether suffering patients have a constitutionally cognizable interest in obtaining relief from the suffering that they may experience in the last days of their lives. There is no dispute that dying patients in Washington and New York can obtain palliative care, even when doing so would hasten their deaths. The difficulty in defining terminal illness and the risk that a dying patient's request for assistance in ending his or her life might not be truly voluntary justifies the prohibitions on assisted suicide we uphold here.

## NOTES

1. The court identified and discussed six state interests: (1) preserving life; (2) preventing suicide; (3) avoiding the involvement of third parties and use of arbitrary, unfair, or undue influence; (4) protecting family members and loved ones; (5) protecting the integrity of the medical profession; and (6) avoiding future movement toward euthanasia and other abuses. 79 F.3d 816–832.

2. Respondents also admit the existence of these interests, Brief for Respondents 28–39, but contend that Washington could better promote and protect them through regulation, rather than prohibition, of physician-assisted suicide. Our inquiry, however, is limited to the question whether the State's prohibition is rationally related to legitimate state interests.

*JUSTICE GINSBURG concurs in the Court's judgments substantially for the reasons stated in this opinion. JUSTICE BREYER joins this opinion except insofar as it joins the opinion of the Court.

*Landmark Legislation and Legal Cases*

# BALLOT MEASURE 16: THE OREGON DEATH WITH DIGNITY ACT

## Proposed by Initiative Petition to be Voted on at the General Election, November 8, 1994

ALLOWS TERMINALLY ILL ADULTS TO OBTAIN PRESCRIPTION FOR LETHAL DRUGS

*Question.* Shall law allow terminally ill adult patients voluntary informed choice to obtain physician's prescription for drugs to end life?

Excerpted from Office of the Secretary of State, State of Oregon, Official 1994 General Election Voters' Pamphlet, pp. 123–134. Available at http://library.state.or.us/repository /2010/201003011350161/ORVPGenMari1994.pdf. Accessed 24 August 2012.

*Summary.* Adopts law. Allows terminally ill adult Oregon residents voluntary informed choice to obtain physician's prescription for drugs to end life. Removes criminal penalties for qualifying physician-assisted suicide. Applies when physicians predict patient's death within 6 months. Requires:

15-day waiting period;
2 oral, 1 written request;
second physician's opinion; counseling if either physician believes patient has mental disorder, impaired judgment from depression.

Person has choice whether to notify next of kin. Health care providers immune from civil, criminal liability for good faith compliance. . . .

• • •

## SECTION 2: WRITTEN REQUEST FOR MEDICATION TO END ONE'S LIFE IN A HUMANE AND DIGNIFIED MANNER

### § 2.01 WHO MAY INITIATE A WRITTEN REQUEST FOR MEDICATION

An adult who is capable, is a resident of Oregon, and has been determined by the attending physician and consulting physician to be suffering from a terminal disease, and who has voluntarily expressed his or her wish to die, may make a written request for medication for the purpose of ending his or her life in a humane and dignified manner in accordance with this Act. . . .

## SECTION 3: SAFEGUARDS

### § 3.01 ATTENDING PHYSICIAN RESPONSIBILITIES

The attending physician shall:

1. Make the initial determination of whether a patient has a terminal disease, is capable, and has made the request voluntarily;
2. Inform the patient of:
   (a) his or her medical diagnosis;
   (b) his or her prognosis;
   (c) the potential risks associated with taking the medication to be prescribed;
   (d) the probable result of taking the medication to be prescribed;
   (e) the feasible alternatives, including, but not limited to, comfort care, hospice care and pain control.
3. Refer the patient to a consulting physician for medical confirmation of the diagnosis, and for a determination that the patient is capable and acting voluntarily;
4. Refer the patient for counseling if appropriate pursuant to Section 3.03;
5. Request that the patient notify next of kin;

6. Inform the patient that he or she has an opportunity to rescind the request at any time and in any manner, and offer the patient an opportunity to rescind at the end of the 15-day waiting period pursuant to Section 3.06;
7. Verify, immediately prior to writing the prescription for medication under this Act, that the patient is making an informed decision;
8. Fulfill the medical record documentation requirements of Section 3.09;
9. Ensure that all appropriate steps are carried out in accordance with this Act prior to writing a prescription for medication to enable a qualified patient to end his or her life in a humane and dignified manner.

### § 3.02 CONSULTING PHYSICIAN CONFIRMATION

Before a patient is qualified under this Act, a consulting physician shall examine the patient and his or her relevant medical records and confirm, in writing, the attending physician's diagnosis that the patient is suffering from a terminal disease, and verify that the patient is capable, is acting voluntarily and has made an informed decision.

### § 3.03 COUNSELING REFERRAL

If in the opinion of the attending physician or the consulting physician a patient may be suffering from a psychiatric or psychological disorder, or depression causing impaired judgment, either physician shall refer the patient for counseling. No medication to end a patient's life in a humane and dignified manner shall be prescribed until the person performing the counseling determines that the patient is not suffering from a psychiatric or psychological disorder, or depression causing impaired judgment. . . .

### § 3.06 WRITTEN AND ORAL REQUESTS

In order to receive a prescription for medication to end his or her life in a humane and dignified manner, a qualified patient shall have made an oral request and a written request, and reiterate the oral request to his or her attending physician no less than fifteen (15) days after making the initial oral request. At the time the qualified patient makes his or her second oral request, the attending physician shall offer the patient an opportunity to rescind the request.

### § 3.07 RIGHT TO RESCIND REQUEST

A patient may rescind his or her request at any time and in any manner without regard to his or her mental state. No prescription for medication under this Act may be written without the attending physician offering the qualified patient an opportunity to rescind the request.

### § 3.08 WAITING PERIODS

No less than fifteen (15) days shall elapse between the patient's initial oral request and the writing of a prescription under this Act. No less than 48 hours shall elapse between the patient's written request and the writing of a prescription under the Act. . . .

### § 3.11 REPORTING REQUIREMENTS

1. The Health Division shall annually review a sample of records maintained pursuant to this Act.
2. The Health Division shall make rules to facilitate the collection of information regarding compliance with this Act. The information collected shall not be a public record and may not be made available for inspection by the public.
3. The Health Division shall generate and make available to the public an annual statistical report of information collected under Section 3.11(2) of this Act. . . .

### § 3.13 INSURANCE OR ANNUITY POLICIES

The sale, procurement, or issuance of any life, health, or accident insurance or annuity policy or the rate charged for any policy shall not be conditioned upon or affected by the making or rescinding of a request, by a person, for medication to end his or her life in a humane and dignified manner. Neither shall a qualified patient's act of ingesting medication to end his or her life in a humane and dignified manner have an effect upon a life, health, or accident insurance or annuity policy.

### § 3.14 CONSTRUCTION OF ACT

Nothing in this Act shall be construed to authorize a physician or any other person to end a patient's life by lethal injection, mercy killing or active euthanasia. Actions taken in accordance with this Act shall not, for any purpose, constitute suicide, assisted suicide, mercy killing or homicide, under the law.

## SECTION 4: IMMUNITIES AND LIABILITIES

### § 4.01 IMMUNITIES

Except as provided in Section 4.02:

1. No person shall be subject to civil or criminal liability or professional disciplinary action for participating in good faith compliance with this Act. This includes being present when a qualified patient takes the prescribed medication to end his or her life in a humane and dignified manner.
2. No professional organization or association, or health care provider, may subject a person to censure, discipline, suspension, loss of license, loss of privileges, loss of membership or other penalty for participating or refusing to participate in good faith compliance with this Act.
3. No request by a patient for or provision by an attending physician of medication in good faith compliance with the provisions of this Act shall constitute neglect for any purpose of law or provide the sole basis for the appointment of a guardian or conservator. . . .

### § 4.02 LIABILITIES

1. A person who without authorization of the patient willfully alters or forges a request for medication or conceals or destroys a rescission of that request with the intent or effect of causing the patient's death shall be guilty of a Class A felony.

2. A person who coerces or exerts undue influence on a patient to request medication for the purpose of ending the patient's life, or to destroy a rescission of such a request, shall be guilty of a Class A felony. . . .

## SECTION 6: FORM OF THE REQUEST

### § 6.01 FORM OF THE REQUEST

A request for medication as authorized by this act shall be in substantially the following form:

---

**REQUEST FOR MEDICATION TO END MY LIFE IN A HUMANE AND DIGNIFIED MANNER**

I, _____, am an adult of sound mind.

   I am suffering from _____, which my attending physician has determined is a terminal disease and which has been medically confirmed by a consulting physician.

   I have been fully informed of my diagnosis, prognosis, the nature of medication to be prescribed and potential associated risks, the expected result, and the feasible alternatives, including comfort care, hospice care and pain control.

   I request that my attending physician prescribe medication that will end my life in a humane and dignified manner.

**INITIAL ONE:**

_____ I have informed my family of my decision and taken their opinions into consideration.

_____ I have decided not to inform my family of my decision.

_____ I have no family to inform of my decision.

I understand that I have the right to rescind this request at any time.

I understand the full import of this request and I expect to die when I take the medication to be prescribed.

I make this request voluntarily and without reservation, and I accept full moral responsibility for my actions.

Signed:_____

Dated: _____

**DECLARATION OF WITNESSES**

We declare that the person signing this request:

   (a) Is personally known to us or has provided proof of identity;

   (b) Signed this request in our presence;

   (c) Appears to be of sound mind and not under duress, fraud or undue influence;

   (d) Is not a patient for whom either of us is attending physician.

_____ Witness 1/Date

_____ Witness 2/Date

NOTE: One witness shall not be a relative (by blood, marriage or adoption) of the person signing this request, shall not be entitled to any portion of the person's estate upon death and shall not own, operate or be employed at a health care facility where the person is a patient or resident. If the patient is an inpatient at a health care facility, one of the witnesses shall be an individual designated by the facility.

# ALBERTO R. GONZALES, ATTORNEY GENERAL ET AL. v. OREGON ET AL.

## United States Supreme Court, 2006
### ON WRIT OF CERTIORARI TO THE UNITED STATES COURT OF APPEALS FOR THE NINTH CIRCUIT

JUSTICE KENNEDY delivered the opinion of the Court.

The question before us is whether the Controlled Substances Act allows the United States Attorney General to prohibit doctors from prescribing regulated drugs for use in physician-assisted suicide, notwithstanding a state law permitting the procedure. As the Court has observed, "Americans are engaged in an earnest and profound debate about the morality, legality, and practicality of physician-assisted suicide." *Washington v. Glucksberg*, 521 U.S. 702, 735 (1997). The dispute before us is in part a product of this political and moral debate, but its resolution requires an inquiry familiar to the courts: interpreting a federal statute to determine whether Executive action is authorized by, or otherwise consistent with, the enactment.

In 1994, Oregon became the first State to legalize assisted suicide when voters approved a ballot measure enacting the Oregon Death With Dignity Act (ODWDA). Ore. Rev. Stat. §127.800 *et seq.* (2003). ODWDA, which survived a 1997 ballot measure seeking its repeal, exempts from civil or criminal liability state-licensed physicians who, in compliance with the specific safeguards in ODWDA, dispense or prescribe a lethal dose of drugs upon the request of a terminally ill patient.

The drugs Oregon physicians prescribe under ODWDA are regulated under a federal statute, the Controlled Substances Act (CSA or Act). 84 Stat.

1242, as amended, 21 U.S.C. §801 *et seq.* The CSA allows these particular drugs to be available only by a written prescription from a registered physician. In the ordinary course the same drugs are prescribed in smaller doses for pain alleviation.

A November 9, 2001 Interpretive Rule issued by the Attorney General addresses the implementation and enforcement of the CSA with respect to ODWDA. It determines that using controlled substances to assist suicide is not a legitimate medical practice and that dispensing or prescribing them for this purpose is unlawful under the CSA. The Interpretive Rule's validity under the CSA is the issue before us. . . .

The present dispute involves controlled substances listed in Schedule II, substances generally available only pursuant to a written, nonrefillable prescription by a physician. 21 U.S.C. §829(a). A 1971 regulation promulgated by the Attorney General requires that every prescription for a controlled substance "be issued for a legitimate medical purpose by an individual practitioner acting in the usual course of his professional practice." 21 CFR §1306.04(a) (2005).

To prevent diversion of controlled substances with medical uses, the CSA regulates the activity of physicians. To issue lawful prescriptions of Schedule II drugs, physicians must "obtain from the Attorney General a registration issued in accordance with the rules and regulations promulgated by him." 21 U.S.C. §822(a)(2). The Attorney General may deny, suspend, or revoke this registration if, as relevant here, the physician's registration would be "inconsistent with the public interest." §824(a)(4); §822(a)(2). When deciding whether a practitioner's

Excerpted from 546 U.S. 243 (2006). Notes and some references omitted.

registration is in the public interest, the Attorney General "shall" consider:

"1. The recommendation of the appropriate State licensing board or professional disciplinary authority.
"2. The applicant's experience in dispensing, or conducting research with respect to controlled substances.
"3. The applicant's conviction record under Federal or State laws relating to the manufacture, distribution, or dispensing of controlled substances.
"4. Compliance with applicable State, Federal, or local laws relating to controlled substances.
"5. Such other conduct which may threaten the public health and safety." §823(f).

The CSA explicitly contemplates a role for the States in regulating controlled substances, as evidenced by its preemption provision. . . .

The reviewing physicians must keep detailed medical records of the process leading to the final prescription, §127.855, records that Oregon's Department of Human Services reviews, §127.865. Physicians who dispense medication pursuant to ODWDA must also be registered with both the State's Board of Medical Examiners and the federal Drug Enforcement Administration (DEA). §127.815(1)(L). In 2004, 37 patients ended their lives by ingesting a lethal dose of medication prescribed under ODWDA. Oregon Dept. of Human Servs., Seventh Annual Report on Oregon's Death with Dignity Act 20 (Mar. 10, 2005). . . .

On November 9, 2001, without consulting Oregon or apparently anyone outside his Department, the Attorney General issued an Interpretive Rule announcing his intent to restrict the use of controlled substances for physician-assisted suicide. Incorporating the legal analysis of a memorandum he had solicited from his Office of Legal Counsel, the Attorney General ruled

"assisting suicide is not a 'legitimate medical purpose' within the meaning of 21 CFR 1306.04 (2001), and that prescribing, dispensing, or administering federally controlled substances to assist suicide violates the Controlled Substances Act. Such conduct by a physician registered to dispense controlled substances may 'render his registration . . . inconsistent with the public interest' and therefore subject to possible suspension or revocation under 21 U.S.C. 824(a)(4). The Attorney General's conclusion applies regardless of whether state law authorizes or permits such conduct by practitioners or others and regardless of the condition of the person whose suicide is assisted." 66 Fed. Reg. 56608 (2001).

There is little dispute that the Interpretive Rule would substantially disrupt the ODWDA regime. Respondents contend, and petitioners do not dispute, that every prescription filled under ODWDA has specified drugs classified under Schedule II. A physician cannot prescribe the substances without DEA registration, and revocation or suspension of the registration would be a severe restriction on medical practice. Dispensing controlled substances without a valid prescription, furthermore, is a federal crime. . . .

In response the State of Oregon, joined by a physician, a pharmacist, and some terminally ill patients, all from Oregon, challenged the Interpretive Rule in federal court. The United States District Court for the District of Oregon entered a permanent injunction against the Interpretive Rule's enforcement.

A divided panel of the Court of Appeals for the Ninth Circuit granted the petitions for review and held the Interpretive Rule invalid. . . . It reasoned that, by making a medical procedure authorized under Oregon law a federal offense, the Interpretive Rule altered the "usual constitutional balance between the States and the Federal Government" without the requisite clear statement that the CSA authorized such action. . . .

The Government first argues that the Interpretive Rule is an elaboration of one of the Attorney General's own regulations, 21 CFR § 1306.04 (2005), which requires all prescriptions be issued "for a legitimate medical purpose by an individual practitioner acting in the usual course of his professional practice." . . .

The regulation uses the terms "legitimate medical purpose" and "the course of professional practice," *ibid.*, but this just repeats two statutory phrases and attempts to summarize the others. It gives little or no instruction on a central issue in this case: Who decides whether a particular activity is in "the course of professional practice" or done for a "legitimate medical purpose"? Since the regulation gives no indication how to decide this issue, the Attorney General's effort to decide it now cannot be considered an interpretation of the regulation. . . .

Turning first to the Attorney General's authority to make regulations for the "control" of drugs, this delegation cannot sustain the Interpretive Rule's attempt to define standards of medical practice. . . .

It is not enough that the terms "public interest," "public health and safety," and "Federal law" are used in the part of the statute over which the Attorney General has authority. The statutory terms "public interest" and "public health" do not call on the Attorney General, or any other Executive official, to make an independent assessment of the meaning of federal law. The Attorney General did not base the Interpretive Rule on an application of the five-factor test generally, or the "public health and safety" factor specifically. Even if he had, it is doubtful the Attorney General could cite the "public interest" or "public health" to deregister a physician simply because he deemed a controversial practice permitted by state law to have an illegitimate medical purpose. . . .

The importance of the issue of physician-assisted suicide, which has been the subject of an "earnest and profound debate" across the country, *Glucksberg*, 521 U.S., at 735, makes the oblique form of the claimed delegation all the more suspect. Under the Government's theory, moreover, the medical judgments the Attorney General could make are not limited to physician-assisted suicide. Were this argument accepted, he could decide whether any particular drug may be used for any particular purpose, or indeed whether a physician who administers any controversial treatment could be deregistered. This would occur, under the Government's view, despite the statute's express limitation of the Attorney General's authority to registration and control, with attendant restrictions on each of those functions, and despite the statutory purposes to combat drug abuse and prevent illicit drug trafficking. . . .

In deciding whether the CSA can be read as prohibiting physician-assisted suicide, we look to the statute's text and design. The statute and our case law amply support the conclusion that Congress regulates medical practice insofar as it bars doctors from using their prescription-writing powers as a means to engage in illicit drug dealing and trafficking as conventionally understood. Beyond this, however, the statute manifests no intent to regulate the practice of medicine generally. . . .

Oregon's regime is an example of the state regulation of medical practice that the CSA presupposes. Rather than simply decriminalizing assisted suicide, ODWDA limits its exercise to the attending physicians of terminally ill patients, physicians who must be licensed by Oregon's Board of Medical Examiners. . . .

In the face of the CSA's silence on the practice of medicine generally and its recognition of state regulation of the medical profession it is difficult to defend the Attorney General's declaration that the statute impliedly criminalizes physician-assisted suicide. . . . A prescription, the Government argues, necessarily implies that the substance is being made available to a patient for a legitimate medical purpose. The statute, in this view, requires an anterior judgment about the term "medical" or "medicine." The Government contends ordinary usage of these words ineluctably refers to a healing or curative art, which by these terms cannot embrace the intentional hastening of a patient's death. It also points to the teachings of Hippocrates, the positions of prominent medical organizations, the Federal Government, and the judgment of the 49 States that have not legalized physician-assisted suicide as further support for the proposition that the practice is not legitimate medicine. . . .

On its own, this understanding of medicine's boundaries is at least reasonable. The primary problem with the Government's argument, however, is its assumption that the CSA impliedly authorizes an Executive officer to bar a use simply because it may be inconsistent with one reasonable understanding of medical practice. . . .

The Government, in the end, maintains that the prescription requirement delegates to a single Executive officer the power to effect a radical shift of authority from the States to the Federal Government to define general standards of medical practice in every locality. The text and structure of the CSA show that Congress did not have this far-reaching intent to alter the federal–state balance and the congressional role in maintaining it.

The judgment of the Court of Appeals is

*Affirmed.*

JUSTICE SCALIA, with whom CHIEF JUSTICE ROBERTS and JUSTICE THOMAS join, dissenting.

The Court concludes that the Attorney General lacked authority to declare assisted suicide illicit under the Controlled Substances Act (CSA), because the CSA is concerned only with *"illicit drug dealing and trafficking,"* *ante*, at 23 (emphasis added). This question-begging conclusion is obscured by a flurry of arguments that distort the statute and disregard settled principles of our interpretive jurisprudence. . . .

The [Attorney General's] Directive . . . purports to do three distinct things: (1) to interpret the phrase "legitimate medical purpose" in the Regulation to exclude physician-assisted suicide; (2) to determine that prescribing, dispensing, and administering federally controlled substances to assist suicide violates the CSA; and (3) to determine that participating in physician-assisted suicide may render a practitioner's registration "inconsistent with the public interest" within the meaning of 21 U.S.C.

§§ 823(f) and 824(a)(4) (which incorporates § 823(f) by reference). The Court's analysis suffers from an unremitting failure to distinguish among these distinct propositions in the Directive. . . .

It is beyond dispute . . . that a "prescription" under § 829 must issue for a "legitimate medical purpose." . . .

The Directive is assuredly valid insofar as it interprets "prescription" to require a medical purpose that is "legitimate" as a matter of *federal* law—since that is an interpretation of "prescription" that we ourselves have adopted. *Webb v. United States*, 249 U.S. 96 (1919), was a prosecution under the Harrison Act of a doctor who wrote prescriptions of morphine "for the purpose of providing the user with morphine sufficient to keep him comfortable by maintaining his customary use," *id.*, at 99. The dispositive issue in the case was whether such authorizations were "prescriptions" within the meaning of §2(b) of the Harrison Act, predecessor to the CSA. *Ibid.* We held that "to call such an order for the use of morphine a physician's prescription would be so plain a perversion of meaning that no discussion of the subject is required." *Id.*, at 99–100. Like the Directive, this interprets "prescription" to require medical purpose that is legitimate as a matter of federal law. And the Directive is also assuredly valid insofar as it interprets "legitimate medical purpose" as a matter of federal law to exclude physician-assisted suicide, because that is not only a permissible but indeed the most natural interpretation of that phrase. . . .

In sum, the Directive's construction of "legitimate medical purpose" is a perfectly valid agency interpretation of its own regulation; and if not that, a perfectly valid agency interpretation of the statute. No one contends that the construction is "plainly erroneous or inconsistent with the regulation." . . . In fact, as explained below, the Directive provides *the most natural* interpretation of the Regulation and of the statute. The Directive thus definitively establishes that a doctor's order authorizing the dispensation of a Schedule II substance for the purpose of assisting a suicide is not a "prescription" within the meaning of § 829. . . .

Virtually every relevant source of authoritative meaning confirms that the phrase "legitimate medical purpose"* does not include intentionally assisting suicide. "Medicine" refers to "[t]he science and art dealing with the prevention, cure, or alleviation of disease." Webster's Second 1527. The use of the word "legitimate" connotes an *objective* standard of "medicine," and our presumption that the CSA creates a uniform federal law regulating the dispensation of controlled substances, see *Mississippi Band of Choctaw Indians v. Holyfield*, 490 U.S. 30, 43 (1989), means that this objective standard must be a federal one. As recounted in detail in the memorandum for the Attorney General that is attached as an appendix to the Directive (OLC Memo), virtually every medical authority from Hippocrates to the current American Medical Association (AMA) confirms that assisting suicide has seldom or never been viewed as a form of "prevention, cure, or alleviation of disease," and (even more so) that assisting suicide is not a "legitimate" branch of that "science and art." See OLC Memo, App. to Pet. for Cert. 113a–130a. Indeed, the AMA has determined that "[p]hysician-assisted suicide is fundamentally incompatible with the physician's role as a healer." . . . "[T]he overwhelming weight of authority in judicial decisions, the past and present policies of nearly all of the States and of the Federal Government, and the clear, firm and unequivocal views of the leading associations within the American medical and nursing professions, establish that assisting in suicide . . . is not a legitimate medical purpose." . . .

---

*This phrase appears only in the Regulation and not in the relevant section of the statute. But as pointed out earlier, the Court does not contest that this is the most reasonable interpretation of the section—regarding it, indeed, as a mere "parroting" of the statute.

The only explanation for such a distortion is that the Court confuses the *normative* inquiry of what the boundaries of medicine *should be*—which it is laudably hesitant to undertake—with the *objective* inquiry of what the accepted definition of "medicine" is. The same confusion is reflected in the Court's remarkable statement that "[t]he primary problem with the Government's argument . . . is its assumption that the CSA impliedly authorizes an Executive officer to bar a use simply because it may be inconsistent with *one reasonable understanding* of medical practice." *Ibid.* (emphasis added). The fact that many in Oregon believe that the boundaries of "legitimate medicine" *should be* extended to include assisted suicide does not change the fact that the overwhelming weight of authority (including the 49 States that condemn physician-assisted suicide) confirms that they have not yet been so extended. Not even those of our Eighth Amendment cases most generous in discerning an "evolution" of national standards would have found, on this record, that the concept of "legitimate medicine" has evolved so far. See *Roper v. Simmons*, 543 U.S. 551, 564–567 (2005).

The Court contends that the phrase "legitimate medical purpose" *cannot* be read to establish a broad, uniform federal standard for the medically proper use of controlled substances. *Ante*, at 22. But it also rejects the most plausible alternative proposition, urged by the State, that any use authorized under state law constitutes a "legitimate medical purpose." . . .

Even assuming, however, that the *principal* concern of the CSA is the curtailment of "addiction and recreational abuse," there is no reason to think that this is its *exclusive* concern. We have repeatedly observed that Congress often passes statutes that sweep more broadly than the main problem they were designed to address. "[S]tatutory prohibitions often go beyond the principal evil to cover reasonably comparable evils, and it is ultimately the provisions of our laws rather than the principal concerns of our legislators by which we are governed." *Oncale v. Sundowner Offshore Services, Inc.*, 523 U.S. 75, 79 (1998). See also *H. J. Inc. v. Northwestern Bell Telephone Co.*, 492 U.S. 229, 248 (1989). . . .

Even if we could rewrite statutes to accord with sensible "design," it is far from a certainty that the Secretary, rather than the Attorney General, ought to control the registration of physicians. Though registration decisions sometimes require judgments about the legitimacy of medical practices, the Department of Justice has seemingly had no difficulty making them. See *In re Harline*, 65 Fed. Reg. 5665; *In re Tecca*, 62 Fed. Reg. 12842; *In re Roth*, 60 Fed. Reg. 62262. But unlike decisions about whether a substance should be scheduled or whether a narcotics addiction treatment is legitimate, registration decisions are not exclusively, or even primarily, concerned with "medical [and] scientific" factors. See 21 U.S.C. § 823(f). Rather, the decision to register, or to bring an action to deregister, an individual *physician* implicates all the policy goals and competing enforcement priorities that attend any exercise of prosecutorial discretion. It is entirely reasonable to think (as Congress evidently did) that it would be easier for the Attorney General occasionally to make judgments about the legitimacy of medical practices than it would be for the Secretary to get into the business of law enforcement. It is, in other words, perfectly consistent with an intelligent "design of the statute" to give the Nation's chief law enforcement official, not its chief health official, broad discretion over the substantive standards that govern registration and deregistration. That is *especially* true where the contested "scientific and medical" judgment at issue has to do with the legitimacy of physician-assisted suicide, which ultimately rests, not on "science" or "medicine," but on a naked value judgment. It no more depends upon a "quintessentially medical judgmen[t]," *ante*, at 20, than does the legitimacy of polygamy or eugenic infanticide. And it requires no particular *medical* training to undertake the objective inquiry into how the continuing traditions of Western medicine have consistently treated this subject. See OLC Memo, App. to Pet. for Cert. 113a–130a. The Secretary's supposedly superior "medical expertise" to make "medical judgments," *ante*, at 19–20, is strikingly irrelevant to the case at hand. . . .

In sum, the Directive's first conclusion—[(1)] namely that physician-assisted suicide is not a "legitimate medical purpose"—is supported both by the deference we owe to the agency's interpretation of its own regulations and by the deference we owe to its interpretation of the statute. The other two conclusions— (2) that prescribing controlled drugs to assist suicide violates the CSA, and (3) that such conduct is also "inconsistent with the public interest"—are inevitable consequences of that first conclusion. Moreover, the third conclusion, standing alone, is one that the Attorney General is authorized to make.

The Court's decision today is perhaps driven by a feeling that the subject of assisted suicide is none of the Federal Government's business. It is easy to sympathize with that position. The prohibition or deterrence of assisted suicide is certainly not among the enumerated powers conferred on the United States by the Constitution, and it is within the realm of public morality (*bonos mores*) traditionally addressed by the so-called police power of the States. But then, neither is prohibiting the recreational use of drugs or discouraging drug addiction among the enumerated powers. From an early time in our national history, the Federal Government has used its enumerated powers, such as its power to regulate interstate commerce, for the purpose of protecting public morality—for example, by banning the interstate shipment of lottery tickets, or the interstate transport of women for immoral purposes. See *Hoke v. United States*, 227 U.S. 308, 321–323 (1913); *Lottery Case*, 188 U.S. 321, 356 (1903). Unless we are to repudiate a long and well-established principle of our jurisprudence, using the federal commerce power to prevent assisted suicide is unquestionably permissible. The question before us is not whether Congress *can* do this, or even whether Congress *should* do this; but simply whether Congress *has* done this in the CSA. I think there is no doubt that it has. If the term "*legitimate* medical purpose" has any meaning, it surely excludes the prescription of drugs to produce death.

For the above reasons, I respectfully dissent from the judgment of the Court.

---

# CRUZAN v. DIRECTOR, MISSOURI DEPARTMENT OF HEALTH

## United States Supreme Court, 1990

CHIEF JUSTICE REHNQUIST delivered the opinion of the Court.

Petitioner Nancy Beth Cruzan was rendered incompetent as a result of severe injuries sustained during an

Excerpted from 110 Sup. Ct. Rptr. 2841 (1990). Notes and some references omitted.

automobile accident. Co-petitioners Lester and Joyce Cruzan, Nancy's parents and co-guardians, sought a court order directing the withdrawal of their daughter's artificial feeding and hydration equipment after it became apparent that she had virtually no chance of recovering her cognitive faculties. The Supreme Court of Missouri held that because there was no clear and convincing evidence of Nancy's desire to have life-sustaining treatment withdrawn under such circumstances, her parents lacked authority to effectuate such a request. . . .

She now lies in a Missouri state hospital in what is commonly referred to as a persistent vegetative state: generally, a condition in which a person exhibits motor reflexes but evinces no indications of significant cognitive function.[1] The State of Missouri is bearing the cost of her care.

After it had become apparent that Nancy Cruzan had virtually no chance of regaining her mental facilities her parents asked hospital employees to terminate the artificial nutrition and hydration procedures. All agree that such a removal would cause her death. The employees refused to honor the request without court approval. The parents then sought and received authorization from the state trial court for termination. The court found that a person in Nancy's condition had a fundamental right under the State and Federal Constitutions to refuse or direct the withdrawal of "death prolonging procedures." App to Pet for Cert A99. The court also found that Nancy's "expressed thoughts at age twenty-five in somewhat serious conversation with a housemate friend that if sick or injured she would not wish to continue her life unless she could live at least halfway normally suggest that given her present condition she would not wish to continue with her nutrition and hydration." Id.

The Supreme Court of Missouri reversed by a divided vote. The court recognized a right to refuse treatment embodied in the common-law doctrine of informed consent, but expressed skepticism about the application of that doctrine in the circumstances of this case. *Cruzan v. Harmon* (Mo 1988) (en banc). The court also declined to read a broad right of privacy into the State Constitution which would "support the right of a person to refuse medical treatment in every circumstance," and expressed doubt as to whether such a right existed under the United States Constitution. Id. It then decided that the Missouri Living Will statute, Mo Rev Stat § 459.010 et seq. (1986), embodied a state policy strongly favoring the preservation of life. The court found that Cruzan's statements to her roommate regarding her desire to live or die under certain conditions were "unreliable for the purpose of determining her intent," id., "and thus insufficient to support the co-guardians claim to exercise substituted judgment on Nancy's behalf." Id.

It rejected the argument that Cruzan's parents were entitled to order the termination of her medical treatment, concluding that "no person can assume that choice for an incompetent in the absence of the formalities required under Missouri's Living Will statutes or the clear and convincing, inherently reliable evidence absent here." Id. The court also expressed its view that "[b]road policy questions bearing on life and death are more properly addressed by representative assemblies" than judicial bodies. Id. . . .

[The] notion of bodily integrity has been embodied in the requirement that informed consent is generally required for medical treatment. Justice Cardozo, while on the Court of Appeals of New York, aptly described this doctrine: "Every human being of adult years and sound mind has a right to determine what shall be done with his own body; and a surgeon who performs an operation without his patient's consent commits an assault, for which he is liable in damages." *Schloendorff v. Society of New York Hospital* (1914). The informed consent doctrine has become firmly entrenched in American tort law. . . .

The common-law doctrine of informed consent is viewed as generally encompassing the right of a competent individual to refuse medical treatment. Beyond that, [court] decisions demonstrate both similarity and diversity in their approach to decision of what all agree is a perplexing question with unusual strong moral and ethical overtones. State courts have available to them for decision a number of sources—state constitutions, statutes, and common law—which are not available to us. In this Court, the question is simply and starkly whether the United States Constitution prohibits Missouri from choosing the rule of decision which it did. This is the first case in which we have been squarely presented with the issue of whether the United States Constitution grants what is in common parlance referred to as a "right to die." . . .

The Fourteenth Amendment provides that no State shall "deprive any person of life, liberty, or property, without due process of law." The principle that a competent person has a constitutionally protected liberty interest in refusing unwanted medical treatment may be inferred from our prior decisions. . . .

But determining that a person has a "liberty interest" under the Due Process Clause does not end the inquiry; "whether respondent's constitutional rights have been violated must be determined by balancing his liberty interests against the relevant state interests." *Youngberg v. Romeo* (1982). See also *Mills v. Rogers* (1982).

Petitioners insist that under the general holdings of our cases, the forced administration of life-sustaining medical treatment, and even of artificially delivered food and water essential to life, would implicate a competent person's liberty interest. . . . The dramatic consequences involved in refusal of treatment would inform the inquiry as to whether the deprivation of the interest is constitutionally permissible. But for purposes of this case, we assume that the United States Constitution would grant a competent person a constitutionally protected right to refuse lifesaving hydration and nutrition.

Petitioners go on to assert that an incompetent person should possess the same right in this respect as is possessed by a competent person. . . .

The difficulty with petitioners' claim is that in a sense it begs the question: an incompetent person is not able to make an informed and voluntary choice to exercise a hypothetical right to refuse treatment or any other right. Such a "right" must be exercised for her, if at all, by some sort of surrogate. Here, Missouri has in effect recognized that under certain circumstances a surrogate may act for the patient in electing to have hydration and nutrition withdrawn in such a way as to cause death, but it has established a procedural safeguard to assure that the action of the surrogate conforms as best it may to the wishes expressed by the patient while competent. Missouri requires that evidence of the incompetent's wishes as to the withdrawal of treatment be proved by clear and convincing evidence. The question, then, is whether the United States Constitution forbids the establishment of this procedural requirement by the State. We hold that it does not.

Whether or not Missouri's clear and convincing evidence requirement comports with the United States Constitution depends in part on what interests the State may properly seek to protect in this situation. Missouri relies on its interest in the protection and preservation of human life, and there can be no gain-saying this interest. . . .

But in the context present here, a State has more particular interests at stake. The choice between life and death is a deeply personal decision of obvious and overwhelming finality. We believe Missouri may legitimately seek to safeguard the personal element of this choice through the imposition of heightened evidentiary requirements. It cannot be disputed that the Due Process Clause protects an interest in life as well as an interest in refusing life-sustaining medical treatment. Not all incompetent patients will have loved ones available to serve as surrogate decision makers. And even where family members are present "[t]here will, of course, be some unfortunate situations in which family members will not act to protect a patient.". . . Finally, we think a State may properly decline to make judgments about the "quality" of life that a particular individual may enjoy, and simply assert an unqualified interest in the preservation of human life to be weighed against the constitutionally protected interests of the individual.

In our view, Missouri has permissibly sought to advance these interests through the adoption of a "clear and convincing" standard of proof to govern such proceedings. "The function of a standard of proof, as that concept is embodied in the Due Process Clause and in the realm of factfinding, is to 'instruct the factfinder concerning the degree of confidence our society thinks he should have in the correctness of factual conclusions for a particular type of adjudication.'" . . .

There is no doubt that statutes requiring wills to be in writing, and statutes of frauds which require that a contract to make a will be in writing, on occasion frustrate the effectuation of the intent of a particular decedent, just as Missouri's requirement of proof in this case may have frustrated the effectuation of the not-fully-expressed desires of Nancy Cruzan. But the Constitution does not require general rules to work faultlessly; no general rule can. . . .

The Supreme Court of Missouri held that in this case the testimony adduced at trial did not amount to clear and convincing proof of the patient's desire to have hydration and nutrition withdrawn. In so doing, it reversed a decision of the Missouri trial court which had found that the evidence "suggest[ed]" Nancy Cruzan would not have desired to continue such measures, but which had not adopted the standard of "clear and convincing evidence" enunciated by the Supreme Court. The testimony adduced at trial consisted primarily of Nancy Cruzan's statements made to a housemate about a year before her accident that she would not want to live should she face life as a "vegetable," and other observations to the same effect. The observations did not deal in terms with withdrawal of medical treatment or of hydration and nutrition. We cannot say that the Supreme Court of Missouri committed constitutional error in reaching the conclusion that it did. . . .

No doubt is engendered by anything in this record but that Nancy Cruzan's mother and father are loving and caring parents. If the States were required by the United States Constitution to repose a right of "substituted judgment" with anyone, the Cruzans would surely qualify. But we do not think the Due Process Clause requires the State to repose judgment on these matters with anyone but the patient herself. Close family members may have a strong feeling— a feeling not at all ignoble or unworthy, but not entirely disinterested, either—that they do not wish to witness the continuation of the life of a loved one which they regard as hopeless, meaningless, and even degrading. But there is no automatic assurance that the view of close family members will necessarily be the same as the patient's would have been had she been confronted with the prospect of her situation while competent. All of the reasons previously discussed for allowing Missouri to require clear and convincing evidence of the patient's wishes lead us to conclude that the State may choose to defer only to those wishes, rather than confide the decision to close family members.

The judgment of the Supreme Court of Missouri if affirmed.

## SEPARATE OPINIONS

### JUSTICE O'CONNOR, CONCURRING.

[T]he Court does not today decide the issue whether a State must also give effect to the decisions of a surrogate decisionmaker. . . . In my view, such a duty may well be constitutionally required to protect the patient's liberty interest in refusing medical treatment. Few individuals provide explicit oral or written instructions regarding their intent to refuse medical treatment should they become incompetent. States which decline to consider any evidence other than such instructions may frequently fail to honor a patient's intent. Such failures might be avoided if the State considered an equally probative source of evidence: the patient's appointment of a proxy to make

health care decisions on her behalf. Delegating the authority to make medical decisions to a family member or friend is becoming a common method of planning for the future. . . .

Today's decision, holding only that the Constitution permits a State to require clear and convincing evidence of Nancy Cruzan's desire to have artificial hydration and nutrition withdrawn, does not preclude a future determination that the Constitution requires the States to implement the decisions of a patient's duly appointed surrogate. Nor does it prevent States from developing other approaches for protecting an incompetent individual's liberty interest in refusing medical treatment. As is evident from the Court's survey of state court decisions, . . . no national consensus has yet emerged on the best solution for this difficult and sensitive problem. Today we decide only that one State's practice does not violate the Constitution; the more challenging task of crafting appropriate procedures for safeguarding incompetents' liberty interests is entrusted to the "laboratory" of the States, *New State Ice Co. v. Liebmann* (1932) (Brandeis, J., dissenting), in the first instance.

### JUSTICE BRENNAN, WITH WHOM JUSTICE MARSHALL AND JUSTICE BLACKMUN JOIN, DISSENTING

. . . .A grown woman at the time of the accident, Nancy had previously expressed her wish to forgo continuing medical care under circumstances such as these. Her family and her friends are convinced that this is what she would want. A guardian ad litem appointed by the trial court is also convinced that this is what Nancy would want. See 760 SW2d at 444 (Higgins, J., dissenting from denial of rehearing). Yet the Missouri Supreme Court, alone among state courts deciding such a question, has determined that an irreversibly vegetative patient will remain a passive prisoner of medical technology—for Nancy, perhaps for the next 30 years. . . . Because I believe that Nancy Cruzan has a fundamental right to be free of unwanted artificial nutrition and hydration, which right is not outweighed by any interests of the State, and because I find that the improperly biased procedural obstacles imposed by the Missouri Supreme Court impermissibly burden that right, I respectfully dissent. Nancy Cruzan is entitled to choose to die with dignity. . . .

# I

. . . .The right to be free from medical attention without consent, to determine what shall be done with one's own body, is deeply rooted in this Nation's traditions, as the majority acknowledges. . . . This right has long been "firmly entrenched in American tort law" and is securely grounded in the earliest common law. . . . "'Anglo-American law starts with the premise of thoroughgoing self determination. It follows that each man is considered to be master of his own body, and he may, if he be of sound mind, expressly prohibit the performance of lifesaving surgery, or other medical treatment.'" *Natanson v. Kline* (1960) . . . .

No material distinction can be drawn between the treatment to which Nancy Cruzan continues to be subject—artificial nutrition and hydration—and any other medical treatment. . . .

Artificial delivery of food and water is regarded as medical treatment by the medical profession and the Federal Government. According to the American Academy of Neurology, "[t]he artificial provision of nutrition and hydration is a form of medical treatment . . . analogous to other forms of life-sustaining treatment, such as the use of the respirator. When a patient is unconscious, both a respirator and an artificial feeding device serve to support or replace normal bodily functions that are compromised as a result of the patient's illness." . . .

# II

## A

The right to be free from unwanted medical attention is a right to evaluate the potential benefit of treatment and its possible consequences according to one's own values and to make a personal decision whether to subject oneself to the intrusion. For a patient like Nancy Cruzan, the sole benefit of medical treatment is being kept metabolically alive. . . .

There are also affirmative reasons why someone like Nancy might choose to forgo artificial nutrition and hydration under these circumstances. Dying is personal. And it is profound. For many, the thought of an ignoble end, steeped in decay, is abhorrent. A quiet, proud death, bodily integrity intact, is a matter of extreme consequence. "In certain, thankfully rare, circumstances the burden of maintaining the corporeal

existence degrades the very humanity it was meant to serve." *Brophy v. New England Sinai Hospital, Inc.* (1986). . . .

Such conditions are, for many, humiliating to contemplate, as is visiting a prolonged and anguished vigil on one's parents, spouse, and children. A long, drawn-out death can have a debilitating effect on family members. . . .

## B

Although the right to be free of unwanted medical intervention, like other constitutionally protected interests, may not be absolute, no State interest could outweigh the rights of an individual in Nancy Cruzan's position. Whatever a State's possible interests in mandating life-support treatment under other circumstances, there is no good to be obtained here by Missouri's insistence that Nancy Cruzan remain on life-support systems if it is indeed her wish not to do so. Missouri does not claim, nor could it, that society as a whole will be benefited by Nancy's receiving medical treatment. No third party's situation will be improved and no harm to others will be averted.

The only state interest asserted here is a general interest in the preservation of life. But the State has no legitimate general interest in someone's life, completely abstracted from the interest of the person living that life, that could outweigh the person's choice to avoid medical treatment. . . . Thus, the State's general interest in life must accede to Nancy Cruzan's particularized and intense interest in self-determination in her choice of medical treatment. There is simply nothing legitimately within the State's purview to be gained by superseding her decision.

Moreover, there may be considerable danger that Missouri's rule of decision would impair rather than serve any interest the State does have in sustaining life. Current medical practice recommends use of heroic measures if there is a scintilla of a chance that the patient will recover, on the assumption that the measures will be discontinued should the patient improve. When the President's Commission in 1982 approved the withdrawal of life support equipment from irreversibly vegetative patients, it explained that "[a]n even more troubling wrong occurs when a treatment that might save life or improve health is not started because the health care personnel are afraid that they will find it very difficult to stop the treatment if, as is fairly likely, it proves to be of little benefit and greatly burdens the patient." President's Commission 75. . . .

### III

. . . Missouri may constitutionally impose only those procedural requirements that serve to enhance the accuracy of a determination of Nancy Cruzan's wishes or are at least consistent with an accurate determination. The Missouri "safeguard" that the Court upholds today does not meet that standard. The determination needed in this context is whether the incompetent person would choose to live in a persistent vegetative state on life-support or to avoid this medical treatment. Missouri's rule of decision imposes a markedly asymmetrical evidentiary burden. Only evidence of specific statements of treatment choice made by the patient when competent is admissible to support a finding that the patient, now in a persistent vegetative state, would wish to avoid further medical treatment. Moreover, this evidence must be clear and convincing. No proof is required to support a finding that the incompetent person would wish to continue treatment. . . .

Even more than its heightened evidentiary standard, the Missouri court's categorical exclusion of relevant evidence dispenses with any semblance of accurate factfinding. The court adverted to no evidence supporting its decision, but held that no clear and convincing, inherently reliable evidence had been presented to show that Nancy would want to avoid further treatment. In doing so, the court failed to consider statements Nancy had made to family members and a close friend. The court also failed to consider testimony from Nancy's mother and sister that they were certain that Nancy would want to discontinue artificial nutrition and hydration, even after the court found that Nancy's family was loving and without malignant motive. The court also failed to consider the conclusions of the guardian ad litem, appointed by the trial court, that there was clear and convincing evidence that Nancy would want to discontinue medical treatment and that this was in her best interests. The court did not specifically define what kind of evidence it would consider clear and

convincing, but its general discussion suggests that only a living will or equivalently formal directive from the patient when competent would meet this standard. . . .

The Missouri Court's disdain for Nancy's statements in serious conversations not long before her accident, for the opinions of Nancy's family and friends as to her values, beliefs and certain choice, and even for the opinion of an outside objective factfinder appointed by the State evinces a disdain for Nancy Cruzan's own right to choose. The rules by which an incompetent person's wishes are determined must represent every effort to determine those wishes. The rule that the Missouri court adopted and that this Court upholds, however, skews the result away from a determination that as accurately as possible reflects the individual's own preferences and beliefs. It is a rule that transforms human beings into passive subjects of medical technology. . . .

That Missouri and this Court may truly be motivated only by concern for incompetent patients makes no matter. As one of our most prominent jurists warned us decades ago: "Experience should teach us to be most on our guard to protect liberty when the government's purposes are beneficent. . . . The greatest dangers to liberty lurk in insidious encroachment by men of zeal, well meaning but without understanding." *Olmstead v. United States* (1928) (Brandeis, J., dissenting).

I respectfully dissent.

*Editor's Note:* The concurring opinion of JUSTICE SCALIA and the dissenting opinion of JUSTICE STEVENS are omitted.

### NOTE

1. See 2 President's Commission for the Study of Ethical Problems in Medicine and Biomedical and Behavioral Research, Making Health Care Decision 241–242 (1982) (36% of those surveyed gave instructions regarding how they would like to be treated if they ever became too sick to make decisions: 23% put those instructions in writing) (Lou Harris Poll, September 1982); American Medical Association Surveys of Physicians and Public Opinion on Health Care Issues 29–30 (1988) (56% of those surveyed had told family members their wishes concerning the use of life-sustaining treatment if they entered an irreversible coma; 15% had filled out a living will specifying those wishes).

## Terri Schiavo

Michael Schiavo claimed that around four in the morning on February 26, 1990, he was awakened by a dull thud. Startled, he jumped out of bed, and it was then that he discovered his wife Terri sprawled on the floor. Michael knelt down and spoke to her, but she was obviously unconscious. He called 911, but by the time the paramedics arrived and resuscitated Terri, she had suffered damage from which she would never recover.

Teresa Marie Schindler was born on December 31, 1963, in Huntingdon Valley, Pennsylvania. Although overweight during her childhood, she lost fifty pounds in her senior year in high school, and most of the rest of her life she struggled to keep her weight down. She and Michael Schiavo met when she was in her second semester at Bucks County Community College. They married in 1984 and soon moved to St. Petersburg, Florida. Michael worked as a restaurant manager, and Terri got a job as a clerk with an insurance company. Terri's parents, Robert and Mary Schindler, also moved to Florida to be near their daughter and son-in-law. Relations between the parents and the young couple were friendly.

After Terri collapsed at home, she was rushed to the nearest hospital and treated for an apparent heart attack. A blood assay done at the hospital showed that she was suffering from a potassium imbalance, and her doctors thought that this had probably triggered the heart attack. The potassium imbalance, some physicians later suggested, might have been the result of bulimia, the eating disorder that had troubled her life since high school. The cycle of overeating, purging, and dieting characteristic of the disorder can produce a change in the electrolytes in the blood. Because this change disrupts the electrical signals controlling the heart, it may produce cardiac arrest. Terri had continued to work at losing weight in Florida, and at the time of her collapse she weighed only 120 pounds.

## Diagnosis

Whatever the reason for Terri's collapse, she failed to regain consciousness. Once she was out of immediate danger, the hospital neurologists performed a series of tests and examinations: Did she respond to a simple command like "Squeeze my hand"? Did her eyes track moving objects? Did her pupils respond to light? Did she show any sign of recognizing Michael or her parents? The answers to these questions were always no.

Terri's neurological responses were distinctly abnormal, and she showed no signs of cognitive functioning. In addition, CT scans of her brain revealed that the disruption of the oxygen supply to her brain caused by the cardiac arrest had damaged the cerebral cortex. The more primitive parts of her brain were undamaged, but the parts responsible for even the most basic forms of thinking and self-awareness had been destroyed.

The neurologists, after reviewing all the evidence, reached the conclusion that Terri Schiavo had suffered damage to her brain that was both severe and irreversible. She was diagnosed as being in a persistent vegetative state.

## Persistent Vegetative State

Persistent vegetative state (PVS) is a specific diagnosis, not to be confused with brain death. People diagnosed with PVS have damaged or dysfunctional cerebral

hemispheres, and this results in their not being aware of themselves or their surroundings. They are incapable of thinking and of deliberate or intentional movement. When the brain stem is undamaged, as it was in Terri's case, the autonomic nervous system and a range of bodily reflexes remain intact. (See the Social Context "When the Diagnosis Is Death," in this chapter.)

PVS patients are still able to breathe and excrete; their hearts beat, and their muscles behave reflexively. The patients cycle through regular sleep–wake patterns, but although their eyelids may blink and their eyes move, they lack the brain capacity to see. (They resemble a digital camera with a functioning optical system but no microprocessor—information is supplied, but it can't be used.) Some PVS patients may smile or tears may run down their cheeks, but these events are reflexive and thus are connected with circumstances in which smiling or crying would be appropriate only in an accidental way.

If a patient's brain is injured but not substantially destroyed, the patient may remain in a vegetative state for only a short time. Such a recovery is unusual, however. After a vegetative state lasts four weeks, neurologists consider it *persistent.* In most cases of PVS, if a change for the better has not occurred after three months, it's not likely to occur at all. When PVS lasts for six months, only about half of those with the diagnosis ever acquire any sort of interactive consciousness. Even then, it is only interactive consciousness of the "Squeeze my hand" variety. Such higher functions as talking or answering questions do not occur. (A study by Cambridge University scientists in September 2006 showed that MRI images might be used to make more reliable diagnoses. The study obtained images of conscious people asked to imagine walking around a room in their house or watching a tennis match, then compared them with the images of a brain of a patient who was given the same instructions. The same areas of the patient's brain lighted up. This suggested that her brain was responding to the command, but whether she was having any subjective experience can't be known. Nor is it clear whether the patient or others like her are likely to recover any interactive abilities.)

After six months, PVS patients virtually never recover even the most rudimentary form of consciousness. They remain vegetative as long as they live, which may be for decades. (Karen Quinlan lived almost ten years after lapsing into unconsciousness: see the Case Presentation

"Karen Quinlan: The Debate Begins," in this chapter.) PVS patients require complete care, including feeding through a gastric tube surgically implanted in the stomach and hydration through an IV line, for the remainder of their lives. Because they are prone to infections, they must be carefully monitored and given IV antibiotics prophylactically. They must be kept on special mattresses and moved regularly to prevent the development of bedsores, ulcers caused by the breakdown of the skin and underlying tissue from the constant pressure of the body's weight on the same area.

## Neither Brain Dead nor Minimally Conscious

PVS patients have no higher level brain functioning, but they are not brain dead. To be considered brain dead, a patient must be diagnosed as lacking in any detectable brain activity. This means that even the brain stem (which keeps the heart beating and the lungs functioning) must show no functional or electrical activity.

PVS patients are also not in a *minimally conscious state*. Those who fit into this diagnostic category show at least some episodes of awareness. Their eyes may track movement from time to time, though not always. They may respond to commands like "Squeeze my hand for yes" by squeezing for no.

Neurologists consider this category an appropriate diagnosis when the available evidence supports the idea that the patient displays some glimmer of consciousness at least some of the time. Brain scans of minimally conscious patients, for example, show that their language areas respond when a loved one speaks to them. PVS patients display none of these characteristics. Also, minimally conscious patients have a much higher expectation of recovering more consciousness than do PVS patients. Even so, the expectation of any recovery is low, and if any recovery does occur, it is likely to be only slight.

## Michael as Guardian

Michael Schiavo, as Terri's husband, became her legal guardian as soon as she was diagnosed as mentally incompetent. In 1992, he sued his wife's gynecologists for malpractice to get the money to pay for her private care. The theory behind the suit was that they had failed to detect the potassium imbalance that led to her heart attack, which, in turn, led to the loss of oxygen that caused her brain damage. (After Terri Schiavo died, an autopsy showed no evidence that she had suffered a heart attack.) Michael won the suit. He was awarded $750,000 earmarked for Terri's extended care and another $300,000 to compensate him for his loss and suffering.

In 1993, a year later, Michael and his wife's parents, Robert and Mary Schindler, had a disagreement over the care Terri was receiving. Michael later claimed that the disagreement was really over money and that the Schindlers wanted to force him to give them a share of his $300,000 malpractice award. They filed a suit asking the court to remove Michael as Terri's guardian and appoint them in his place. The court found no reason to hold that the care Michael was providing Terri was inadequate, and the suit against him was dismissed.

## Treatment Decisions: The Legal Battles

The course of events involving the struggle over the fate of Terri Schiavo became intricate and confusing after the falling-out between Michael and the Schindlers. The clearest way to follow the dispute is to consider the events in chronological order.

**1994.** Four years after Terri's PVS diagnosis, Michael met with the doctors taking care of her to ask about the likelihood of her ever regaining consciousness. He learned from them that this was unlikely ever to happen. Michael then told the long-term care facility where she was a patient that he didn't want her to be resuscitated if she suffered a heart attack or if some other life-threatening event occurred. (This is known as a "do not resuscitate," or DNR, order.)

Relations between Michael and the Schindlers continued to deteriorate, particularly after Michael and his girlfriend Jodi Centonze had two children together. (The Schindlers had originally encouraged Michael to move on with his life, and he started a relationship with Centonze only after Terri had been in a nursing home for four years.) Supporters of the Schindlers denounced Michael as an adulterer who was not fit to act as Terri's guardian.

**1998–2003.** Four years after Michael had authorized the DNR order and eight years after Terri was diagnosed as being in a PVS, Michael, in his role as Terri's guardian, filed a petition asking Florida's Pinellas–Pasco Circuit Court to authorize him to order the removal of her gastric tube and allow her to die. Michael argued that, even though Terri had left no written instructions, several times she had expressed to him the view that she would not want to be kept alive in her present condition. Robert and Mary Schindler opposed Michael's petition, claiming that Terri was capable of recovering consciousness.

The court found in favor of Michael, but between 1998 and 2003 the Schindlers continued to engage in legal maneuvers to block Michael's efforts to allow Terri to die. They filed civil suits against him, as well as accusations of abuse. They sought support from prolife groups and members of the religious right, urging them to appeal to elected officials for help in keeping Terri alive. In violation of a court order, they showed a videotape of Terri that convinced many viewers that she had some cognitive function.

When Terri's feeding tube was removed under court order on October, 15, 2003, the Florida state legislature quickly passed "Terri's Law" allowing the governor to order the tube replaced. Governor Jeb Bush signed the order, and President George Bush made a public statement praising the action.

Religious conservatives claimed that Terri's Law was the result of their prayer vigils, broadcasts on Christian radio, and thousands of email messages to Florida legislators. Some saw the result as a model for an approach they might take to get laws passed in other states to forbid removing feeding tubes, to allow prayer in school, and to post the Ten Commandments in courts and other public places. Terri's Law, some said, was a victory for conservatives nationally, for it showed that it was possible to use legislation to take away much of the power of the courts.

Vigils and demonstrations continued around Woodside Hospice, where Terri was a patient. Fundamentalist religious conservatives, both Catholic and Protestant, vied for media attention. Most had special agendas, some connected with promoting religious values, others with promoting disability rights. Still others seemed to focus only on Terri and the prospect of her death. Very few counterdemonstrators appeared in what was often a hostile, angry environment. Michael Schiavo was compared to Hitler and called a murderer.

Starting in 2001, the Schindlers began to file accusations of abuse against Michael. From 2001 to 2004, they made nine accusations that included neglect of hygiene, denial of dental care, poisoning, and physical harm. All were investigated by the Florida Department of Children and Families. (Agency reports released in 2005 concluded that there were no indications of any harm, abuse, or neglect.) The Schindlers continued to make clear their opinion that Terri's condition was not the result of a heart attack. In their view, Michael tried to strangle her but failed to kill her. They offered no evidence for this view, other than their speculation that Michael eventually established a relationship with another woman.

**2005.** When Terri's Law was ruled unconstitutional by a state court, the Florida attorney general appealed the case to the Florida Supreme Court, which upheld the lower court ruling. When the Schindlers appealed the decision to the U.S. Supreme Court, the case was again refused. On March 18, 2005, the Florida Circuit Court once more ordered the gastric tube removed.

Various members of the U.S. Congress were approached by a number of members of the religious right and asked to intervene in the Florida case. Speaker of the House Tom DeLay, a Texas Republican, said that the removal of Terri's feeding tube would be "an act of medical terrorism." One of the Schindlers' spiritual advisors said, "We pray that this modern-day crucifixion will not happen."

**March 16.** Congress initiated a debate over what could be done to allow the Schindlers to prevent Terri's feeding tube from being removed. The White House indicated that if Congress passed such a bill, the president would sign it.

**March 18.** While the debate was proceeding, Terri's feeding tube was removed, for the third time, in accordance with Judge Greer's order. The Schindlers visited Terri in the hospice afterward. They were accompanied by one of their spiritual advisors, Father Malinowski, who later said he had taken a scrap from a robe worn by Mother Teresa and touched Terri's throat, forehead, and cheek with it.

**March 21.** The House and Senate passed a bill that allowed the Schindlers' case against removing Terri's feeding tube to be heard in a federal court. They were thus given another opportunity to achieve what they had failed to accomplish in the state courts. "Every hour is incredibly important to Terri Schiavo," said House Majority Leader DeLay.

Senator Bill Frist, Republican of Tennessee, the Senate majority leader, said that Congress had to act on the bill because "These are extraordinary circumstances that center on the most fundamental of human values and virtues: the sanctity of human life." Frist, a transplant surgeon as well as a senator, had earlier claimed to be able to tell from the videotape of Terri that she was not in a persistent vegetative state. He received much criticism from the medical community for making a diagnosis without examining the patient or the medical records.

A number of legislators denounced the legislation. Representative Christopher Shays of Connecticut, one of four Republicans in the House to vote against it, objected that "this Republican party of Lincoln has become a party of theocracy."

President Bush signed the bill into law at his ranch in Texas around one in the morning. The next day, at a public appearance in Tucson, he praised Congress for "voting to give Terri's parents another chance to save their daughter's life." The statement was met with a roar of approval from the crowd of Republican supporters.

**March 23–26.** The bill passed by Congress and signed into law permitted the Schindlers to file a sequence of petitions and appeals in the federal courts. On Wednesday, March 23, they filed an emergency request with the U.S. Supreme Court to replace Terri's feeding tube. Republican leaders of the House and the Senate filed briefs in support of the Schindlers. The brief signed by Senator Frist argued that "the Court cannot permit Mrs. Schiavo to die" before the claims of her parents are reviewed by federal courts. But on Thursday, March 24, the Supreme Court rejected the Schindlers' petition.

In Florida, Governor Bush suggested on Wednesday, March 23, that he might send state agents to forcibly replace Terri's gastric tube. Judge Greer issued an emergency order barring the state from "taking possession of Theresa Marie Schiavo."

On Thursday, March 24, Governor Bush appealed the ruling. In court documents, he charged that Terri's medical condition might be due to abuse by her husband and filed an affidavit by a neurologist claiming that she had been misdiagnosed as being in a persistent vegetative state. The Schindlers also filed a petition on the same grounds.

The court-appointed neurologist who examined Terri rejected the possibility of a misdiagnosis. Judge Greer then turned down the petitions of both Governor Bush and the Schindlers. On the same day, a higher state court and the Florida Supreme Court also rejected appeals of the rulings.

A federal 11th Circuit Court of Appeal panel in Atlanta refused to reconsider the case. Further, Chief Judge J. L. Edmundson, a conservative Republican, wrote that federal courts had no jurisdiction in the case and that the law enacted by Congress and signed by President Bush allowing the Schindlers to seek a federal court review was unconstitutional. "If sacrifices to the independence of the judiciary are permitted today," Judge Edmundson wrote, "precedent is established for the constitutional transgressions of tomorrow." Having been turned down by the Appeals Court, the Schindlers made another emergency appeal to the U.S. Supreme Court. For the fifth time, however, the Supreme Court refused to intervene in the case. The Schindlers had reached the end of the legal line.

**March 27–30.** Reporter Rick Lyman described the mood of the protesters who maintained their post across the street from Woodside Hospice as one that was more somber and subdued than it had been earlier. Not Dead Yet, a disability rights organization that focuses on end-of-life issues, blocked the driveway leading to the hospice. A member of the group said that it hoped to make society change its view that a life with a severe disability is not worth living. One man at the scene blew a ram's horn from time to time, another chanted, and a young woman prayed into her cupped hands, then released the prayer toward the hospice.

Signs expressed in shorthand the views that protesters had often spelled out in interviews and speeches: *Hey, Judge. Who Made You God? Murder Is Legal in America, Hospice or Auschwitz?* Even Governor Bush wasn't immune from criticism, because he had said there was nothing else he could do within the law: *Where's Jeb?* Some protestors became angry, shouting "Nazi!" and "Murder!" but the Schindlers made it known that they wanted the crowd to remain calm.

Several protesters tried to carry cups of water into the hospice to give to Terri, but they were turned back by the police. Because Terri was unable to swallow, the attempts were symbolic. Some protesters continued to hold prayer vigils.

## The End

On the morning of Thursday, March 31, 2005, just after nine o'clock, Terri Schiavo died at Woodside Hospice. Michael was at her bedside and cradled her head as life slipped away and she stopped breathing. At Michael's request, neither her parents nor her brother or sister was present, although all of them had paid her a last visit at the hospice. Thirteen days had passed since Terri's feeding tube had been withdrawn. The end came, as is typical in such cases, as a result of dehydration.

The acrimony toward Michael by the Schindlers and their supporters did not end with Terri's death. "After these recent years of neglect at the hands of those who were supposed to care for her, she is finally at peace with God for eternity," Terri's sister, Suzzane Vitadamo, said in a public statement. "His [Michael's] heartless cruelty continued until the very last moment," said a priest who had sided with the Schindlers.

Michael Schiavo neither appeared in public nor made any statement. His lawyer, speaking on his behalf, said that "Mr. Schiavo's overriding concern here was to provide for Terri a peaceful death with dignity. This death was not for the siblings and not for the spouse and not for the parents. This was for Terri."

## Autopsy

Three months after Terri Schiavo's death, on June 15, 2005, the results of the extensive autopsy that was performed on her body were made public. The results revealed that her brain had shrunk to less than half its normal weight due to the destruction caused by a loss of oxygen ("anoxic-ischemic encephalopathy"). No treatment nor the passage of time could ever have restored Terri to even the lowest level of awareness or motor control. Her brain had shriveled and forever lost those capacities. The autopsy showed that the original diagnosis of persistent vegetative state had been correct.

The autopsy failed to find any signs of trauma or strangulation, undercutting the assertion by the Schindlers that Michael had abused Terri and thus was responsible for her condition. Also, no evidence was found suggesting that she had been neglected or received inadequate or inappropriate care.

What the autopsy could not establish, however, was the cause of the cardiac arrest that resulted in the oxygen deprivation that caused Terri's brain damage. "No one observed her taking diet pills, binging and purging or consuming laxatives," the autopsy report observes, "and she apparently never confessed to her family or friends about having an eating disorder." What is more, says the report, her potassium level was measured only after she had been treated with a number of drugs known to lower potassium in the blood, and this makes suspect the main piece of evidence supporting the idea that she suffered from bulimia. Thus, the evidence that Terri suffered "a severe anoxic brain injury" is certain, but what caused it is not. "The manner of death will therefore be certified as undetermined," the report concludes.

## The Battles Continue

Incredibly, the conflict over Terri Schiavo did not end with her death. The Schindlers attempted to have independent experts witness the autopsy, but the Pinellas County Medical Examiner refused their request. Videotapes, photographs, and tissue samples from the autopsy were made available by the agency's office, however.

The Schindlers also petitioned a court for the right to determine the disposition of their daughter's body. They said that they wanted her to be buried in Pinellas County so that they could visit her grave. The court rejected the petition, holding that Michael Schiavo had the right to make such decisions.

Terri Schiavo's body was cremated on April 1, 2005. Michael's lawyer announced that Michael's plan was to bury Terri's ashes in Huntingdon Valley, Pennsylvania, where she had grown up and where they had met so many years earlier. In January 2006, Michael married Jodi Centonze, the woman he had met in 1994, four years after Terri had been placed in a nursing home. The newly married couple and their two children continued to live in Florida.